Careers in Science & Engineering

Careers in Science & Engineering

Editor
Michael Shally-Jensen, Ph.D.

SALEM PRESS
A Division of EBSCO Information Services, Inc.
Ipswich, Massachusetts

GREY HOUSE PUBLISHING

55445444456345

Publisher's Cataloging-In-Publication Data
(Prepared by The Donohue Group, Inc.)

Careers in science & engineering / editor, Michael Shally-Jensen, Ph.D.
 -- [First edition].

   pages : illustrations ; cm. -- (Careers in--)

   Edition statement supplied by publisher.
   Includes bibliographical references and index.
   Contents: Publisher's note -- Editor's introduction -- Aerospace Engineer -- Agricultural and Food Scientist -- Agricultural Engineer -- Astronomer -- Biological Scientist -- Biomedical Engineer -- Chemical Engineer -- Chemist -- Civil Engineer -- Computer Engineer -- Electrical & Electronics Engineer -- Geologist & Geophysicist -- Industrial Engineer -- Marine Engineer and Naval Architect -- Materials Engineer -- Mathematician -- Mechanical Engineer -- Medical Scientist -- Microbiologist -- Mining and Geological Engineer -- Nuclear Engineer -- Petroleum Engineer -- Physicist -- Veterinarian -- Zoologist -- Appendix A: Holland Code -- Appendix B: Bibliography --Index.
   ISBN: 978-1-61925-860-0 (hardcover)

   1. Science--Vocational guidance--United States. 2. Engineering--Vocational guidance--United States. I. Shally-Jensen, Michael. II. Title: Careers in science and engineering III. Series: Careers in--

Q147 .C375 2015
502.3

First Printing

PRINTED IN THE UNITED STATES OF AMERICA

CONTENTS

PUBLISHER'S NOTE

Careers in Science & Engineering contains twenty-five alphabetically arranged chapters describing specific fields of interest in these broad industry segments. Merging scholarship with occupational development, this single comprehensive guidebook provides students studying various scientific and engineering paths with the necessary insight into potential careers, and provides instruction on what job seekers can expect in terms of training, advancement, earnings, job prospects, working conditions, relevant associations, and more. *Careers in Science & Engineering* is specifically designed for a high school and under-graduate audience and is edited to align with secondary or high school curriculum standards.

Scope of Coverage

Understanding the wide net of jobs in both science and engineering is important for anyone preparing for a career within them. *Careers in Science & Engineering* comprises twenty-five lengthy chapters on a broad range of occupations including traditional and long-established jobs such as Civil Engineer and Chemist, as well as in-demand jobs like Computer Engineer and Mining & Geological Engineer. This excellent reference also presents possible career paths and high-growth and emerging occupations within this field.

Careers in Science & Engineering is enhanced with numerous charts and tables, including projections from the US Bureau of Labor Statistics, and median annual salaries or wages for those occupations profiled. Each chapter also notes those skills that can be applied across broad occupation categories. Interesting enhancements, like **Fun Facts**, **Famous Firsts**, and dozens of photos, add depth to the discussion. A highlight of each chapter is **Conversation With** – a two-page interview with a professional working in a related job. The respondents share their personal career paths, detail potential for career advancement, offer advice for students, and include a "try this" for those interested in embarking on a career in their profession.

Essay Length and Format

Each chapter ranges in length from 3,500 to 4,500 words and begins with a Snapshot of the occupation that includes career clusters, interests, earnings and employment outlook. This is followed by these major categories:

- **Overview** includes detailed discussions on: Sphere of Work; Work Environment; Occupation Interest; A Day in the Life. Also included here is a Profile that outlines working conditions, educational needs, and physical abilities. You will also find the occupation's Holland Interest Score, which matches up character and personality traits with specific jobs.

- **Occupational Specialties** lists specific jobs that are related to the main profile in some way, like Chemical Engineering Technician (Chemical Engineer) and Statistician (Mathematician). Duties and Responsibilities are also included.

- **Work Environment** details the physical, human, and technological environment of the occupation profiled.

- **Education, Training, and Advancement** outlines how to prepare for this field while in high school, and what college courses to take, including licenses and certifications needed. A section is devoted to the Adult Job Seeker, and there is a list of skills and abilities needed to succeed in the job profiled.

- **Earnings and Advancements** offers specific salary ranges, and includes a chart of metropolitan areas that have the highest concentration of the profession.

- **Employment and Outlook** discusses employment trends, and projects growth to 2020. This section also lists related occupations.

- **Selected Schools** list those prominent learning institutions that offer specific courses in the profiles occupations.

- **More Information** includes associations that the reader can contact for more information.

Special Features

Several features continue to distinguish this reference series from other career-oriented reference works. The back matter includes:

- Appendix A: Guide to Holland Code. This discusses John Holland's theory that people and work environments can be classified into six different groups: Realistic; Investigative; Artistic; Social; Enterprising; and Conventional. See if the job you want is right for you!

- Appendix B: General Bibliography. This is a collection of suggested readings, organized into major categories.

- Subject Index: Includes people, concepts, technologies, terms, principles, and all specific occupations discussed in the occupational profile chapters.

Acknowledgments

Special mention is made of editor Michael Shally-Jensen, who played a principal role in shaping this work with current, comprehensive, and valuable material. Thanks are due to Allison Blake, who took the lead in developing "Conversations With," with help from Vanessa Parks, and to the professionals who communicated their work experience through interview questionnaires. Their frank and honest responses provide immeasurable value to *Careers in Science & Engineering*. The contributions of all are gratefully acknowledged.

EDITOR'S INTRODUCTION

Introduction

The acronym STEM is commonly used to refer to occupations in the fields of science, technology, engineering, and mathematics. Without the work of STEM professionals, many new products and discoveries would never be developed. Workers in STEM occupations use science, math, and engineering to solve problems and create new technologies. Because of the ongoing need for STEM professionals, employment in occupations related to science, technology, engineering, and mathematics is projected by the Bureau of Labor Statistics to grow to more than 9 million jobs by 2022—an increase of about a million jobs over 2012 employment levels (when the study was done). This represents a 13-percent increase, which is faster than the 11-percent growth rate projected for all occupations in the coming decade. Currently, STEM occupations make up more than 1 out of every 10 jobs in the United States, and they have wages that stand at nearly twice the U.S. average. Moreover, although STEM fields are generally led by those with advanced degrees, the majority of STEM jobs are available to those with two- or four-year college degrees.

There are a number of different ways to identify and count STEM occupations. Some researchers, for example, count business technology managers and social scientists; others include virtually any occupation that employs science and technology. For our purposes here, we adopt a fairly narrow definition, focusing on basic life sciences, physical sciences, and classical engineering and math. Excluded, for the most part, are occupations in health care, and environmental science and technology, which are covered in separate volumes in the series, *Careers in Health Care*, and *Careers in Environment & Conservation*. Information technology (IT) jobs, similarly, are only touched on here in anticipation of a possible future *Careers in...* volume.

There are many different kinds of work within the STEM category as a whole, even when limited to its core occupations.

Science

Scientists develop experiments in order to test hypotheses and theories and to make discoveries about how the world operates. They oversee and carry out those experiments, analyze the results, and organize the information in research reports that present their findings to other scientists and the public. In short, they use the scientific method to explore the nature of the world and interpret it for others. Science technicians, meanwhile, assist scientists by collecting samples, preparing materials, conducting experiments, and doing other tasks related to the research effort. In 2013, according to the Bureau of Labor Statistics, 28 percent of STEM jobs were in the areas of research, development, and design. About half of those STEM jobs were technologist and technician positions, with more than twice that percentage if the field is widened to include health care and related areas.

Science occupations fall into two broad groups: life scientists and physical scientists. The sciences also can be broken down into general areas of study—biological sciences, earth sciences, chemistry, physics, space science, and so on—and, further, into areas of specialization. For example, someone who studies the physics of the earth may concentrate in oceanography, and may further specialize on the movement of the ocean floor or the dynamics of ocean currents.

Life scientists. Life scientists and life science technicians study living systems, from organisms to ecosystems. Agricultural and food scientists, for example, study the production and distribution of food. They work to increase food quantity, quality, and safety. Biological scientists and technicians study animals, plants, and bacteria. They also analyze metabolic processes and other life elements. Conservation scientists and technicians work to manage natural resources to maximize their long-term economic, recreational, and conservation value. And medical scientists and technicians look for both causes of and treatments for human diseases.

Physical scientists. Physical scientists and physical science technicians study forces and processes in nature lying outside of living systems. They might, for example, examine the makeup of distant planets or the bonds between nuclear particles. Geoscientists study the composition and structure of the earth, often in search of available supplies of natural resources. Materials scientists and engineers conduct research to create new materials or new combinations of existing materials, often to develop new products. Physicists and astronomers explore the fundamental laws governing matter and energy in the universe, modeling the forces of nature by means of mathematics.

Engineering and Technology

Engineers and engineering technicians use math, science, and technology to solve practical problems. Their work typically involves developing systems, structures, products, or materials to use in real-world situations. A civil engineer, for example, might design a new train station to accommodate more passengers. An electrical and electronics engineer might design consumer electronics, electrical robotic devices, or other electrical equipment. A mechanical engineer might design, manufacture, and test tools or other mechanical devices. Meanwhile, engineering technicians build models, do calculations, and perform other engineering tasks. A chemical engineering technician, for example, might be involved in manufacturing—say, by monitoring industrial processes or preparing chemical compounds.

Technology workers, on the other hand, use science and engineering to create and troubleshoot technological devices and computer-based information systems. This category sometimes includes any occupation that requires technical skill, but it most often refers to information technology or computer-related occupations. Workers in these occupations use logic, mathematics, and computer science to make computers function. Some technology workers create new software, design computer systems, and develop databases. Others focus on keeping computers running well.

Mathematics

Many occupations use mathematics, including most of those noted above. Some occupations, however, focus on mathematics more or less exclusively. Mathematicians develop new mathematical theories and tools to solve problems. The work often involves finding patterns in data or abstract logic. For example, an industrial engineer uses math to model production operations to determine the most efficient way to make products, move materials, or meet other management objectives. Statisticians collect, analyze, and interpret data. Some specialists devise or decipher encryption methods to protect confidential information.

STEM Wages

In 2013, the annual average wage for all STEM occupations (including health care and social sciences) was $79,640. This is more than 1.7 times the national annual average wage for all occupations ($46,440). If, moreover, one excludes health care and social sciences (as this volume does), the average annual wage rises to $83,750, about 1.8 times the national average.

There are five general types of wage earners in STEM occupations: 1) researchers/developers; 2) technologists/technicians; 3) teachers/professors; 4) managers; and 5) technical/engineering sales. Of the five types, the highest wages are traditionally found at the management level, with an annual average wage of $122,470 in 2013. The lowest paying types of STEM occupations are the technologist and technician occupations, averaging $49,930—but note that these wages are still higher than the average for all occupations.

Conclusion

STEM occupations have some of the best opportunities for job growth in the future, and many of them continue to be actively promoted by federal agencies such as the National Science Foundation. In general, STEM workers find their jobs intellectually stimulating. They enjoy working collaboratively with those who share their enthusiasm and are happy to work with cutting-edge technology. STEM work can be challenging, and yet it often creates tangible results, leading to job satisfaction. The fact that one can embark on a STEM career with a two-year associate's degree, a four-year college degree, or a more advanced level of training makes the field all the more attractive to a broad array of career seekers.

—Michael Shally-Jensen, Ph.D.

Sources

Bush, Pamela McCauley. *Transforming Your STEM Career through Leadership and Innovation*. Boston: Elsevier, 2013.

Hacker, Andrew. "The Frenzy about High-Tech Talent," *New York Review of Books*, vol. LXII, no. 12, July 9, 2015; 33-35.

Jones, John I. "An Overview of Employment and Wages in Science, Technology, Engineering, and Math (STEM) Groups," *Beyond the Numbers* (Bureau of Labor Statistics), April 2014. http://www.bls.gov/opub/btn/volume-3/an-overview-of-employment.htm

Vilorio, Dennis. "STEM 101: Intro to Tomorrow's Jobs," *Occupational Outlook Quarterly* (Bureau of Labor Statistics), Spring 2014; 1-12.

Aerospace Engineer

Snapshot

Career Cluster: Science, Technology, Engineering & Mathematics

Interests: Engineering, mathematics, physical sciences, flight, jet propulsion

Earnings (Yearly Average): $107,700

Employment & Outlook: Slower Than Average Growth Expected

OVERVIEW

Sphere of Work

Aerospace engineers design, develop, test, maintain, and assist in the manufacture of different types of aircraft, missiles, spacecraft, and other technologically advanced modes of transport. Aerospace engineers in the field of aeronautical engineering work on civilian and military aircraft, which may include helicopters, airliners, fighter jets, missiles, and other airborne craft. Aerospace engineers in the field of astronautical engineering work with satellites, rockets, and similar space-bound technologies. Aerospace engineers focus

on aerodynamics, propulsion, hull composition, communications networks, and electrical systems.

Work Environment

Aerospace engineers typically work in government or business offices, where they manage administrative tasks, design models and schematics, and write reports. They also spend time working in laboratories, industrial plants, and manufacturing facilities, where they work with other technicians to assemble systems and aircraft. Those engineers who work in astronautical engineering also work at launch facilities, while aeronautical engineering typically requires spending time at noisy airfields. Aerospace engineers generally work in several complex and busy locations over the course of a project, with many separate activities taking place simultaneously. They work a regular forty-hour workweek, although longer hours may be required as deadlines draw near.

Profile

Working Conditions: Work Indoors
Physical Strength: Light Work
Education Needs: Bachelor's Degree, Master's Degree, Doctoral Degree
Licensure/Certification: Required
Opportunities For Experience: Internship, Apprenticeship, Military Service, Part-Time Work
Holland Interest Score*: IRE

* See Appendix A

Occupation Interest

Aerospace engineers are part of an exciting industry, one that helps develop high-speed trains, deep-sea vessels, missiles/rockets, commercial airliners, and many other large aircraft and spacecraft. They use the most advanced technology to design, build, test, and maintain these vehicles. Because they have expertise unique to their field and area of specialization, aerospace engineers receive highly competitive salaries. The job market for aerospace engineers is continuously growing, thanks to the sales of new aircraft and missiles, as well as growth in the commercial airline construction industry.

A Day in the Life—Duties and Responsibilities

There are two basic types of aerospace engineers: aeronautical engineers (who focus on aircraft, missiles, and other "earthbound" technologies) and astronautical engineers (who focus on spacecraft and space exploration technologies). Both aeronautical and astronautical engineers further specialize in certain types of products or product features. Aerospace engineers create conceptual designs of aeronautical or astronautical vehicles, instrumentation, defense systems, guidance and navigation systems, and propulsion systems according to the specifications of the client. They also improve the structural design of existing aircraft and spacecraft. Some engineers specialize in innovating more sophisticated production methods. All of these design and development processes include practical steps such as analyzing production costs, developing quality control standards, and testing methodologies, as well as establishing timelines for project development and completion. During the course of construction and/ or assembly, aerospace engineers travel to the production site and conduct inspections and tests on the systems to ensure that they are operating efficiently and according to the needs of the client. Many aerospace engineers assist in the production phase, integrating systems and examining components as they are being built.

When production is complete, the aerospace engineer creates performance and technical reports so that customers have a full knowledge of the vehicle's capabilities. He or she retains copies of such reports for future reference. In the event that the vehicle or a vehicular system malfunctions, aerospace engineers play an important role in the investigation, examining damaged parts and reviewing performance reports and other documentation to determine the cause of the malfunction.

Duties and Responsibilities

- Designing and developing aircraft
- Overseeing the manufacture of prototypes (models)
- Testing prototypes to evaluate their operation
- Estimating the time and cost to complete projects

OCCUPATION SPECIALTIES

Aeronautical Engineers

Aeronautical Engineers design, develop, and test aircraft that operate within the earth's atmosphere. They test models to study how they operate under a variety of conditions in order to make aircraft safe and effective.

Astronautical Engineers

Astronautical Engineers design, develop, and test spacecraft that operate outside the earth's atmosphere. They test models to study how they operate under a variety of conditions in order to make spacecraft safe and effective.

Aerospace Engineering Technicians

Aerospace Engineering Technicians, who usually work under an Aerospace Engineer or other senior staff person, operate and maintain equipment used in developing and testing new aircraft and spacecraft.

WORK ENVIRONMENT

Physical Environment

Aerospace engineers spend long hours working at drawing boards in offices but also spend significant amounts of time working in laboratories, manufacturing facilities, test facilities, and airfields. These locations are generally clean, very well organized, and well ventilated. There are physical risks when working with or in close proximity to machines, electricity, manufacturing chemicals, and engines, so safety protocols are strictly enforced.

Relevant Skills and Abilities

Communication Skills
- Speaking effectively
- Writing concisely

Interpersonal/Social Skills
- Working as a member of a team

Organization & Management Skills
- Paying attention to and handling details
- Performing duties which change frequently

Research & Planning Skills
- Using logical reasoning

Technical Skills
- Applying technology to a task
- Performing scientific, mathematical and technical work

Human Environment

Aerospace engineers work with many other professionals, including engineers with different specialties. They interact with electricians, technicians, construction personnel, forklift and other heavy machinery operators, physicists, chemists, and project managers.

Technological Environment

Aerospace engineers use a variety of analytical tools and sophisticated technology in their daily work. Computer-aided design (CAD) and computer-aided manufacturing (CAM) software, as well as a variety of computer modeling and design programs, are used for planning and design. Analytical and scientific software help aerospace engineers to examine thermal patterns, complex mathematical formulas, and other aspects of systems engineering. At test facilities, engineers use such tools as flow meters, lasers, and vibration testing equipment.

EDUCATION, TRAINING, AND ADVANCEMENT

High School/Secondary

High school students who intend to become aerospace engineers should study mathematics, including algebra, applied mathematics, trigonometry, calculus, and geometry. Physics, chemistry, and other laboratory sciences are equally important. Computer science courses expose high school students to design and analytical software, while industrial arts courses expose them to mechanical equipment, such as engines and electrical systems. High school students interested in the field of aerospace engineering must apply to related college or university programs.

Suggested High School Subjects
- Algebra
- Applied Communication
- Applied Math
- Applied Physics
- Blueprint Reading
- Calculus
- Chemistry
- College Preparatory
- Composition
- Computer Science
- Drafting
- Electricity & Electronics
- English
- Geometry
- Mathematics
- Physics
- Science
- Statistics
- Trigonometry

Famous First

Orville and Wilbur Wright flew the first airplane at Kitty Hawk, NC, in December, 1903. "The Flyer" was designed to reach 23 MPH.

College/Postsecondary

All aerospace engineers must have at least a bachelor's degree in engineering. Most obtain a master's degree or a doctorate in engineering, mathematics, or natural sciences. Some universities and colleges offer two- and four-year degrees in engineering technology. These programs give students direct exposure to applied engineering, which is useful for future design and production work.

Related College Majors
- Aerospace, Aeronautical & Astronautical Engineering
- Drafting, General
- Engineering Design
- Mechanical Drafting

Adult Job Seekers

Qualified aerospace engineers may apply directly to aerospace companies, such as aircraft manufacturers and commercial airlines, or on government agencies, such as NASA. In many cases, applicants to government positions must pass a civil service examination. Many other candidates apply to universities, consulting firms, and research and design companies. Professional associations, such as the Aerospace Industries Association and the American Institute of Aeronautics and Astronautics, provide networking opportunities.

Professional Certification and Licensure

All aerospace engineers are required to pass examinations and register as Professional Engineers (PE). The National Society of Professional Engineers (NSPE) works to establish consistent professional and ethical standards throughout the states. If an aerospace engineer is the lead engineer on a project, he or she must pass additional examinations in the state where the work is conducted.

Additional Requirements

Aerospace engineers must have strong analytical and research skills, with an exceptional ability to understand and solve complex problems. They should be experienced with computer systems and design software. Aerospace engineers must have an eye for detail and scientific and mathematical approach to solving issues. Finally, they must have strong communications skills to coordinate with other professionals and customers.

Fun Fact

The University of Michigan is home to the U.S.'s oldest collegiate aeronautics program, which started in 1914—11 years after the Wright Brothers' first flight at Kitty Hawk, NC.

Source: www.engin.umich.edu/aero/about/facts; www.wright-house.com/wright-brothers/wrights/1903.html

EARNINGS AND ADVANCEMENT

Earnings depend on the individual's education, experience, field of specialization and job duties. According to a salary survey by the National Association of Colleges and Employers, the average starting salary offer to college graduates with a bachelor's degree in aerospace engineering was $61,532 in 2012. Those with a master's degree were offered $70,299, and those with a Ph.D. were offered $83,078. Mean annual earnings of aerospace engineers were $107,700 in 2014. The lowest ten percent earned less than $66,110, and the highest ten percent earned more than $155,240.

Aerospace engineers may receive paid vacations, holidays, and sick days; life and health insurance; and retirement benefits. These are usually paid by the employer.

Metropolitan Areas with the Highest
Employment Level in this Occupation

Metropolitan area	Employment [1]	Employment per thousand jobs	Annual mean wage
Seattle-Bellevue-Everett, WA	8,400	5.63	N/A
Los Angeles-Long Beach-Glendale, CA	4,440	1.09	$122,920
Huntsville, AL	3,040	14.57	$108,800
Washington-Arlington-Alexandria, DC-VA-MD-WV	2,850	1.20	$136,420
Wichita, KS	2,680	9.22	$98,150
Houston-Sugar Land-Baytown, TX	2,510	0.88	$114,850
Fort Worth-Arlington, TX	1,940	2.09	$113,850
Cincinnati-Middletown, OH-KY-IN	1,840	1.82	N/A
Santa Ana-Anaheim-Irvine, CA	1,560	1.05	$112,950
San Diego-Carlsbad-San Marcos, CA	1,550	1.17	$103,570

[1]Does not include self-employed. Source: Bureau of Labor Statistics

EMPLOYMENT AND OUTLOOK

There were approximately 89,000 aerospace engineers employed
nationally in 2012. Employment of aerospace engineers is expected
to grow slower than the average for all occupations through the year
2022, which means employment is projected to increase 3 percent to 9
percent. New designs and new technologies involved in the creation of
commercial and military aircraft will encourage demand for aerospace
engineers.

Employment Trend, Projected 2012–22

Total, All Occupations: 11%

Engineers (all): 9%

Aerospace engineers: 7%

Note: "All Occupations" includes all occupations in the U.S. Economy. Source: U.S. Bureau of Labor
Statistics, Employment Projections Program

Related Occupations
- Electrical & Electronics Engineer
- Mechanical Engineer

Related Military Occupations
- Aerospace Engineer
- Space Operations Officer

Conversation With . . .
JOHN ROSE

Chief of Staff, Boeing Defense Space and Security
Huntington Beach, CA
Aerospace Engineer, 17 years

1. What was your individual career path in terms of education/training, entry-level job, or other significant opportunity?

I've always loved aviation and spaceflight, and originally wanted to be an astronaut. By high school, I knew I wanted to be an aerospace engineer and took AP courses in chemistry and physics. My physics class got to visit the Space Academy in Huntsville, Alabama, which was my second visit there.

I got my B.S. in aerospace from Cal Poly Pomona. In college, I worked part-time on the attractions in the Disneyland Resort and spent a summer interning with Disney's Ride & Show Engineering, Inc., where I later spent two years of my career. I also did two other internships.

As graduation approached, Rockwell International, the builder of the Space Shuttle, asked me to interview. I was thrilled, since working on the Space Shuttle was THE job I wanted. So, my first full-time job in the aerospace industry was in a group supporting the Space Shuttle and International Space Station.

A benefit of working for a large company like Rockwell (which became Boeing) is that they may pay for your advanced degrees. I got my M.S. in aerospace, also from Cal Poly Pomona, and my M.B.A. from the University of Southern California.

I've always leveraged the opportunities at Boeing. In my current role, in the Office of the Vice President of Engineering, Mission Assurance and Product Support, I'm working with top leadership to develop global strategy on our defense side.

2. What are the most important skills and/or qualities for someone in your profession?

Aerospace, particularly defense, can be cyclical, so you need to be adaptable. Contracts come and go, sometimes without much notice. Also, new graduates need to recognize that the way something is done in industry may not be how they learned it in class. Inquisitiveness and passion are also important. In addition, the aerospace industry is typically risk averse, so experience is a highly valued commodity. This means younger engineers must be patient; there isn't always a lot of support for putting untested or inexperienced individuals in a critical role.

3. What do you wish you had known going into this profession?

Aerospace products are a prime target for cybersecurity threats and must be protected from being taken offline or taken control of. Had I known cybersecurity would develop into such an important area, I would have taken related coursework.

Also, I had to learn that it's easy to slip through the cracks at a large company and that it isn't a bad thing to ask about opportunities if they aren't presenting themselves.

4. Are there many job opportunities in your profession? In what specific areas?

Companies like Boeing or Lockheed Martin offer jobs in a wide variety of areas, including business development, finance, software development, manufacturing, structural design, systems engineering and computer science.

Unmanned Aerial Vehicles (UAVs) are fueling a major evolution. Pilotless vehicles can remove human physiological limitations on what a vehicle can do (for example, making sharper turns or diving deeper) as well as spare humans from some dangerous missions. UAVs are adding a new commercial aspect to the industry because they can be made by smaller companies.

5. How do you see your profession changing in the next five years, what role will technology play in those changes, and what skills will be required?

The fact that most products will be tied to the Internet will change how we design and build them, as well as how we approach vulnerabilities relative to such systems as flight controls. Air traffic management is becoming satellite-based, and that's a quickly evolving area of cybersecurity where we need to respond to threats.

Additive manufacturing, or 3D printing, is revolutionizing how things are built. Small, portable machines are building pieces used in rocket engines. The concept is also being used on the International Space Station where a 3D CADD model for a specific part or tool can be designed on earth, emailed up to the ISS, and 'printed' out.

Immersive development—which is kind of a virtual reality that allows us to try out a repair procedure or do a virtual walkaround of a product without the time and expense of travel—will be a bigger part of the design of and customer support for products.

Systems thinking—being able to conceptualize all of the moving pieces and influencers, versus focusing on one piece—will be valuable.

6. What do you enjoy most about your job? What do you enjoy least about your job?

I really love the amazing products that our industry produces. I love going to an airshow with my son and seeing them. I also love that many of our products support our armed forces. And I have amazing opportunities to work on projects in different parts of the United States and the world.

But I also have to deal with non-technical, administrative issues like coordinating meetings that are necessary but not exciting. Another downside is the cyclical nature of being tied to defense and space budgets.

7. Can you suggest a valuable "try this" for students considering a career in your profession?

Try to find an internship. Also, get to an airshow—seeing all the products and watching them fly is great exposure to the amazing things we build.

SELECTED SCHOOLS

Most colleges and universities offer programs in engineering; a variety of them also have concentrations in aeronautical engineering. Some of the more prominent schools in this field are listed below.

California Institute of Technology
1200 East California Boulevard
Pasadena CA, 91125
Phone: (626) 395-6811
http://www.caltech.edu

Georgia Institute of Technology
225 North Avenue NW
Atlanta, GA 30332
Phone: (404) 894-2000
www.gatech.edu

Massachusetts Institute of Technology
77 Massachusetts Avenue
Cambridge, MA 02139
Phone: (617) 253-1000
http://web.mit.edu

Purdue University, West Lafayette
Schleman Hall, 475 Stadium Mall Drive
West Lafayette, IN 47907-2050
Phone: (765) 494-4600
http://www.purdue.edu

Stanford University
450 Serra Mall
Stanford, CA 94305
Phone: (650) 723-2300
https://www.stanford.edu

Texas A&M University
Jack K. Williams Bldg.
College Station, TX 77843
Phone: (979) 845-7541
http://engineering.tamu/aerospace

University of Colorado
422 UCB
Boulder, CO 80309
Phone: (303) 735-4900
www.colorado.edu

University of Illinois, Urbana, Champaign
601 East John Street
Champaign, IL 61820
Phone: 217 333-1000
http://illinois.edu

University of Michigan, Ann Arbor
500 S. State St.
Ann Arbor, MI 48109
Phone: (734) 764-1817
https://www.umich.edu

University of Texas, Austin
Austin, Texas 78712-1111
Phone: (512) 471-3434
http://www.utexas.edu

MORE INFORMATION

Aerospace Industries Association
1000 Wilson Boulevard, Suite 1700
Arlington, VA 22209
703.358.1000
www.aia-aerospace.org

**American Institute of Aeronautics
and Astronautics**
1801 Alexander Bell Drive
Suite 500
Reston, VA 20191-4344
800.639.2422
www.aiaa.org

**National Aeronautics Space
Agency (NASA)**
Suite 5K39
Washington, DC 20546-0001
202.358.0001
www.nasa.gov

SAE International
400 Commonwealth Drive
Warrendale, PA 15096-0001
724.776.4841
www.sae.org

Michael Auerbach/Editor

Agricultural and Food Scientist

Snapshot

Career Cluster: Agriculture; Science, Technology, Engineering & Mathematics

Interests: Agricultural Science, Agronomy, Environmental Science, Biology, Chemistry, Research, Food Science

Earnings (Yearly Average): $66,870

Employment & Outlook: Average Growth Expected

OVERVIEW

Sphere of Work

Agricultural and food scientists study crops, farm animals, and other elements of agriculture and food production to ensure the highest possible degree of productivity and safety. They research ways to maximize crop yields, reduce pest infestations and weed growth, and use resources such as soil and water in an efficient manner. Many of these scientists also study the impacts of agriculture on the natural environment and work towards a better balance between environmental sustainability and production. Others ensure that food is safe and nutritious.

Many agricultural and food scientists are involved in the research and development activities of private agricultural businesses, while others provide consulting services, manage farms, conduct research at educational institutions, or work for government agencies.

Work Environment

Agricultural and food scientists spend a great deal of time in office environments found in private consulting firms, business corporations, agricultural research stations, or government agencies. These settings are clean, well lit, and pleasant. Some scientists also work in laboratory environments, conducting experiments on samples and analyzing data. Agricultural scientists also spend a significant amount of time outdoors to conduct experiments and take samples, measure volumes, and perform other research activities. Some scientists visit dairies or feed lots when examining livestock. When conducting research, agricultural and food scientists may travel into distant farm areas and work in many different types of weather conditions.

Profile

Working Conditions: Work both Indoors and Outdoors
Physical Strength: Light Work
Education Needs: Bachelor's Degree, Master's Degree, Doctoral Degree
Licensure/Certification: Recommended
Opportunities For Experience: Internship, Military Service, Part-time Work
Holland Interest Score*: IRS

* See Appendix A

Occupation Interest

Agricultural and food scientists fulfill a very important role because they help keep agricultural products safe, processing operations efficient, food products pure, and output at maximum sustainable levels. They are also invaluable to the protection of the environment, working to ensure that farms do not pollute the soil or nearby water resources. Agricultural and food scientists should enjoy research and spending time outdoors and around animals. They should find satisfaction in using their knowledge and skills to help people throughout the world access safe and affordable food.

A Day in the Life—Duties and Responsibilities

The daily responsibilities and duties of agricultural and food scientists vary significantly based on their area of expertise and employer. For example, soil scientists primarily analyze the ground in which crops are grown, while biotechnology specialists study ways to increase crop yields. Government agencies may focus on food safety or sustainable development, while private companies tend to concentrate on maximizing profit yields from agricultural business.

In general, agricultural and food scientists work with commercial agricultural firms, government agencies, small farmers, and food manufacturers, performing in-depth research, collecting samples, and providing technical data and advice for clients. They offer public policy guidance for political leaders, sharing information on ways to produce food, safeguard the environment, and ensure long-term soil fertility and water-use sustainability. Agricultural and food scientists collect water, soil, plant, and animal samples, diagnose diseases and nutrient problems among animals and crops, assess the severity of insect infestations, track breeding trends, monitor weed growth, and examine the effectiveness of new farming techniques and food production technologies. Many agricultural and food scientists conduct controlled experiments in laboratories, trying to generate increased crop growth or healthier foods.

Senior agricultural and food scientists train technicians, research assistants, and other members of their teams. They also perform important administrative tasks, such as completing grant applications and editing research papers.

Duties and Responsibilities

- Studying crop production to discover the best methods of planting and harvesting, and studying the food stream for safety and availability of products
- Determining feed requirements of animals and the human use of foods
- Controlling breeding practices to improve strains of animals
- Managing marketing or production operations in companies that produce food products or agricultural supplies and machinery

OCCUPATION SPECIALTIES

Agronomists

Agronomists study how field crops such as corn, wheat and cotton grow. They improve their quality and yield by developing new growth methods and by controlling diseases, pests and weeds.

Animal Scientists

Animal Scientists conduct research on the selection, breeding, feeding, management and health of domestic farm animals.

Dairy Scientists

Dairy Scientists, along with Poultry Scientists, conduct research on the selection, breeding, feeding and management of dairy cattle and poultry.

Food Scientists and Technologists

Food Scientists and Technologists study the food stream and the chemical, physical and biological nature of food to learn how to safely process, preserve, package, distribute and store it.

WORK ENVIRONMENT

Physical Environment

Agricultural and food scientists spend much of their time working in well-organized office environments, but they also must work outdoors on a regular basis at animal or crop farms.

Human Environment

Depending on their areas of specialty, agricultural and food scientists interact and collaborate with a wide range of individuals, including government officials, technologists and technicians,

farmers, environmental scientists, business executives, and food
manufacturers.

Relevant Skills and Abilities

Communication Skills
- Speaking effectively
- Writing concisely

Interpersonal/Social Skills
- Being able to work independently
- Working as a member of a team

Organization & Management Skills
- Paying attention to and handling details

Research & Planning Skills
- Solving problems

Technical Skills
- Performing scientific, mathematical and technical work

Work Environment Skills
- Working in a laboratory setting
- Working outdoors

Technological Environment

Agricultural and food scientists work with a wide array of technologies in the field, in the laboratory, and at the office. They use spectrometers and photometers to break down soil and other natural agricultural materials. They examine bacteria and other potential toxins in food. Soil scoops, water containers, and other sampling equipment are frequently used as well. In the office, agricultural and food scientists use a wide range of databases, scientific and analytical software systems, and general business software, which is used to prepare technical reports and public policy proposals.

EDUCATION, TRAINING, AND ADVANCEMENT

High School/Secondary

High school students should study biology, physics, chemistry, and other natural sciences. Algebra and applied mathematics are extremely useful as well. High school students should take computer science courses and hone their writing and public speaking skills through English and communications classes. Finally, courses that help students understand agricultural and food systems, such as farm equipment, seeding practices, and food production are extremely important. Part-time, seasonal, and internship employment opportunities doing farm work or food research are excellent ways to become familiar with this type of work. Interested high school students may also want to pursue supplemental educational programs or opportunities at their state's land-grant colleges.

Suggested High School Subjects
- Agricultural Education
- Agricultural Mechanization
- Algebra
- Applied Biology/Chemistry
- Applied Math
- Biology
- Chemistry
- College Preparatory
- English
- Forestry
- Landscaping
- Physics

Famous First

The first farm set up for experimentation was established near Savannah, Georgia, in 1735. An experienced botanist was assigned by the town "to collect the seeds of drugs and dying-stuffs in other countries in the same climate, in order to cultivate such of them as shall be found to thrive well in Georgia."

College/Postsecondary

Agricultural and food scientists who plan to work in product development need at least a bachelor's degree in agricultural science or a similar field. Those who wish to secure research or teaching positions must have a master's degree or a doctorate. They may also possess a master's degree or doctorate in biology, physics, engineering, or another field relevant to their area of expertise.

Related College Majors
- Agriculture/Agricultural Sciences, General
- Agronomy & Crop Science
- Animal Sciences, General
- Dairy Science
- Entomology
- Food Sciences & Technology
- Foods & Nutrition Science
- Foods & Nutrition Studies, General
- Horticulture Science
- International Agriculture
- Plant Sciences, General
- Poultry Science
- Soil Sciences
- Zoology, General

Adult Job Seekers

Qualified agricultural and food scientists may apply directly to government agencies, businesses, or educational institutions with open positions. They may also join and network through a professional organization, such as the American Society of Agronomy or the Soil Science Society of America.

Professional Certification and Licensure

Many states require that soil scientists to be licensed. Licensure typically involves obtaining an undergraduate degree, gaining supervised experience in the field, and passing a written exam. Although professional certification as crop advisors or agronomists may not be required, such certifications may enhance a candidate's credentials. The American Society for Agronomy offers certification for agronomists and crop advisors. The National Association of Animal Breeders offers voluntary certification in that field, as does the Institute of Food Technologists. Certifications usually require a combination of education and work experience.

Additional Requirements

Agricultural and food scientists must demonstrate exceptional communications skills as well as research and analytical capabilities. Strong knowledge of computer software is also very useful to these scientists. They should enjoy the outdoors, be comfortable working in close proximity to livestock and other animals, and be able to work under varying conditions.

EARNINGS AND ADVANCEMENT

Earnings and Advancement of agricultural and food scientists depend upon such factors as education, professional experience, individual ability and type of employment. According to a salary survey by the National Association of Colleges and Employers, average annual starting salaries for agricultural and food scientists with a bachelor's degree in agricultural science were $37,916 in 2012. Those with a bachelor's degree in animal science earned $36,860, and those with a bachelor's degree in plant science earned $36,559.

Mean annual earnings of agricultural scientists were $66,870 in 2014. The lowest ten percent earned less than $35,150, and the highest ten percent earned more than $107,810. Agricultural and food scientists may receive paid vacations, holidays, and sick days; life and health insurance; and retirement benefits. These are usually paid by the employer.

States with the Highest Employment Level in this Occupation

State	Employment [1]	Employment per thousand jobs	Annual mean wage
California	2,110	0.14	$65,100
Minnesota	2,020	0.74	$76,680
Texas	900	0.08	$71,600
New Jersey	660	0.17	$72,020
Wisconsin	630	0.23	$68,560

[1]Does not include self-employed. Source: Bureau of Labor Statistics

EMPLOYMENT AND OUTLOOK

There were approximately 38,500 agricultural and food scientists employed nationally in 2012. In addition, several thousand persons held agricultural science faculty positions in colleges and universities around the nation. Employment is expected to grow about as fast as the average for all occupations through the year 2022, which means employment is projected to increase 6 percent to 12 percent. Agricultural and food scientists with a background in biotechnology, food science and technology and agronomy will have the best opportunities.

Employment Trend, Projected 2012–22

Food scientists and technologists: 11%

Total, all occupations: 11%

Agricultural and food scientists: 9%

Animal scientists: 9%

Soil and plant scientists: 8%

Note: "All Occupations" includes all occupations in the U.S. Economy. Source: U.S. Bureau of Labor Statistics, Employment Projections Program

Related Occupations
- Agricultural Engineer
- Biological Scientist
- Biomedical Engineer
- Botanist
- Farm & Home Management Advisor
- Fish & Game Warden
- Forester & Conservation Scientist
- Range Manager
- Science Technician
- Soil Scientist

Related Military Occupations
- Environmental Health & Safety Officer
- Life Scientist

Conversation With . . .
HILLARY MEHL, Ph.D.

Assistant Professor, Plant Pathology
Virginia Tech Tidewater
Agricultural Research & Extension Center
Plant Pathologist, 14 years

1. **What was your individual career path in terms of education/training, entry-level job, or other significant opportunity?**

From a young age, I was fascinated with all aspects of biology; my family would go hiking and camping and collect plants and insects and try to identify them. I majored in botany at Humboldt State University, then went straight into a Ph.D. program at the University of California Davis. I studied plant pathology, which combined my interests of plants, microbiology and fungal biology, and seeks practical ways to manage plant diseases and increase crop yields and quality. As a graduate student, I spent plenty of time in the lab, but I also interacted with growers to identify problems in their crops and conducted field research in grower's fields.

My post-doc was with the U.S. Department of Agriculture in a lab located at the University of Arizona, where I researched biological control of aflatoxin, a toxin produced by a fungus that contaminates food and feed crops. My job here at Virginia Tech is a combination of research and working through the extension service to present the knowledge we gain from research to growers and consultants so they can use it in practice, often through our publications or crop meetings. I'm working on field crops such as peanuts, cotton, soybeans, small grains and corn, and looking at disease management approaches that combine the use of disease resistant crops, chemical control, and different cropping practices that can help minimize disease. I'm trying to understand the biology of specific fungal pathogens so we can better understand what they are, what they're doing to plants, and how we can better control them. For example, we're finding strains of frogeye leaf spot of soybean that are resistant to certain fungicides and are trying to find alternative ways to control the disease.

2. **What are the most important skills and/or qualities for someone in your profession?**

Plant pathology aims to solve real-world problems, so a plant pathologist needs to listen to the needs and concerns of growers and effectively communicate solutions, both verbally and in writing. In addition, analytical skills and curiosity are important to analyze data, make careful observations, and ask good questions.

A plant pathologist who does what I do needs to enjoy being outdoors, working in different weather extremes, and traveling to locations with different field conditions.

3. What do you wish you had known going into this profession?

I feel lucky that I got to do what I wanted to do, but there are only so many jobs in academia. It would be beneficial to be aware of other opportunities as an undergraduate so that scientists can train accordingly, rather than go through a doctoral program—where the emphasis is on academic jobs—and find themselves without necessary skills for industry. Knowing this would have given me additional perspective into the field of plant pathology.

4. Are there many job opportunities in your profession? In what specific areas?

A variety of job opportunities are available in academia, industry, and government. In academia, positions include teaching, research, and extension services, and typically require either an M.S. degree (e.g. extension agents, research technicians) or a Ph.D. (researcher, professor, extension specialist). Industry jobs can be in small companies or big corporations, and can range from work as a private consultant who advises growers to a technical representative or researcher working for a chemical or seed company. Federal and state positions may include working for a regulatory agency or conducting research in a government lab.

5. How do you see your profession changing in the next five years, what role will technology play in those changes, and what skills will be required?

As food safety and security become an increasingly global issue, the need for agricultural scientists, including plant pathologists, will increase, but the focus of the work will be more international. Thus, the ability to communicate with and transfer technologies to other countries, especially those in the developing world, will be increasingly important.

6. What do you enjoy most about your job? What do you enjoy least about your job?

I most enjoy solving problems through careful observation, experiments, and analyses, as well as coming up with solutions to growers' problems and helping to improve plant disease management. I least enjoy the times I am unable to come up with solutions—at least not right away—but in the end, these challenges keep the job interesting.

7. Can you suggest a valuable "try this" for students considering a career in your profession?

High school students can look for opportunities at agricultural extension services, which are usually run by states. Undergraduate students at research universities should be able to find ample opportunities to work in a lab or assist with field work. Private industry offers internships. You could also get experience helping out on a farm for the summer.

Fun Fact

On average, every hour of every day about $6 million in US agricultural products are consigned for shipment for export to foreign markets.

Source: www.cals.ncsu.edu/CollegeRelations/AGRICU.htm

SELECTED SCHOOLS

Many colleges and universities offer programs in agricultural science; a variety of them also have concentrations in food science. Some of the more prominent schools in this field are listed below.

Cornell University
Ithaca, New York 14850
Phone: (607) 254-4636
www.cornell.edu

Harvard University
Cambridge, Massachusetts 02138
Phone: (617) 495-1000
www.harvard.edu

Rutgers State University
96 Davidson Road
Piscataway Township, NJ 08854
Phone: (973) 353-1766
www.rtgers.edu

Tufts University
Medford, Massachusetts 02155
Phone: (617) 628-5000
www.tufts.edu

University of California, Davis
1 Shields Avenue
Davis, California 95616
Phone: (530) 752-1011
www.ucdavis.edu

University of Florida
201 Criser Hall
Gainesville, Florida 32611
Phone: (352) 392-3261
www.ufl.edu

University of Illinois, Urbana, Champaign
601 East. John Street
Champaign, Illinois 61820-5711
Phone: (217) 333-1000
www.illinois.edu

University of Massachusetts, Amherst
Amherst, MA 01002-01003
Phone: (413) 545-0111
www.umass.edu

University of Minnesota, Twin Cities
100 Church Street SE
Minneapolis, Minnesota 55455-0213
Phone: (612) 625-5000
www.umn.edu

University of Wisconsin, Madison
500 Lincoln Drive
Madison, Wisconsin 53708
Phone: (608) 263-2400
www.wisc.edu

MORE INFORMATION

**American Society for
Horticultural Science**
1018 Duke Street
Alexandria, VA 22314-2851
703.836.4606
www.ashs.org

American Society of Agronomy
Career Development & Placement
Services
5585 Guilford Road
Madison, WI 53711
608.273.8080
www.agronomy.org

**Council for Agricultural Science
and Technology**
4420 W. Lincoln Way
Ames, IA 50014-3447
515.292.2125
www.cast-science.org

Food and Drug Administration
10903 New Hampshire Avenue
Silver Springs, MD 20993
888.463.6332
www.fda.gov

**Institute of Food and Agricultural
Sciences**
P.O. Box 110180
Gainesville, FL 32611-0180
352.392.1971
www.ifas.ufl.edu

Institute of Food Technologists
525 W. Van Buren, Suite 1000
Chicago, IL 60607
312.782.8348
www.ift.org

**Soil and Water Conservation
Society**
945 SW Ankeny Road
Ankeny, IA 50021
515.289.2331
www.swcs.org

U.S. Department of Agriculture
Natural Resources Conservation
Service
14th and Independence Avenue SW
Washington, DC 20250
202.720.3210
www.nrcs.usda.gov

Agricultural Engineer

Snapshot

Career Cluster: Agriculture; Science, Technology, Engineering & Mathematics

Interests: Plant biology, mechanical engineering, environmental studies, chemistry, agricultural science

Earnings (Yearly Average): $75,440

Employment & Outlook: Slower Than Average Growth Expected

OVERVIEW

Sphere of Work

Agricultural engineers work to improve the efficiency and efficacy of agricultural practice through scientific innovations in areas such as machinery, crop production, and power systems. Since many agricultural engineers specialize in different areas, they often work with other agricultural engineers to devise solutions to specific problems facing the community. Work Environment Agricultural engineers work in a variety of environments, depending on their specialization. Some may do biological research in laboratories, while others may

work in offices to improve methods of produce transportation or design heavy machinery, oversee processes in a plant or factory, or test new developments in the field.

Profile

Working Conditions: Work both Indoors and Outdoors
Physical Strength: Light Work
Education Needs: Bachelor's Degree, Master's Degree, Doctoral Degree
Licensure/Certification: Required
Opportunities For Experience: Internship, Apprenticeship, Volunteer Work, Part-Time Work
Holland Interest Score*: IRE

* See Appendix A

Occupation Interest

Agricultural engineering is an ideal job for somebody with an interest in both science and agricultural production. The diversity of available jobs allows agricultural engineers to pursue very specialized areas of interest, meaning that someone with a preference for mechanical engineering could work on heavy machinery, while someone interested in plant biology could work toward improving the health of crops and soil.

A Day in the Life—Duties and Responsibilities

Agricultural engineers working on mechanical issues spend much of their time designing and testing heavy-duty machinery in order to improve overall efficiency. They might work for a company such as John Deere, building large machines for agricultural uses such as threshing and plowing. Other agricultural engineers might be more appropriately called biological engineers, since they use their knowledge of plant and animal biology to develop better methods of maintaining healthy livestock and crops, and might also work to improve crop yields or find alternative uses for agricultural waste products.

Alternatively, they may work in a related capacity, conducting research and working on sales or marketing issues for a company whose focus is agricultural engineering. The field of agricultural engineering is ultimately a collaborative one, with engineers often working together to create solutions that will be enacted by farmers and laborers whom they will never meet.

Duties and Responsibilities

- Designing machinery, equipment and systems to perform agricultural tasks better, faster and more economically
- Designing, developing and testing agricultural structures and controlled environments for plants and animals
- Designing and using special equipment to study particular problems, such as the effects of temperature, humidity and light on plants or animals
- Designing waste management programs for rural areas

OCCUPATION SPECIALTIES

Agricultural-Research Engineers

Agricultural-Research Engineers conduct research to develop agricultural machinery and equipment.

Agricultural Equipment Engineers

Agricultural Equipment Engineers design and test agricultural machinery and equipment.

Agricultural Engineering Technicians

Agricultural Engineering Technicians, who usually work under an agricultural engineer or other senior staff person, prepare the original layouts and complete detailed drawings of agricultural machinery and equipment, such as farm machinery, irrigation, power and electrification systems, soil and water conservation equipment and agricultural harvesting and processing equipment.

WORK ENVIRONMENT

Physical Environment

Agricultural engineers work in a variety of physical settings depending on their specialization. Laboratory and office settings are most common, although some outdoor work may be required as well.

Relevant Skills and Abilities

Communication Skills
- Speaking effectively
- Writing concisely

Organization & Management Skills
- Making decisions
- Paying attention to and handling details
- Performing duties which change frequently

Research & Planning Skills
- Creating ideas
- Developing evaluation strategies
- Using logical reasoning

Technical Skills
- Performing scientific, mathematical and technical work
- Working with machines, tools or other objects

Human Environment

Due to the variety of specializations within the field, agricultural engineers can expect to work collaboratively with other engineers. They also interact with coworkers, supervisors, and, occasionally, the agricultural professionals who will benefit from their work.

Technological Environment

Agricultural engineers who specialize in power and design often work with large machinery and heavy equipment. Others may do more work in laboratories or offices, using computer-aided design (CAD) software, office suites, and graphics imaging programs.

EDUCATION, TRAINING, AND ADVANCEMENT

High School/Secondary

Aspiring agricultural engineers should take mathematics classes such as algebra, geometry, calculus, and statistics, and science classes such as physics, biology, and chemistry. They should also try to gain some experience working in the agricultural industry in whatever subfield of agricultural engineering interests them, such as mechanical engineering or plant biology. Even working as a laborer on a farm could be helpful and informative.

Suggested High School Subjects
- Agricultural Education
- Agricultural Mechanization
- Applied Communication
- Applied Math
- Applied Physics
- Blueprint Reading
- College Preparatory
- Computer Science
- Drafting
- English
- Mechanical Drawing

Famous First

The first state agricultural experimental station was established in Connecticut in 1875. Orange Judd, owner and editor of *American Agriculturalist* magazine, supplied $1,000, Wesleyan University provided the use of its chemical laboratory, and the state legislature appropriated $2,800 per year for two years. The program's goal was to research difficulties and improvements in food production.

College/Postsecondary

College students interested in becoming agricultural engineers should expect to major in agricultural or biological engineering, which will entail courses in environmental sciences, biology, mathematics, and mechanical engineering. While in college, students should pursue internships in one or more professions where their degree will be applicable. At this point, students should seek whatever job experience they can find, even if it does not directly relate to what they hope to pursue, since the nature of agricultural engineering involves the work of a large number of people who make the agriculture industry run smoothly on a variety of levels.

Related College Majors
- Agricultural Mechanization, General
- Agricultural Engineering
- Engineering, General

Adult Job Seekers

Adults seeking jobs in agricultural engineering should have some experience in their prospective field, as an intern or otherwise. Due to the scientific nature of mechanical and biological engineering, jobs in these fields will be difficult to obtain without a postsecondary degree in a relevant subject. Experience working in a laboratory in a different field may translate well into certain aspects of agricultural engineering.

Professional Certification and Licensure

Certification and licensure requirements vary by specialization and by state. Agricultural engineers working in areas related to civil engineering, such as irrigation or drainage systems, should be licensed as a Professional Engineer in their state, a process which usually entails four years of experience and two written exams. Those who work with livestock or with certain biological or chemical materials may need to acquire separate certification. Agricultural engineers should investigate the licensing requirements for their location that pertain to their particular interest.

Additional Requirements

Agricultural engineers should have naturally inquisitive minds and be interested in various aspects of farming. They should also be comfortable working in a laboratory setting.

EARNINGS AND ADVANCEMENT

Earnings depend on personal ability, education and experience, the type, size and location of the employer, and the duties and responsibilities of the position. Since many jobs are in rural communities where the cost of living tends to be lower, agricultural engineers generally receive lower salaries than other engineers. According the National Association of Colleges and Employers, the average annual salary offer to college graduates with a bachelor's degree in agricultural engineering was $59,392 in 2012. Master's degree candidates were offered an average annual salary of $63,258.

Mean annual earnings of agricultural engineers were $75,440 in 2014. The lowest ten percent earned less than $45,940, and the highest ten percent earned more than $112,700.

Agricultural engineers may receive paid vacations, holidays, and sick days; life and health insurance; and retirement benefits. These are usually paid by the employer.

States with the Highest Employment Level in this Occupation

State	Employment [1]	Employment per thousand jobs	Annual mean wage
Iowa	320	0.21	$78,620
California	250	0.02	$86,640
Florida	160	0.02	$49,610
Virginia	150	0.04	n/a
Georgia	140	0.03	$73,840

[1]Does not include self-employed. Source: Bureau of Labor Statistics

EMPLOYMENT AND OUTLOOK

There were approximately 2,600 agricultural engineers employed nationally in 2012. Employment is expected to grow slower than the average for all occupations through the year 2022, which means employment is projected to increase 3 percent to 7 percent. Demand for agricultural engineers will grow as the need for increased crop production to feed the world's population and to create renewable energy sources continues.

Employment Trend, Projected 2012–22

Total, all occupations: 11%

Engineers: 9%

Agricultural engineers: 5%

Note: "All Occupations" includes all occupations in the U.S. Economy. Source: U.S. Bureau of Labor Statistics, Employment Projections Program

Related Occupations
- Agricultural Scientist
- Biomedical Engineer
- Botanist
- Chemical Engineer
- Environmental Engineer
- Environmental Science Technician
- Farm & Home Management Advisor
- Forester & Conservation Scientist
- Medical Scientist
- Water & Wastewater Engineer
- Wind Energy Engineer

SELECTED SCHOOLS

A variety of colleges and universities offer programs in agricultural engineering. Some of the more prominent schools in this field are listed below.

Iowa State University
100 Enrollment Services Center
Ames, IA 50011
Phone: (800) 262-3810
https://www.iastate.edu/

North Carolina State University, Raleigh
Box 7001
Raleigh, NC 27695
Phone: (919) 515-2011
https://www.ncsu.edu/

Ohio State University, Columbus
154 W. 12th Avenue
Columbus, OH 43210
Phone: (614) 292-6446
https://www.osu.edu/

Purdue University, West Lafayette
Schleman Hall 475
Stadium Mall Drive
West Lafayette, IN 47907-2050
Phone: (765) 494-4600
http://www.purdue.edu/

Texas A&M University, College Station
401 Joe Routt Boulevard
College Station, TX 77843
Phone: (979) 845-3211
https://www.tamu.edu/

University of California, Davis
1 Shields Avenue
Davis CA 95616
Phone: (530) 752-1011
http://ucdavis.edu/

University of Nebraska, Lincoln
14th and R Streets
Lincoln, NE 68588
Phone: (402) 472-7211
http://www.unl.edu/

University of Florida
201 Criser Hall
Gainesville, FL 32611
Phone: (352) 392-3261
http://www.ufl.edu/

University of Illinois, Urbana, Champaign
601 E. John Street
Champaign, IL 61820-5711
Phone: (217) 333-1000
http://illinois.edu/

Virginia Tech
Blacksburg, VA 24061
Phone: (549) 231-6000
https://www.vt.edu/

MORE INFORMATION

American Society for Engineering Education
1818 N Street NW, Suite 600
Washington, DC 20036
202.331.3500
www.asee.org

American Society of Agricultural & Biological Engineers
2950 Niles Road
St. Joseph, MI 49085
269.429.0300
www.asabe.org

National Action Council for Minorities in Engineering
440 Hamilton Avenue, Suite 302
White Plains, NY 10601-1813
914.539.4010
www.nacme.org

National Society of Black Engineers
205 Daingerfield Road
Alexandria, VA 22314
703.549.2207
www.nsbe.org

National Society of Professional Engineers
1420 King Street
Alexandria, VA 22314
703.684.2800
www.nspe.org

Society of Hispanic Professional Engineers
13181 Crossroads Parkway North, Suite 450
City of Industry, CA 91746-3497
323.725.3970
www.shpe.org

Society of Women Engineers
203 N. La Salle Street, Suite 1675
Chicago, IL 60601
877.793.4636
www.swe.org

Technology Student Association
1914 Association Drive
Reston, VA 20191-1540
703.860.9000
www.tsaweb.org

Mark Boccard//Editor

Astronomer

Snapshot

Career Cluster: Science, Technology, Engineering & Mathematics
Interests: Mathematics, physics, chemistry, engineering, research, appreciation of the unknown
Earnings (Yearly Average): $107,140
Employment & Outlook: Average Growth Expected

OVERVIEW

Sphere of Work

An astronomer is a scientist who studies celestial objects such as planets, moons, stars, and entire galaxies. Astronomers also study natural space phenomena such as black holes, sunspots, and solar winds, as well as interstellar medium such as dust, gases, and cosmic rays. An astronomer conducts a great deal of research, using theoretical models and equipment such as telescopes and radio observatories. These professionals write and publish scholarly papers and present their findings at government agencies, within the academic community, and at scientific conferences.

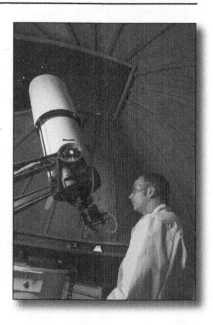

Work Environment

Astronomers generally work in two locations: in a laboratory setting or at a remote location with minimal light pollution. In a laboratory setting, an astronomer might use computer models and technologies to analyze data, formulate theories, and record their findings. At a dark sky location or observatory, typically in a remote location, an astronomer will study space-based objects and phenomena through telescopes and other technologies. At such remote observatories, it is common for astronomers to work long hours at night, when light pollution is at its lowest levels. Astronomers may also work in teams, collaborating on research studies.

Profile

Working Conditions: Work Indoors
Physical Strength: Light Work
Education Needs: Bachelor's Degree, Master's Degree, Doctoral Degree
Licensure/Certification: Usually Not Required
Opportunities For Experience: Military Service, Volunteer Work, Part-time Work
Holland Interest Score*: IRE

* See Appendix A

Occupation Interest

Individuals interested in pursuing astronomy must be highly capable in understanding and applying the principles of mathematics, physics, chemistry, and engineering. They must have strong analytical skills and demonstrate an ability to study and keep track of large amounts of complex information and data. Astronomers typically have advanced degrees beyond the undergraduate level, including both postgraduate and doctoral degrees. People who are interested in becoming astronomers must also possess a strong appreciation for the unexplained and unknown phenomena within the universe. Through persistence, such phenomena can begin to be explained—even if, sometimes, only in small steps.

A Day in the Life–Duties and Responsibilities

Much of the typical work day for an astronomer is spent in the laboratory conducting research and studying data. They may conduct experiments using particle accelerators, lasers, and radio systems in order to create models for and formulate theories on space phenomena. Using the concepts of mathematics and physics, astronomers will attempt to discover new objects, study cosmic forces, and further chart the universe. In addition to laboratory work, astronomers may also spend weeks or longer in remote locations, operating equipment such as large optical and radio telescopes to supplement their research. In addition to conducting experiments, collecting and compiling data, and formulating theories, astronomers must write scholarly papers on their findings and submit them to scientific journals, government agencies (such as NASA), and other scientific bodies or organizations. Astronomers must often present their findings and theories to their peers—and, to an extent, the general public—an activity that often occurs at universities, astronomy-oriented conferences, or within the organization at which the astronomer is employed. In light of this responsibility, an astronomer must be able to communicate clearly and demonstrate strong presentation skills.

Along with their research pursuits, many astronomers have more managerial and technical responsibilities. Some astronomers, for example, work in planetariums, where they are responsible for providing non-technical presentations on space to students and other visitors. Other astronomers must maintain research equipment, a responsibility which includes cleaning optical telescope lenses, calibrating radio dishes, and coordinating satellite-based technologies.

Duties and Responsibilities

- Developing theories, projects and ways to test them
- Testing theories through observation and analysis of results
- Developing conclusions based on test results
- Teaching classes in astronomy and/or physics
- Developing mathematical tables and charts for navigational and other purposes
- Designing new optical instruments for observation

WORK ENVIRONMENT

Physical Environment

Most of the work of the astronomer is performed at laboratories and observatories. In both of these settings, the environment must be clean and well-organized in order to prevent corruption of data and/or equipment malfunctions and facility accidents.

Relevant Skills and Abilities

Communication Skills
- Speaking effectively
- Writing concisely

Interpersonal/Social Skills
- Being able to work independently

Organization & Management Skills
- Making decisions
- Paying attention to and handling details

Research & Planning Skills
- Creating ideas

Technical Skills
- Performing scientific, mathematical and technical work
- Working with data or numbers

Plant Environment

Astronomers work in small, medium, and large laboratories, observatories, and similar facilities. These research facilities may be based in academia, such as at a research university or college, where astronomers are also responsible for bringing in grant money and teaching and supervising students, or at government-funded labs and national observatories. They also work in planetariums and museums.

Human Environment

Astronomers must work with a number of other team members, collaborating on research and operating equipment. Astronomers will work with fellow astronomers, engineers, physicists, and mathematicians. They will also work with other non-scientific personnel, such as facilities managers and directors. Furthermore, professional astronomers may be joined by interns, university students, and computer scientists. Astronomers employed as professors at research universities or teaching colleges must interact with the students they are teaching and advising.

Technological Environment

Astronomers use a wide range of technological equipment to aid them in their research and experiments. They will operate optical and radio telescopes, lasers, particle accelerators, and other large-scale equipment. Additionally, they will use computers to collect and compile data and to manage the collection of information from satellite-based technology located in orbit.

EDUCATION, TRAINING, AND ADVANCEMENT

High School/Secondary

High school students who wish to become astronomers can best prepare by studying mathematics through pre-calculus levels. Such math training helps lay the groundwork for the complex mathematics they will study in college. Additionally, high schoolers should take courses in chemistry and physics. Many students take physics and mathematics at the advanced placement (AP) level, although such training is not required. To further their early understanding of astronomy, students should also consider joining science-related groups at their school, participating in a state-sponsored junior academy of science, or simply contacting their local amateur astronomy club or organization. Lastly, students should also familiarize themselves with what they can see at night, be it constellations, planets, or any other object commonly seen in the nighttime sky.

Suggested High School Subjects
- Algebra
- Applied Math
- Applied Physics
- Calculus
- Chemistry
- Earth Science
- English
- Mathematics

- Physical Science
- Physics
- Science
- Trigonometry

Famous First

The first scientific program aimed at identifying advanced extraterrestrial life was SETI (Search for Extraterrestrial Intelligence) in 1960 at the National Radio Astronomy Observatory in Green Bank, W. Va. Intelligent life was found, and subsequent programs continued, culminating in 1992 in NASA's Microwave Observing Program, which was soon cancelled under Congressional mandate. In 1995 it was revived under the non-profit SETI Institute of Mountain View, Calif. Despite efforts by experienced astronomers, no signs of intelligent life were identified and the program was closed in 2004.

College/Postsecondary

Because astronomy is often considered a subfield of physics, students at the collegiate and postgraduate levels will study other subsets or branches within this field, including magnetism, atomic and nuclear physics, thermodynamics, statistical mechanics, and quantum physics and theory. College students should also continue to build on their mathematical skills, including courses in advanced algebra, calculus, and trigonometry. Additionally, the fact that twenty-first-century astronomy relies on computers for data collection and model building means that undergraduate college students must study computer science to help them explore new concepts in this field. As there are a number of applications for astronomy, some students may choose to study geology as well.

After the undergraduate level, students must pursue their master's degree and doctorate (PhD), although some astronomers will enter into professional practice after receiving their master's degree. In addition to the continuation of core courses in physics, astronomy, and astrophysics, much of the work at this level is research-oriented, and students must design and pursue their own individual projects under the supervision of faculty members

Related College Majors
- Astronomy
- Astrophysics
- Chemistry, General
- Earth & Planetary Sciences
- Physics, General

Adult Job Seekers

People become astronomers after many years of educational training. Provided that they have such backgrounds, adults seeking to enter this field may do so by collaborating with their peers. These fellow astronomers may recommend them to the faculties on which they work, or to the observatory or research facility for which they work. Professional associations such as the American Astronomical Society (AAS) and similar regional organizations often provide networking opportunities and grant resources.

Professional Certification and Licensure

Astronomers may not be required to receive professional certification beyond a Ph.D. and other postsecondary degrees. However, in order to operate and maintain some astronomical equipment, such as radio telescopes, some facilities require technical certification.

Additional Requirements

Astronomy requires the constant pursuit of knowledge related to the fundamentals of the universe. Astronomers must therefore be intellectually curious, willing to invest significant time to investigate often very difficult and elusive information, and should be open to accepting new theories in the fields of physics and astronomy. In addition to this exploratory mindset, astronomers must be patient, sometimes working long nights at a remote observatory or spending years trying to validate a theory. Science and mathematics, though, are the main tools for astronomers in this pursuit

Fun Fact

If you travel at the speed of light, you will still need more than four years to reach the Sun's nearest star.

Source: http://astro.cornell.edu/quotes/category

EARNINGS AND ADVANCEMENT

Advancement opportunities for astronomers can be limited because of the small size of this field. Professional positions with universities or the government probably offer the greatest number of opportunities for study and research. Education and experience provide the greatest advancement opportunities in observatories or private industry. Mean annual earnings of astronomers were $107,140 in 2014. The lowest ten percent earned less than $51,160, and the highest ten percent earned more than $162,630. Average annual earnings for astronomers employed by the federal government were $133,800 in 2014.

Astronomers may receive paid vacations, holidays, and sick days; life and health insurance; and retirement benefits. These are usually paid by the employer.

Metropolitan Areas with the Highest Employment Level in this Occupation

Metropolitan area	Employment	Employment per thousand jobs	Annual mean wage
Washington-Arlington-Alexandria, DC-VA-MD-WV	370	0.16	$122,510
Honolulu, HI	50	0.10	$145,780
Houston-Sugar Land-Baytown, TX	40	0.01	$122,120

Source: Bureau of Labor Statistics

EMPLOYMENT AND OUTLOOK

Astronomers held about 2,700 jobs nationally in 2012. Astronomers work for research, development, and testing laboratories. The federal government employs a large number of astronomers, mostly in the Department of Defense, but also in the National Aeronautics and Space Administration (NASA), the Department of Commerce, the Department of Health and Human Services, and the Department of Energy. Some work for aerospace firms, noncommercial research laboratories, electrical equipment manufacturers, engineering services firms, and the transportation equipment industry. In addition, astronomers held faculty positions in colleges and universities across the country.

Employment of astronomers is expected to grow about as fast as the average for all occupations through the year 2022, which means employment is projected to increase 8 percent to 12 percent. Federal funding for physical sciences is on the increase and will result in job opportunities for astronomers.

Employment Trend, Projected 2012–22

Total, all occupations: 11%

Physicists and astronomers: 10%

Astronomers: 10%

Note: "All Occupations" includes all occupations in the U.S. Economy. Source: U.S. Bureau of Labor Statistics, Employment Projections Program

Related Occupations
- College Faculty Member
- Meteorologist
- Physicist

Conversation With . . .
PATRICK BREYSSE

Ph.D. candidate, Johns Hopkins University
Dept. of Physics and Astronomy
Astronomer, 3 years

1. **What was your individual career path in terms of education/training, entry-level job, or other significant opportunity?**

Both of my parents are scientists; my mother in industrial hygiene and my father in environmental and public health. The summer after fifth grade, I read a book about black holes and decided I wanted to be an astrophysicist. I took a lot of physics in high school. I was a double major in physics and astronomy at Penn State. I have finished three years of graduate school at Johns Hopkins in Baltimore and will probably graduate with a Ph.D. In two more. From there, I'll apply for postdoctoral positions.

I do theory work, like Sheldon on "The Big Bang Theory." I stand in front of a blackboard and come up with equations, then tell the computer to figure it out. I am studying cosmology, which is studying the universe on its largest scale. I'm working on a way to study far-away galaxies by looking for galaxies that have a lot of carbon monoxide. These galaxies form a lot of stars, so you can look back in time to see how the stars evolve in time.

2. **What are the most important skills and/or qualities for someone in your profession?**

You need to know a lot of math and have reasonable programming knowledge. You need to know basic physics and be able to teach yourself the things you don't know. You also need to think creatively about problems and find ways to solve them that no one has thought of yet. You really need to love the work. Specifically, you have to love research, which can be really frustrating. Someone with a similar skill set can go into industry instead of academia and make a considerably higher salary. But, one of the nice things about doing a Ph.D. is that after a year or two as a student, you're getting paid to do science, the kind of work you want to do for the rest of your career.

3. **What do you wish you had known going into this profession?**

I wish I'd known more programming. It's becoming more and more important and I only took one basic programming class in college. I've done all right teaching myself, but it's not easy. I would have been better off with some advanced courses under my belt.

4. **Are there many job opportunities in your profession? In what specific areas?**

The standard career progression in astronomy academia looks something like this: Get a Ph.D. (five-ish years), do two postdocs (two or three years each), get an assistant professorship, then tenure. Unfortunately, getting a position at each successive level gets more difficult, so a small fraction of Ph.D.s end up as professors. The good news is that most Ph.D.'s can find jobs either in industry or in government, in labs such as those at NASA. Also, the math/programming/problem-solving skills that physics/astronomy Ph.D.'s give you translate to other areas. I've heard of astronomy Ph.D.'s getting jobs doing analysis for big financial companies. They tend to make a LOT of money.

5. **How do you see your profession changing in the next five years, what role will technology play in those changes, and what skills will be required?**

In day-to-day work, computing will become ever more important. New telescopes produce more complicated data sets, and new theories almost always involve more difficult math—much of which can only be solved on a computer.

The next five years are going to be very exciting in astronomy. The James Webb Space Telescope, the successor to the Hubble, is scheduled to launch in 2018. We're discovering thousands of planets orbiting around other stars, and in our own solar system we just got our first look at Pluto. Several major telescopes seem to be on the verge of finding signals from moments after the big bang.

6. **What do you enjoy most about your job? What do you enjoy least about your job?**

The best part of my job is when things work. Doing research means spending many, many hours trying to solve an equation or trying to get some piece of code to run properly. It's a great feeling when everything works and you get a result, especially since, fairly often, that result is something no one has seen before.

My least favorite part is debugging code. Usually during the "many, many hours" I mentioned above, I'll have written code that outputs nonsense. Digging back through lines and lines of code to find whatever mistake or typo I missed can be really frustrating.

7. **Can you suggest a valuable "try this" for students considering a career in your profession?**

The most important thing is to do some research in college. There should be a number of professors who would be happy to let you volunteer in their research groups. This will give you a feel for what this job is really like and let you figure out if you enjoy it or not. If you apply to graduate school, having research experience provides a big boost to your application.

SELECTED SCHOOLS

Most colleges and universities offer programs in physics and/or astronomy. Some of the more prominent schools in this field are listed below.

California Institute of Technology
1200 E. California Boulevard
Pasadena, CA 91125
Phone: (626) 395-6811
http://www.caltech.edu

Cornell University
Ithaca NY, 14853
Phone: (607) 255-2000
https://www.cornell.edu

Harvard University
Gordon Hall, Room 005
Boston, MA 02115
Phone: (617) 432-0884
http://www.harvard.edu

Pennsylvania State University, University Park
208 Muller Laboratory
University Park, PA 16802-5301
Phone: (814) 863-0278
http://www.psu.edu

Princeton University
Guyot Hall
Princeton, NJ 08544-1014
Phone: (609) 258-3658
http://www.princeton.edu/main

Stanford University
450 Serra Mall
Stanford, CA 94305
Phone: (650) 723-2300
https://www.stanford.edu

University of California, Berkeley
307 McCone Hall
Berkeley, CA 04720-4767
Phone: (510) 642-5574
http://www.berkeley.edu

University of California, Santa Barbara
1006 Webb Hall
Santa Barbara, CA 93106-9630
Phone: (805) 893-3329
http://www.ucsb.edu

University of Chicago
924 E. 57th Street
Chicago, IL 60637-5419
Phone: (773) 702-1234
http://www.uchicago.edu

University of Texas, Austin
1 University Station, A6500
Austin, TX 78712-0182
Phone: (512) 232-3691
http://www.utexas.edu

University of Wisconsin, Milwaukee
PO Box 413
Milwaukee WI, 53201
Phone: (414) 229-1122
http://www4.uwm.edu

MORE INFORMATION

American Association of Amateur Astronomers
P.O. Box 7981
Dallas, TX 75209-0981
www.astromax.com

American Astronomical Society
2000 Florida Avenue, NW, Suite 400
Washington, DC 20009-1231
202.328.2010
www.aas.org

National Aeronautics and Space Administration
NASA Headquarters, Suite 5K39
Washington, DC 20546-0001
202.358.0001
www.nasa.gov

***Sky and Telescope* Magazine**
Sky Publishing
90 Sherman Street
Cambridge, MA 02140
617.864.7360
www.skyandtelescope.com

Michael Auerbach/Editor

Biological Scientist

Snapshot

Career Cluster: Science, Technology, Engineering & Mathematics
Interests: Biological sciences, laboratory research, mathematics
Earnings (Yearly Average): $77,920
Employment & Outlook: Average Growth Expected

OVERVIEW

Sphere of Work

Biological scientists, commonly called biologists, study plants, animals, bacteria, protozoa, and fungi, as well as the relationships between these living organisms and their natural environments. Biologists perform basic and applied research in the field and in the laboratory. The goal of basic research is to acquire greater knowledge, while applied research studies are done in pursuit of solving a specific problem. Biologists typically specialize in a subfield of biological science, such as biochemistry, marine biology, microbiology, or botany.

Work Environment

Biological scientists are employed as basic researchers by educational institutions, corporations, and government agencies. Applied research positions are more prevalent in private industry. Biologists spend a great deal of time in the laboratory, conducting experiments and studying live organisms and tissue samples. Laboratories are usually clean, brightly lit, well ventilated, and highly organized. Outside the laboratory, many biologists spend long periods conducting research in the field, which often requires travel to isolated areas for prolonged periods. In these environments, they may endure rough terrain or seas, extreme weather conditions, and the risk of physical injury. Some office or classroom work is also common among biological scientists.

Profile

Working Conditions: Work both Indoors and Outdoors
Physical Strength: Light Work
Education Needs: Bachelor's Degree, Master's Degree, Doctoral Degree
Licensure/Certification: Usually Not Required
Opportunities For Experience: Military Service, Part-time Work
Holland Interest Score*: ISR

* See Appendix A

Occupation Interest

Biologists experience and study nature firsthand. Some applied biological researchers work to discover new treatments for disease or develop safeguards for food supplies. Other biologists seek alternative energy sources, such as biofuels, in an effort to reduce greenhouse gases. The field of biological science is extremely broad, providing countless disciplines in which biologists may specialize.

A Day in the Life—Duties and Responsibilities

The daily responsibilities and duties of biological scientists vary based on the specialty field in which they work. For example, marine biologists may spend a great deal of time at sea, studying and tracking animal behavior, while botanists often work in botanical gardens and greenhouses. Their activities also depend on the type of research being conducted. Basic research may entail observational practices, such as monitoring a species in its natural environment and carefully logging its activities and behavior; applied research, on the other hand, often involves taking a sample of a species (such as a leaf, insect venom, or blood) and conducting experiments to gauge its reaction to certain chemicals, stimuli, or environmental conditions.

At the center of every biological scientist's job is research. They collect and analyze samples and biological data in order to study the origins, anatomy, basic functions, and physical development of the organisms in question. Such research may involve conducting population surveys, tracking selected animals, dissecting carcasses, and analyzing waste. Biologists also study the organisms' environments, breaking down soil and water samples, assessing radioactivity and pollution levels, and measuring rainfall and other climate conditions. They use the data collected in the laboratory and the field to write technical reports, scholarly papers, and articles, which they present to the organizations for which they work, or at public events and scientific conferences.

Duties and Responsibilities

- Studying the nature and characteristics of plant and animal life
- Identifying and classifying plants and animals
- Examining the effects of environmental factors on plant and animal growth
- Investigating the mechanics and chemistry of plant and animal life processes
- Developing new applications of scientific knowledge

OCCUPATION SPECIALTIES

Botanists

Botanists study plants, including their growth, diseases, and structure.

Biochemists

Biochemists study the chemical composition of living things and try to understand the complex chemical combinations and reactions involved in metabolism, reproduction, growth and heredity.

Geneticists

Geneticists perform experiments to determine how traits inherited from genes are transmitted from one generation to the next.

Microbiologists

Microbiologists study microorganisms such as bacteria, viruses, algae, fungi, and some types of parasites.

Ecologists

Ecologists study ecostystems, which include all relationships between organisms and their surrounding environments.

Wildlife Biologists

Wildlife Biologists study animals and other wildlife and how they interact with their environments.

WORK ENVIRONMENT

Physical Environment

Biological scientists work predominantly in laboratories, which are highly organized and very clean. Some laboratory work may require the use of safety equipment to prevent exposure to toxins or biohazards. Most biologists perform some research in the field, in remote or heavily forested locations or at sea. When writing reports and other documents, they work in offices at government agencies, universities, corporations, research centers, and nonprofit organizations.

Relevant Skills and Abilities

Interpersonal/Social Skills
- Cooperating with others
- Working as a member of a team

Organization & Management Skills
- Paying attention to and handling details
- Performing duties which change frequently

Research & Planning Skills
- Analyzing information
- Developing evaluation strategies

Technical Skills
- Performing scientific, mathematical and technical work

Human Environment

Depending on their areas of specialty, biological scientists interact and collaborate with a wide range of individuals. Their colleagues may include government officials, engineers, university professors, research assistants, business executives, and other scientists. In some cases, they may also oversee laboratory assistants and technicians.

Technological Environment

Biological scientists work with a wide array of technologies in the field, in the lab, and at the office. With spectrometers and photometers, they gauge conditions in which organisms live. They use nets to collect aquatic specimens and microtomes to remove extremely thin slices of material, which they then examine under many different types of microscopes, such as electron microscopes and dissecting microscopes. In the office, they must use a wide range of databases, scientific and analytical software systems, and photo imaging programs, as well as office suites to prepare technical reports, articles, papers, and grant proposals.

EDUCATION, TRAINING, AND ADVANCEMENT

High School/Secondary

High school students should study biology, chemistry, and physics. In addition, more specialized subjects such as anatomy, physiology, zoology, and environmental sciences can help students understand the relationship between humanity and the natural world. Mathematics, including algebra, calculus, and geometry, are also highly useful, as are computer science courses. Students should hone their writing and public speaking skills through English and communications classes.

Suggested High School Subjects
- Agricultural Education
- Algebra
- Applied Biology/Chemistry
- Applied Math
- Biology
- Chemistry
- College Preparatory
- English
- Forestry
- Ornamental Horticulture
- Physics
- Science

Famous First

The first college course in biology was given at Bryn Mawr College, pictured, in 1885. The course involved the study of general biology, including taxonomy, unicellular and multicellular organisms, growth and development in plants and animals, and reproduction, and was given by Edmund Beecher Wilson, a pioneer in the field of cell biology.

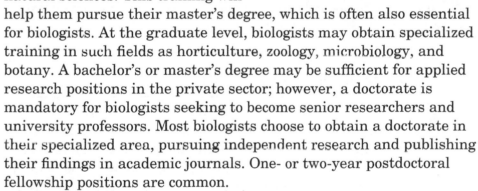

College/Postsecondary

Biologists must have at least a bachelor's degree in the biological or natural sciences. This training will help them pursue their master's degree, which is often also essential for biologists. At the graduate level, biologists may obtain specialized training in such fields as horticulture, zoology, microbiology, and botany. A bachelor's or master's degree may be sufficient for applied research positions in the private sector; however, a doctorate is mandatory for biologists seeking to become senior researchers and university professors. Most biologists choose to obtain a doctorate in their specialized area, pursuing independent research and publishing their findings in academic journals. One- or two-year postdoctoral fellowship positions are common.

Related College Majors
- Agronomy & Crop Science
- Biochemistry
- Biology, General
- Biophysics
- Botany
- Cell Biology
- Ecology
- Entomology
- Environmental Health
- Marine/Aquatic Biology
- Microbiology/Bacteriology
- Molecular Biology

- Plant Sciences, General
- Toxicology
- Zoology, General

Adult Job Seekers

For most biologist positions, the primary qualification is a doctorate. Qualified biologists may find employment through university placement offices or with the assistance of biology professors. Universities, research centers, government agencies, and private companies may also post their openings for biological scientists on their websites. Biology-related academic and professional organizations and societies also offer networking opportunities for job seekers.

Professional Certification or Licensure

Professional certification and licensure are not necessary for biological scientists. Some biological scientist positions in federal government agencies may require successful completion of a civil service examination.

Additional Requirements

Biological scientists must have an appreciation of the natural world. They should be able to analyze complex systems and environments. Research is often painstaking and exhaustive; biologists must be patient and careful in their study approaches. In addition to strong research skills, biological scientists should also demonstrate exceptional communication and writing skills, which are necessary both when presenting study findings and when seeking grants and other funding assistance. A passion for lifelong learning is essential, since biologists must stay current with the latest developments in their field.

Fun Fact

A red blood cell takes 20 seconds to circulate around the human body.
Source: www.sciensational.com/biology.html

EARNINGS AND ADVANCEMENT

Earnings depend on the employer, geographic location and employee's education and level of responsibility. According to a salary survey by the National Association of Colleges and Employers, the average beginning salary offer to college graduates with a bachelor's degree in biological and life sciences was $36,338 in 2012. Mean annual earnings of biological scientists were $77,920 in 2014. The lowest ten percent earned less than $42,480, and the highest ten percent earned more than $115,260.

Biological scientists may receive paid vacations, holidays, and sick days; life and health insurance; and retirement benefits. These are usually paid by the employer.

Metropolitan Areas with the Highest
Employment Level in this Occupation

Metropolitan area	Employment [1]	Employment per thousand jobs	Annual mean wage
Bethesda-Rockville-Frederick, MD	2,720	4.80	$97,460
Boston-Cambridge-Quincy, MA	1,450	0.81	$92,980
San Diego-Carlsbad-San Marcos, CA	1,080	0.82	$74,310
Sacramento--Arden-Arcade--Roseville, CA	1,030	1.20	$76,770
San Francisco-San Mateo-Redwood City, CA	1,020	0.94	$89,220
Oakland-Fremont-Hayward, CA	930	0.91	$99,190
Santa Ana-Anaheim-Irvine, CA	830	0.56	$101,220
Washington-Arlington-Alexandria, DC-VA-MD-WV	820	0.34	$103,720
Seattle-Bellevue-Everett, WA	660	0.44	$77,410
Baltimore-Towson, MD	500	0.38	$87,260

[1]Does not include self-employed. Source: Bureau of Labor Statistics

EMPLOYMENT AND OUTLOOK

Biological scientists held about 70,000 jobs in 2014. About 40 percent of all biological scientists were employed by federal, state, and local governments. Federal biological scientists worked mainly for the U.S. Departments of Agriculture, Interior, and Defense, and for the National Institutes of Health. Employment is expected to grow as fast as the average for all occupations through the year 2022, which means employment is projected to increase 5 percent to 15 percent.

The rapid growth of the biotechnology industry will create the most demand for biological scientists. In addition, more biological scientists and medical scientists will be needed to determine the environmental impact of industry and government actions and to prevent or correct environmental problems. Expected expansion in research related to health issues, such as AIDS, cancer, and Alzheimer's disease, should also result in growth.

Employment Trend, Projected 2012–22

Total, all occupations: 11%

Life, physical, and social science occupations: 10%

Biological scientists: 8%

Note: "All Occupations" includes all occupations in the U.S. Economy. Source: U.S. Bureau of Labor Statistics, Employment Projections Program

Related Occupations
- Agricultural Scientist
- Biomedical Engineer
- Botanist
- College Faculty Member
- Environmental Engineer
- Environmental Science Technician
- Fish & Game Warden
- Forester & Conservation Scientist
- Hazardous Waste Manager
- Marine Biologist
- Medical Scientist
- Microbiologist
- Oceanographer
- Science Technician
- Water & Wastewater Engineer
- Wildlife Biologist
- Wind Energy Engineer
- Zoologist

Related Military Occupations
- Life Scientist

Conversation With . . .
SAMUEL J. LANDRY, PhD

Professor, Tulane University School of Medicine
Department of Biochemistry and Molecular Biology
Biological Scientist, 22 years

1. What was your individual career path in terms of education/training, entry-level job, or other significant opportunity?

My father, his father and my mother's father were all engineers, so engineering seemed like the thing to do when I was in high school. Then my roommate at Louisiana State University (LSU) was going to go to medical school, so I got it in my head that I was going to go on to med school. I was not as disciplined a student as he, so, when the time came, I wasn't going to med school. I earned a bachelor's degree in zoology, took a few more courses, and then went back to LSU. I had minored in chemistry and was going to do a chemical engineering degree. I took a biochemistry class the first semester and fell in love. I knew it was for me. I got my PhD at LSU in biochemistry, did my post-doc at Southwest Medical Center in Dallas, and then became an assistant, associate, and eventually full professor at Tulane University in New Orleans.

My research is in protein-structure function and immunology, although I've always been interested in the chemical and biophysical aspects of protein. When I started out, I worked with a researcher at LSU who was working on how proteins get into a plant cell's chloroplast. The proteins have to be transported across a membrane, and at the time nobody had a clue how it worked. That led me to a group of molecular chaperones, which, basically, are proteins that keep other proteins out of trouble. Now I also work on vaccine research related to CD4-positive T-cells. To me, these areas are about protein structure: the transfer problem, how chaperones work, and then, with T-cells, why does the immune system go after this and not that?

I typically teach two classes per semester.

2. What are the most important skills and/or qualities for someone in your profession?

Nearly all-consuming curiosity is necessary for a career in research. It is difficult to be successful and have outside interests or raise a family. The tasks and roles that professors play at universities, or even in industry, are so diverse that your particular skills and talents can find their usefulness and you can be successful with them. These include precision in the lab, creativity, written and oral communication, personnel management, statistics, and computation–whether programming or finding applications that apply to your work. At some point, you have to be quantitative; you can't be completely without mathematics.

3. What do you wish you had known going into this profession?

Regrettably, that pedigree matters a lot. By this I mean the reputation and/or quality of the undergraduate and graduate schools a scientist attends.

4. Are there many job opportunities in your profession? In what specific areas?

Yes, there is a steady supply of academic jobs, although the pool is affected by federal funding levels and is in slow decline due to the lengthening of a typical career. Someone with my training might also work in the private sector doing research or biotech jobs, such as production, management, intellectual property, or sales. Academic jobs are maybe a third of total jobs; all in all there are a lot more jobs in the biotech industry–although in the last 10 years that has leveled off from a previous period of growth.

5. How do you see your profession changing in the next five years, what role will technology play in those changes, and what skills will be required?

Bioinformatics, which develops methods and software for understanding biological data, will play an increasing role. It's become very cheap to do a genetic sequence of a person or their tumor. Based on a person's DNA, we can predict chances of certain diseases or neurological conditions. There will be many others, and the industry will collect huge amounts of data and mine it for subtle indicators. That is routine now, during, say, a hospital visit when they take any routine measurement. Collaborative projects are more common than before, requiring interpersonal skills. The notion of the "independent investigator" is becoming less valid.

6. What do you enjoy most about your job? What do you enjoy least about your job?

I enjoy analysis of new data the most. My least favorite task is bookkeeping and bureaucratic paperwork.

7. Can you suggest a valuable "try this" for students considering a career in your profession?

To see what the research life is like, take a job as a technician during college. When you go to graduate school, if you are going to be successful, it will take complete dedication.

SELECTED SCHOOLS

Most colleges and universities offer programs in biology; many of them offer specializations in various areas of biological science. Some of the more prominent schools in this field are listed below.

Cornell University
Graduate Field of Biochemistry,
Molecular and Cell Biology
107 Biotechnology Building
Ithaca, NY 14853-2703
Phone: (607) 255-2703
https://www.cornell.edu

Harvard University
Programs in Biological and
Biomedical Sciences
Gordon Hall, Room 005
Boston MA, 02115
Phone: (617) 432-0884
http://www.harvard.edu

John Hopkins University
Biology Department
3400 N. Charles Street
Baltimore, MD 21218
Phone: (410) 516-7330
https://www.jhu.edu

Massachusetts Institute of Technology
Department of Biology
77 Massachusetts Avenue, 68-132
Cambridge, MA 02139
Phone: (617) 253-4701
http://web.mit.edu

Princeton University
Department of Molecular Biology
Washington Road
Princeton, NJ 08544-1014
Phone: (609) 258-3658
http://www.princeton.edu/main

Scripps Research Institute
Kellogg School of Science and
Technology
10550 N. Torrey Pines Road
La Jolla CA, 90237
Phone: (858) 784-8469
http://www.scripps.edu

Stanford University
Department of Biology
Gilbert Hall
Stanford, CA 04305-5020
Phone: (650) 723-2413
https://www.stanford.edu

University of California, Berkeley
College of Letters and Sciences
201 Campbell Hall
Berkeley, CA 94720-2920
Phone: (510) 642-5113
http://www.berkeley.edu

University of California, San Francisco
1675 Owens Street
San Francisco 94143-0523
Phone: (415) 476-2310
https://www.ucsf.edu

Yale University
Combined Program in Biological and
Biomedical Sciences
PO Box 208084
New Haven, CT 06520-8084
Phone: (203) 785-5663
http://www.yale.edu/

MORE INFORMATION

American Physiological Society Education Office
9650 Rockville Pike
Bethesda, MD 20814-3991
301.634.7164
www.the-aps.org

American Society for Biochemistry and Molecular Biology
11200 Rockville Pike, Suite 302
Bethesda, MD 20852-3110
240.283.6600
www.asbmb.org

American Society for Cell Biology
8120 Woodmont Avenue, Suite 750
Bethesda, MD 20814-2762
301.347.9300
www.ascb.org

American Society for Horticultural Science
1018 Duke Street
Alexandria, VA 22314-2851
703.836.4606
www.ashs.org

American Society for Microbiology
1752 N Street NW
Washington, DC 20036-2904
202.737.3600
www.asm.org

American Society of Plant Biologists
15501 Monona Drive
Rockville, MD 20855-2768
301.251.0560
www.aspb.org

Biotechnology Industry Organization
1201 Maryland Avenue, SW
Suite 900
Washington, DC 20024
202.962.9200
www.bio.org

Botanical Society of America
P.O. Box 299
St. Louis, MO 63166-0299
314.577.9566
www.botany.org

Ecological Society of America
1990 M Street, NW, Suite 700
Washington, DC 20006-3915
202.833.8773
www.esa.org

Nature Conservancy
4245 North Fairfax Drive, Suite 100
Arlington, VA 22203-1606
800.628.6860
nature.org

Society for Conservation Biology
1017 O Street NW
Washington, DC 20001-4229
202.234.4133
www.conbio.org

Society for Developmental Biology
9650 Rockville Pike
Bethesda, MD 20814-3998
301.634.7815
www.sdbonline.org

Society for Integrative and Comparative Biology
1313 Dolley Madison Boulevard
Suite 402
McLean, VA 22101
800.955.1236
www.sicb.org

Michael Auerbach/Editor

Biomedical Engineer

Snapshot

Career Cluster: Health Science; Science, Technology, Engineering & Mathematics

Interests: Science, engineering, mathematics, solving problems

Earnings (Yearly Average): $91,760

Employment & Outlook: Faster Than Average Growth Expected

OVERVIEW

Sphere of Work

Biomedical engineering is very broad, combining engineering techniques with human biology to develop medically relevant technologies. Research in the field centers on prosthetic limbs, joint replacement devices, rehabilitation and assistive technologies, medical imaging, and genetic, tissue, and cellular engineering. The field is constantly spreading into new areas. Most of this expansion is linked to the needs of an aging population and the increased demand for medical devices and equipment designed by biomedical engineers.

Biomedical engineers often cross over into multidisciplinary skill sets and collaborate with mechanical engineers, physicists, biologists, and clinicians.

Work Environment

Working with scientists in and out of the lab is especially important for biomedical engineers. Communication skills are critical for collaboration with specialists across disciplines. Engineers, researchers, and clinicians use different approaches and technical languages, and ongoing communication facilitates day-to-day and project-specific communication.

It is also important for biomedical engineers to be mindful of a holistic, patient-focused approach, beyond the machines or technology at hand, and toward the patient who will benefit from the work.

Profile

Working Conditions: Work Indoors
Physical Strength: Light Work
Education Needs: Bachelor's Degree, Master's Degree, Doctoral Degree
Licensure/Certification: Required
Opportunities For Experience: Internship, Military Service
Holland Interest Score*: IRE

* See Appendix A

Occupation Interest

Biomedical engineering covers a diverse body of scientific knowledge and skills, and attracts graduates and professionals who have strong foundations in the sciences, engineering, or mathematics. Biomedical engineers are pragmatic, problem-solving people who are also enthusiastic about working in different scientific arenas.

Many universities also offer specific undergraduate and postgraduate programs in biomedical engineering, but engineers enter the field from a true variety of science disciplines.

A Day in the Life—Duties and Responsibilities

Biomedical engineers, like all engineers, are problem solvers. The medical application of their work is focused on making people's lives better, and requires a strong desire to collaborate.

A biomedical engineer's day can vary widely, depending on the area of specialty. Meetings and classes relating to medical safety issues may be held, and schedules outlined. Design and testing usually dominate daily work.

Some engineers may interact directly with surgeons who are looking for better technologies to improve surgery. The engineers will set about brainstorming design ideas that are safe and effective. Engineers in this area may also observe surgeries to better understand the limits and difficulties of a surgical procedure that requires design help.

Sometimes, the work centers on reworking manufacturing flaws in a design, and the engineer will work with a manufacturing specialist onsite or by phone to correct the problem. Other biomedical engineers might work one-on-one with patients using a rehabilitative device, such as a prosthetic limb, in order to improve the design and deliver higher performance or comfort. This will occur daily for those engineers in specific patient-centered practice, or on those occasions when clinical trials begin to test a new device with patients.

In an academic setting, biomedical engineers work with students at the undergraduate, graduate, doctoral, and post-doctoral level. Biomedical engineers might also work with entrepreneurs and manufacturers interested in building and marketing devices and technologies the engineer has created

Duties and Responsibilities

- Conducting research concerning behavioral, biological, psychological, or life systems
- Designing and developing new medical instruments and techniques, such as artificial organs, cardiac pacemakers, or ultrasonic imaging devices
- Recommending equipment design changes
- Studying engineering aspects of biomedical systems of humans
- Assisting medical personnel in observing or treating physical ailments or deformities

OCCUPATION SPECIALTIES

Biomedical Equipment Technicians

Biomedical Equipment Technicians, who usually work under a biomedical engineer or other senior staff member, install, repair and maintain medical equipment and instruments used in the health-care delivery field. They inspect and install medical and related technical equipment in medical and research facilities for use by physicians, nurses, scientists or engineers involved in researching or treating physical ailments.

WORK ENVIRONMENT

Physical Environment

Laboratory and office settings predominate. Research and design work relating to biomedical engineering may involve contact with human or animal tissue, and biomedical safety practices will be observed.

Plant Environment

Biomedical engineers can work in a variety of settings, from laboratories and hospitals, to corporate offices and university campuses.

Human Environment

Biomedical engineering requires strong collaboration skills. Depending on the field of biomedical engineering, professionals in this field interact with students and colleagues in fields across the scientific spectrum, as well as with technicians, managers, directors, patients, and in some cases, business specialists.

Relevant Skills and Abilities

Communication Skills
- Speaking effectively
- Writing concisely

Organization & Management Skills
- Coordinating tasks
- Making decisions
- Managing people/groups
- Paying attention to and handling details

Research & Planning Skills
- Creating ideas
- Using logical reasoning

Technical Skills
- Performing scientific, mathematical and technical work
- Working with your hands

Technological Environment

Biomedical engineers use technologies that range from telephone, e-mail, and web conferencing, to computer design software, to increasingly complex and highly calibrated diagnostic tools and machinery.

EDUCATION, TRAINING, AND ADVANCEMENT

High School/Secondary

High school students can best prepare for a career in biomedical engineering with courses in algebra, calculus, geometry, trigonometry, biology, chemistry, physics, and computers. Advanced placement (AP) classes in these subjects are especially recommended. Drafting and art classes can also serve as precursors for future design work. Communication and problem-solving skills are vital for success in this occupation, so English and writing courses are also important.

Creating projects for science fairs and science clubs gives students the opportunity to design, invent, and learn from others prior to graduation. Summer programs and internships reinforce the fundamentals, and introduce students to the field and its impact on the world. Many universities in the United States and abroad offer science or technology camps to high school students.

Suggested High School Subjects
- Algebra
- Applied Biology/Chemistry
- Applied Communication
- Applied Math
- Applied Physics
- Biology
- Blueprint Reading
- Chemistry
- College Preparatory
- Composition
- Computer Science
- English
- Geometry
- Mathematics
- Science
- Trigonometry

Famous First

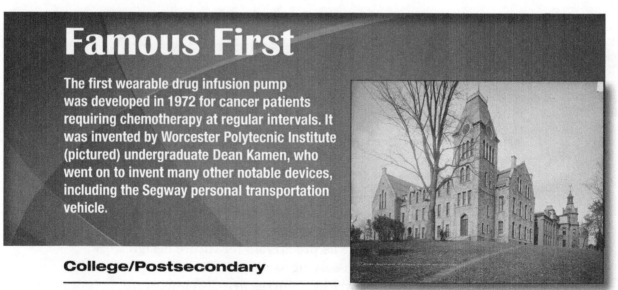

The first wearable drug infusion pump was developed in 1972 for cancer patients requiring chemotherapy at regular intervals. It was invented by Worcester Polytecnic Institute (pictured) undergraduate Dean Kamen, who went on to invent many other notable devices, including the Segway personal transportation vehicle.

College/Postsecondary

This occupation has evolved from a variety of medical and technical disciplines, but is primarily based in engineering. Most biomedical engineers have an undergraduate degree and Ph.D. in engineering, mathematics, or a related field.

Over 120 colleges and universities in the United States offer bioengineering or biomedical engineering programs. Typical coursework or research includes instruction in the fundamentals of biofluid mechanics, engineering electrophysiology, diagnostic imaging physics, neuroengineering, and drug design, development, and delivery. In addition to core courses, students can take electives related to their ultimate career goals.

University programs offer co-op study and internships. These programs offer concrete opportunities to work while gaining both academic credit and professional experience before graduation. They also represent concrete sources for industry contacts. Ph.D. internships and other research positions provide graduate students and graduates opportunities to work on engineering projects in an academic setting.

College and university students from bachelor's candidates to Ph.D. levels are highly encouraged to make use of their academic career centers, and to actively approach professors as advisors and mentors with questions and ideas relating to these and other career and study opportunities.

Biomedical engineers in academia move from instructor to assistant professor, professor, and department chair by demonstrating consistency, excellence, and innovation in research, teaching, and departmental collaboration. Full professors almost always possess a doctoral degree.

Related College Majors
- Bioengineering/Biomedical Engineering
- Biomedical Engineering-Related Technology
- Engineering Mechanics
- Engineering Physics
- Engineering Science
- Engineering, General

Adult Job Seekers

Economic conditions and personal and family responsibilities can require professionals to take time away from active engineering work. A return to employment requires transition time. Updated resume credentials in education and research facilitate the transition period, and can take the form of continuing education, fellowships, scholarships, grants, or employment at a different level than previously held. Professional associations are often good sources for transition contacts and opportunities. For example, the Association for Women in Science (AWIS) has several fellowships for women returning to science.

Networking and interviewing are critical. Pursuing employment with a multidisciplinary approach can also broaden opportunities.

Professional Certification and Licensure

Engineers are encouraged to acquire certification or licensing according to national, state, and district regulations. Specialists whose work affects the health or safety of the public must hold this credential.

Additional Requirements

A strong commitment to study and learning are the hallmarks of aspiring biomedical engineers. Because they are experts in a highly specialized field, they have pursued long years of education in math and science. The recurring advice engineers give newcomers is to be proactive, ask questions, know the science, and stick with it.

Fun Fact

Biomedical engineering is a relatively new name for a long-standing field. One of the first biomedical devices was invented in 1816 when a French physician, who thought it improper to place his ear on a young woman's chest to hear her heartbeat, listened through a rolled up newspaper, the first stethoscope.

Source: www.timetoast.com/timelines/biomedical-engineering

EARNINGS AND ADVANCEMENT

Earnings depend on the type, size and location of the employer and the employee's education, experience, capabilities and responsibilities. According to a salary survey by the National Association of Colleges and Employers, biomedical engineers with a bachelor's degree earned a starting salary of $59,180 in 2012. Biomedical engineers with a master's degree were offered $69,111 annually.

Mean annual earnings of biomedical engineers were $91,760 in 2014. The lowest ten percent earned less than $52,680, and the highest ten percent earned more than $139,350.

Biomedical engineers may receive paid vacations, holidays and sick days; life and health insurance; and retirement benefits. These are usually paid by the employer.

Metropolitan Areas with the Highest Employment Level in this Occupation

Metropolitan area	Employment [1]	Employment per thousand jobs	Annual mean wage
Boston-Cambridge-Quincy, MA	1,410	0.78	$91,090
Santa Ana-Anaheim-Irvine, CA	1,150	0.78	$118,440
San Jose-Sunnyvale-Santa Clara, CA	820	0.84	$117,620
Minneapolis-St. Paul-Bloomington, MN-WI	810	0.44	$112,960
San Diego-Carlsbad-San Marcos, CA	630	0.48	$80,290
San Francisco-San Mateo-Redwood City, CA	610	0.57	$104,890
Philadelphia, PA	590	0.32	$77,800
New York-White Plains-Wayne, NY-NJ	560	0.10	$101,180
Los Angeles-Long Beach-Glendale, CA	510	0.13	$89,390
Oakland-Fremont-Hayward, CA	450	0.44	$108,390

[1]Does not include self-employed. Source: Bureau of Labor Statistics

EMPLOYMENT AND OUTLOOK

There were approximately 19,500 biomedical engineers employed nationally in 2012. Employment of biomedical engineers is expected to grow much faster than the average for all occupations through the year 2022, which means employment is projected to increase 25 percent or more. The aging of the population and the focus on health care issues will increase demand for better medical devices and equipment designed by biomedical engineers.

Employment Trend, Projected 2012–22

Biomedical engineers: 27%

Total, all occupations: 11%

Engineers (all): 9%

Note: "All Occupations" includes all occupations in the U.S. Economy. Source: U.S. Bureau of Labor Statistics, Employment Projections Program

Related Occupations
- Agricultural Engineer
- Agricultural Scientist
- Biological Scientist
- Marine Biologist
- Medical Scientist

Related Military Occupations
- Electrical Products Repairer
- Electronic Instrument Repairer
- Environmental Health & Safety Officer

Conversation With . . .
BEN NOE

Research & Development Project Manager
Medtronic, Boulder, CO
Biomedical Engineer, 2½ years

1. What was your individual career path in terms of education/training, entry-level job, or other significant opportunity?

I have a Bachelor of Science in mechanical engineering from the University of Colorado at Boulder and a certification in project management through the Project Management Institute. Even though my formal training is in mechanical engineering, biomedical engineering was my focus in college. My college didn't have a formal degree program in it. I had considered becoming a doctor or a physical therapist, but as a freshman or sophomore in college, I came to understand my strengths were in engineering and business.

My entry-level job is as an Associate Project Manager with Medtronic's Minimally Invasive Therapies Group. I had been a project management intern at Covidien and transitioned into full-time. I was lucky in that there was a need for my specific position when I graduated and I was hired right out of college. Medtronic acquired Covidien, so now I work for Medtronic. I'm heading my own fairly large project right now and I'm pretty excited about it—an electrosurgical generator that controls electrical cutting and coagulation instruments in surgery.

Another significant opportunity was my involvement with the Biomedical Engineering Society. I started a university chapter of the society when I was in college. That helped with me get my internship because I made contact with a lot of local companies. Also, leading that team helped in my interview for the internship. Now I've moved up to Industry Committee Chair and am on the Board of Directors for the society.

2. What are the most important skills and/or qualities for someone in your profession?

I think the most important skills are the ability to understand processes and regulations that are the framework in which we're working. The medical device industry, and really biomedicine in general, is heavily regulated. Also, the ability to work together in a team to come up with innovative solutions is a very important skill.

3. What do you wish you had known going into this profession?

I wish I had a better background in quality processes/quality control, regulations and restrictions, and then manufacturing. Some universities do offer these types of classes, for example, "Design Control in Medical Devices" or "The Regulatory Environment in the Biomedical Field." They're very specialized classes.

4. Are there many job opportunities in your profession? In what specific areas?

Absolutely. It's a quickly growing field. The majority of biomedical engineering positions are in academia and industry. There are some government jobs, for instance with the Food and Drug Administration (FDA) or National Institutes of Health (NIH).

5. How do you see your profession changing in the next five years? What role will technology play in those changes, and what skills will be required?

I see three key things in terms of the profession changing. One is the consolidation of companies into several large companies. A lot of the smaller and mid-size companies, and even some larger companies, are being gobbled up by a few major companies. The second thing is integration with high tech. There's been a huge push to work with Apple or Google on things like personalized health information on an iPhone. And the third one would be a move toward more automation and robotic procedures, even in an operating room, where everything might be controlled from an iPad. The benefit can be a lot more precision and the possibility of eliminating human error.

6. What do you enjoy most about your job? What do you enjoy least about your job?

What I enjoy most, honestly, is seeing the product in action and seeing the impact our products have on patients' lives. Working in electrosurgery, where you can cut and cauterize tissue with better efficiency than a suture and scalpel, seeing the results for patients in terms of faster recovery time and less pain has been a rewarding experience.

What I enjoy least is probably the conflict management part of the job. A lot of the conflict is around interpretation of and different approaches to applying standards and regulations. Many of the standards are somewhat vague—actually, intentionally somewhat vague—and there can be disagreement over how they apply to our products.

7. Can you suggest a valuable "try this" for students considering a career in your profession?

My advice would be to try to get an internship. You could also start a club or seek out a mentor program. Reach out to someone in the field, just to be able to get on a job for one day. Some companies offer what they call an externship, where you can shadow an engineer for a day.

SELECTED SCHOOLS

Most colleges and universities offer programs in engineering; a variety of them have concentrations in biomedical engineering. Some of the more prominent schools in this field are listed below.

Duke University
2138 Campus Drive
Box 90586
Durham, NC 27708
Phone: (919) 684-8111
https://duke.edu

Georgia Institute of Technology
225 North Avenue NW
Atlanta, GA 30332
Phone: (404) 894-2000
http://www.gatech.edu

John Hopkins University
3400 N. Charles Street
Baltimore, MD 21218
Phone: (410) 516-8000
https://www.jhu.edu

Massachusetts Institute of Technology
77 Massachusetts Avenue
Cambridge, MA 02139
Phone: (617) 253-1000
http://web.mit.edu

Rice University
PO Box 1892
Houston, TX 77251-1892
Phone: (713) 348-0000
http://www.rice.edu

Stanford California
450 Serra Mall
Stanford, CA 94305
Phone: (650) 723-2300
https://www.stanford.edu

University of Michigan, Ann Arbor
500 S. State St.
Ann Arbor, MI 48109
Phone: (734) 764-1817
https://www.umich.edu

University of California, Berkeley
110 Sproul Hall
Berkeley, CA 94720-5800
Phone: (510) 642-6000
http://www.berkeley.edu

University of California, San Diego
9500 Gilman Drive
La Jolla, CA 92093
Phone: (858) 534-2230
https://ucsd.edu

University of Washington
Seattle, WA 98195
Phone: (206) 543-2100
http://www.washington.edu

MORE INFORMATION

Association for Women in Science
1442 Duke Street
Alexandria, VA 22314
703.372.4380
www.awis.org

Biomedical Engineering Society
8401 Corporate Drive, Suite 1125
Landover, MD 20785-2224
301.459.1999
www.bmes.org

National Action Council for Minorities in Engineering
440 Hamilton Avenue, Suite 302
White Plains, NY 10601-1813
914.539.4010
www.nacme.org

National Society of Black Engineers
205 Daingerfield Road
Alexandria, VA 22314
703.549.2207
www.nsbe.org

Society of Hispanic Professional Engineers
13181 Crossroads Parkway North, Suite 450
City of Industry, CA 91746-3497
323.725.3970
www.shpe.org

Society of Women Engineers
203 N. La Salle Street, Suite 1675
Chicago, IL 60601
877.793.4636
www.swe.org

Technology Student Association
1914 Association Drive
Reston, VA 20191-1540
703.860.9000
www.tsaweb.org

Try Engineering
445 Hoes Lane
Piscataway, NJ 08854-4141
tryengineering.org

Women in Biomedical Careers National Institutes of Health
9000 Rockville Pike
Bethesda, MD 20892
womeninscience.nih.gov/women_scientist/kuoc.asp

Bill Rickards/Editor

Chemical Engineer

Snapshot

Career Cluster: Manufacturing; Science, Technology, Engineering & Mathematics

Interests: : Chemistry, mathematics, analyzing data

Earnings (Yearly Average): $103,590

Employment & Outlook: Slower Than Average Growth Expected

OVERVIEW

Sphere of Work

Chemical engineers assist in the manufacture of chemicals or chemical products, such as plastics, gasoline, cement, paper, detergents, and artificial fibers. They invent new processes for using chemicals and design, manufacture, and operate equipment used in laboratories or factories. Chemical engineers frequently provide support to manufacturing facilities that use the equipment or processes they design, and they may assist in developing related safety measures. They are also typically responsible for compiling reports and adhering to budgets.

Work Environment

Chemical engineers work in factories, laboratories, energy plants, government agencies, and educational institutions. The environment in which a chemical engineer works often depends on his or her area of specialty. For example, engineers who focus on pollution control may travel to various locations in order to study the effects of factory emissions on soil, plants, and water, while petrochemical engineers may spend a great deal of time in the laboratory. Chemical engineers generally work a forty-hour week, although approaching deadlines may necessitate extended hours. Chemical engineers risk physical injury and illness from exposure to toxic chemicals and fumes, so it is vital that they follow all protocols regarding safety and chemical use, storage, and disposal.

Profile

Working Conditions: Work Indoors
Physical Strength: Light Work
Education Needs: Bachelor's Degree, Master's Degree, Doctoral Degree
Licensure/Certification: Required
Opportunities For Experience: Internship, Apprenticeship
Holland Interest Score*: IRE, SEC

* See Appendix A

Occupation Interest

Individuals drawn to a career in chemical engineering have a strong affinity for science and mathematics. They enjoy exploring the practical applications of chemistry and have a desire to solve complex real-world problems—the work they perform has great impact on consumers, industry, and the environment. Aspiring chemical engineers should be precise, analytical, mechanically adept, and committed to safety.

A Day in the Life—Duties and Responsibilities

Chemical engineers develop processes whereby chemical compounds are utilized for manufacturing or energy-generating purposes. Working in laboratories, they experiment with new uses for chemicals as well as ways to perform existing industrial processes more efficiently. Chemical engineers consider factors such as chemical properties, temperature, density, and pressure in their experimental designs. They often design equipment, and in many cases, entire buildings and production systems, to facilitate such processes as polymerization, heat distillation, drying, crushing, and mixing.

Frequently, chemical engineers aid in the construction and operation of the equipment, providing support when issues arise.

Additional responsibilities vary based on the individual's area of expertise. For example, some engineers spend some of their time in the field, conducting research and taking samples for analysis. Others may spend the majority of their time in a manufacturing facility, monitoring equipment productivity and energy usage. Some chemical engineers work as consultants and travel between facilities as needed.

In addition to their scientific work, chemical engineers are responsible for monitoring costs, efficiency, and output. Chemical engineers must periodically report their progress and expenditures to their supervisors or clients and assess the operational status of chemical processes and the equipment that generates them. Furthermore, chemical engineers ensure that their production facilities have up-to-date licenses and permits and are in full compliance with all state and federal regulations.

Duties and Responsibilities

- Conducting research to develop new chemical manufacturing processes
- Determining the best method for operations, like mixing, crushing, heat transfer, distillation and oxidation
- Making recommendations to management concerning new manufacturing processes, location and/or design of a new plant or modification of an existing plant

Fun Fact

The automotive industry seeks chemical engineers to create products such as ultra-strong fibers, fabrics and adhesives for vehicles.

Source: www.acs.org/content/acs/en/careers/college-to-career/chemistry-careers/chemical-engineering.html

OCCUPATION SPECIALTIES

Chemical-Engineering Technicians

Chemical-Engineering Technicians, who usually work under a
chemical engineer or other senior staff person, apply chemical
engineering principles and technical skills to assist chemical engineers
in developing, improving and testing chemical-plant processes,
products and equipment. They prepare charts and diagrams, and
record engineering data to clarify design data.

WORK ENVIRONMENT

Physical Environment

Chemical engineers work in scientific laboratories as well as factories,
energy plants, and other production facilities. Some may travel to
visit manufacturing plants or perform research. Chemical engineers
risk physical injury or illness caused by exposure to chemicals and
equipment, so strict safety and operational protocols, including the
wearing of protective clothing and eyewear, must be observed at all
times.

Human Environment

Chemical engineers may work with a wide range of individuals,
including other chemical engineers, engineers in other disciplines, line
workers, government officials, laboratory technicians, construction
personnel, and machine operators. Consequently, they must be able to
convey scientific and technical concepts to individuals from different
professional backgrounds.

Relevant Skills and Abilities

Communication Skills
- Speaking effectively
- Writing concisely

Interpersonal/Social Skills
- Being patient
- Having good judgment

Organization & Management Skills
- Initiating new ideas

Managing time
- Meeting goals and deadlines

Research & Planning Skills
- Creating ideas
- Developing evaluation strategies
- Solving problems

Technical Skills
- Performing scientific, mathematical and technical work

Unclassified Skills
- Using set methods and standards in your work

Technological Environment

In addition to any equipment that they may design themselves, chemical engineers may use freeze dryers, heat exchangers, laboratory mixers, spectrometers, and microscopes of various sizes. They also frequently use computer-aided design (CAD) software, scientific and analytical programs, databases, and basic office software.

EDUCATION, TRAINING, AND ADVANCEMENT

High School/Secondary

High school students interested in pursuing a career in chemical engineering must study chemistry, physics, biology, and environmental science. They should also study mathematics, including geometry, calculus, trigonometry, and algebra. Industrial arts classes that build mechanical and drafting skills are highly useful as well.

Suggested High School Subjects
- Algebra
- Applied Communication
- Applied Math
- Applied Physics
- Blueprint Reading
- Calculus
- Chemistry
- College Preparatory
- Composition
- Computer Science
- Drafting
- English
- Geometry
- Humanities
- Mathematics
- Physics
- Science
- Social Studies
- Trigonometry

Famous First

The first chemical engineer to be awarded the Priestly Medal, the highest honor conferred by the American Chemical Society, was Warren Lewis, pictured, of the Massachusetts Institute of Technology in 1947. Lewis was honored for his work in advancing the catalytic cracking of petroleum, a process that helped enlarge the supply of gasoline during World War II.

College/Postsecondary

At a minimum, chemical engineers should hold a bachelor's degree in engineering, although advanced degrees are frequently required for higher-level positions. Some chemical engineers choose to pursue master's degrees in business management. Postsecondary students may significantly benefit from completing internships, which can potentially lead to full-time work after graduation.

Related College Majors
- Chemical Engineering
- Environmental & Pollution Control Technology
- Industrial/Manufacturing Technology
- Mining & Petroleum Technologies
- Polymer/Plastics Engineering
- Textile Sciences & Engineering

Adult Job Seekers

Qualified candidates may apply directly to employers who post openings online or in print. Professional chemical engineering associations, such as the American Institute of Chemical Engineers (AIChE), may offer career resources and networking opportunities.

Professional Certification and Licensure

Chemical engineers whose work directly affects the public must pass an examination to become licensed Professional Engineers (PEs). The licensing process frequently requires continuing education and licensure renewal, so chemical engineers must educate themselves about the legal requirements in the state or states in which they work.

Trade associations, such as the National Certification Commission in Chemistry and Chemical Engineering (NCCCE), frequently offer specialized certification for chemical engineers. Education or work experience and ongoing participation in professional development activities are typically required. Chemical engineers interested in becoming certified should consult credible professional associations within the field and follow professional debate as to the relevancy and value of any voluntary certification program.

Additional Requirements

Chemical engineers working in certain fields may require a driver's license, security clearance, or other specific qualification.

EARNINGS AND ADVANCEMENT

Earnings of chemical engineers depend on educational background, experience, ability, and on the type, size and location of the employing organization. According to a salary survey by the National Association of Colleges and Employers, chemical engineers with a bachelor's degree earned an annual starting salary of $70,920 in 2012. Chemical engineers with a master's degree earned $77,167 per year, while those with a Ph.D. earned an average annual salary of $82,913.

Mean annual earnings of chemical engineers were $103,590 in 2014. The lowest ten percent earned less than $59,480, and the highest ten percent earned more than $156,980.

Chemical engineers may receive paid vacations, holidays, and sick days; life and health insurance; and retirement benefits. These are usually paid by the employer.

Metropolitan Areas with the Highest Employment Level in this Occupation

Metropolitan area	Employment [1]	Employment per thousand jobs	Annual mean wage
Houston-Sugar Land-Baytown, TX	4,320	1.52	$128,380
Baton Rouge, LA	1,320	3.45	$119,640
Washington-Arlington-Alexandria, DC-VA-MD-WV	810	0.34	$134,400
Chicago-Joliet-Naperville, IL	810	0.21	$103,810
Wilmington, DE-MD-NJ	770	2.27	$125,800
Philadelphia, PA	760	0.41	$101,270
Newark-Union, NJ-PA	740	0.77	$112,670
Los Angeles-Long Beach-Glendale, CA	710	0.17	$89,180
Dallas-Plano-Irving, TX	630	0.28	$102,590
New York-White Plains-Wayne, NY-NJ	600	0.11	$96,710

[1]Does not include self-employed. Source: Bureau of Labor Statistics

EMPLOYMENT AND OUTLOOK

There were about 33,000 chemical engineers employed nationally in 2012. Employment of chemical engineers is expected to grow slower than the average for all occupations through the year 2022, which means employment is projected to increase 2 percent to 6 percent. Chemical companies will continue to research and develop new chemicals and more efficient processes to increase output of existing chemicals, resulting in new jobs for chemical engineers. Among manufacturing industries, pharmaceuticals may provide the best job opportunities. Much of the projected growth, however, will be in non-manufacturing industries, especially service industries, particularly for research in energy and the developing fields of biotechnology and nanotechnology. Many job openings will result from the need to replace chemical engineers who transfer to other occupations.

Employment Trend, Projected 2012–22

Total, all occupations: 11%

Engineers: 9%

Chemical engineers: 4%

Note: "All Occupations" includes all occupations in the U.S. Economy. Source: U.S. Bureau of Labor Statistics, Employment Projections Program

Related Occupations
- Agricultural Engineer
- Ceramic Engineer
- Chemist
- Environmental Engineer
- Environmental Science Technician
- Hazardous Waste Manager
- Medical Scientist
- Petroleum Engineer
- Water & Wastewater Engineer
- Wind Energy Engineer

Conversation With . . .
ANDREW ZYDNEY

Distinguished Professor, Chemical Engineering
Pennsylvania State University
Chemical Engineer, 35 years

1. What was your individual career path in terms of education/training, entry-level job, or other significant opportunity?

I received my B.S. in Chemical Engineering from Yale University, then went to M.I.T. for my Ph.D. in Chemical Engineering. I had always been interested in—and good at—science and math, and thought engineering might be a good fit. I didn't know much about the field, but took an "Introduction to Chemical Engineering" course as a sophomore, and did so well that the instructor offered me a position as a research assistant in his lab. I loved doing research, and I became hooked on the discipline as a career path. I've never regretted that. I enjoy applying the principles of chemistry to solve problems, as well as the combination of mathematics with chemistry.

In graduate school, I was involved in a research project looking at the use of membrane filtration to remove toxic plasma proteins from blood, which was being considered as a treatment for diseases ranging from cancer to rheumatoid arthritis to lupus. I really enjoyed learning the fundamentals of membrane separations and was excited about the impact the work could have on human health. I have continued to do research in both membranes and health-related technology. I'm currently working on projects ranging from the purification of polysaccharide-based vaccines, to the use of novel membranes for the purification of plasmid DNA for gene therapy, to the analysis of virus removal filtration processes used to ensure the safety of a wide range of therapeutics.

2. What are the most important skills and/or qualities for someone in your profession?

My roles as chemical engineer and professor each have a somewhat different, although overlapping, skill set. Chemical engineers need a solid foundation in chemistry, physics, and the life sciences, as well as a strong background in math. They need to be good problem solvers who see the big picture.

As a professor, I have significant responsibilities in research and teaching. Both require strong communication skills, although the nature of the communications is very different. Research requires creativity and insight, including the ability to draw connections between ideas. As a researcher, I spend a tremendous amount of time writing manuscripts, funding proposals, and progress reports.

Teaching requires an ability to recognize that everyone has his or her own learning style. My responsibility is to try to connect with each student and effectively communicate complex material in a way that expands each student's understanding.

3. What do you wish you had known going into this profession?

I initially had no idea of the field's breadth. Chemical engineers provide a unique perspective to the industries in which they're involved, with a focus on the chemical and/or biological reactions involved in making and purifying products and the molecular characteristics of novel materials and products.

I also did not appreciate the importance of strong communications skills; I naively thought all I needed was a strong technical base.

4. Are there many job opportunities in your profession? In what specific areas?

Chemical engineers find jobs in the pharmaceutical and biotechnology industries, medicine, electronics, plastics, the food industry, consumer products, consulting, the environment, biofuels and renewable energy, nanotechnology, process safety, and the chemical and petroleum industries. Recent natural gas finds in the U.S. have created exciting new opportunities in energy.

5. How do you see your profession changing in the next five years, what role will technology play in those changes, and what skills will be required?

Developing more sustainable sources of energy and converting life sciences discoveries into cost-effective approaches for improving human health are key challenges. Solutions will require an ability to function effectively on interdisciplinary teams of individuals with very different backgrounds. In addition, chemical engineers will need a greater appreciation of economic constraints, policy and regulatory issues, and public perceptions.

6. What do you enjoy most about your job? What do you enjoy least about your job?

Chemical engineering is a vibrant field that builds directly on developments in the basic sciences and helps convert those discoveries into solutions to major societal challenges. To me, research and the challenge of working on a problem that no one has ever solved before is incredibly exciting. Teaching can be hugely satisfying as well; it's wonderful to see a student have that "a ha" moment when everything falls into place after having struggled with a complex concept.

To be successful in research, one must write proposals that will generate external funding to support a research program. It's time-consuming and often frustrating; competition is high and most grant proposals are rejected—so that's probably the least enjoyable part of my job.

7. Can you suggest a valuable "try this" for students considering a career in your profession?

Playing with a good chemistry set is a great way to see if you enjoy chemistry. Do number puzzles and brainteasers to see if you enjoy solving problems because chemical engineers must be excellent problem solvers. Entering a science fair will give you a feel for what research is all about. As for teaching, help other students with difficult problems or concepts to see if you have a natural ability to teach and communicate.

SELECTED SCHOOLS

Most colleges and universities offer programs in chemistry; a variety of them also have concentrations in chemical engineering. Some of the more prominent schools in this field are listed below.

California Institute of Technology
1200 E. California Boulevard
Pasadena, CA 91125-4400
Phone: (626) 395-6811
http://www.caltech.edu

Georgia Institute of Technology
225 North Avenue
Atlanta, GA 30332-0360
Phone: (404) 894-2000
http://www.gatech.edu

Massachusetts Institute of Technology
77 Massachusetts Avenue
Room 1-206
Cambridge, MA 02139-4307
Phone: (617) 253-1000
http://web.mit.edu

Princeton University
C230 Engineering Quadrangle
Princeton, NJ 08544-5263
Phone: (609) 258-3000
http://www.princeton.edu/main

Stanford University
Huang Engineering Center, Suite 226
Stanford, CA 94305-4121
Phone: (650) 723-2300
https://www.stanford.edu

University of California, Berkeley
320 McLaughlin Hall #1700
Berkeley, CA 94720-1700
Phone: (510) 642-6000
http://www.berkeley.edu

University of California, Santa Barbara
Harold Frank Hall 1038
Santa Barbara, CA 93106-5130
Phone: (805) 893-8000
http://www.ucsb.edu

University of Minnesota, Twin Cities
117 Pleasant Street SE
Minneapolis, MN 55455
Phone: (612) 625-5000
https://twin-cities.umn.edu

University of Texas, Austin (Cockrell)
301 E. Dean Keeton, St.
Stop C2100
Austin, TX 78712-2100
Phone: (512) 471-3434
http://www.engr.utexas.edu

University of Wisconsin, Madison
2610 Engineering Hall
Madison, WI 53706
Phone: (608) 263-2400
http://www.wisc.edu

MORE INFORMATION

American Chemical Society
Education Division
Career Education Program
1155 16th Street, NW
Washington, DC 20036
800.227.5558
www.chemistry.org

American Institute of Chemical Engineers
3 Park Avenue
New York, NY 10016-5991
800.242.4363
www.aiche.org

American Institute of Chemists
315 Chestnut Street
Philadelphia, PA 19106-2702
215.873.8224
www.theaic.org

Association of Energy Engineers (AEE)
4025 Pleasantdale Road, Suite 420
Atlanta, GA 30340
770.447.5083
www.aeecenter.org

Electrochemical Society (ECS)
65 South Main Street, Building D
Pennington, NJ 08534-2839
609.737.1902
www.electrochem.org

National Action Council for Minorities in Engineering
440 Hamilton Avenue, Suite 302
White Plains, NY 10601-1813
914.539.4010
www.nacme.org

National Society of Black Engineers
205 Daingerfield Road
Alexandria, VA 22314
703.549.2207
www.nsbe.org

North American Catalysis Society (NACS)
nacatsoc@gmail.com
www.nacatsoc.org

Society of Hispanic Professional Engineers
13181 Crossroads Parkway North, Suite 450
City of Industry, CA 91746-3497
323.725.3970
www.shpe.org

Society of Women Engineers
203 N. La Salle Street, Suite 1675
Chicago, IL 60601
877.793.4636
www.swe.org

Technology Student Association
1914 Association Drive
Reston, VA 20191-1540
703.860.9000
www.tsaweb.org

Michael Auerbach/Editor

Chemist

Snapshot

Career Cluster: Science, Technology, Engineering & Mathematics
Interests: Mathematics, science, technology, working with your hands, research
Earnings (Yearly Average): $79,140
Employment & Outlook: Slower Than Average Growth Expected

OVERVIEW

Sphere of Work

Chemists apply scientific principles and techniques and use specialized instruments to measure, identify, and manipulate changes in the composition of matter and improve the way the world lives.

They study the composition, structure, and properties of substances and the interactions between them and put this knowledge to profitable or helpful use. Chemists work in a wide range of industries, including the environmental, forensics, industrial, hygiene, food, cosmetic, and medical fields, among others. Many chemists engage in research and development

to help create new or better products. Others work as professors, teachers, or consultants to government agencies.

Work Environment

Most chemists work in laboratories and offices where they document findings from the lab. Sometimes they work outdoors, especially when involved in collecting samples from the environment or from crime scenes. Others work in factories where they teach plant workers which ingredients to use to make a specific chemical. When working around dangerous chemicals, many chemists must wear protective clothing and follow strict safety rules. The field of chemistry is generally a well-compensated one but may require periodic travel for work-related conferences.

Profile

Working Conditions: Work Indoors
Physical Strength: Light Work
Education Needs: Bachelor's Degree, Master's Degree, Doctoral Degree
Licensure/Certification: Usually Not Required
Opportunities For Experience: Military Service, Part-Time Work
Holland Interest Score*: IRE

* See Appendix A

Occupation Interest

A strong interest in and aptitude for math and science is essential to chemists in their day-to-day work. Individuals attracted to the chemistry profession like working with their hands, performing scientific experiments, and creating computer models. Chemistry can be an exciting field because it involves making discoveries that affect everyday life, especially in the sub-field of research and development for chemical manufacturing companies and departments of the US government. For example, the work of chemists can lead to finding a new medicine to cure a disease or developing a chemical product that keeps the environment clean.

A Day in the Life—Duties and Responsibilities

Typical daily tasks of chemists vary by area of specialization and education level. Some branches of chemistry include analytical chemistry, organic chemistry, inorganic chemistry, physical and theoretical chemistry, macromolecular chemistry, medicinal chemistry, and materials chemistry. The very nature of chemistry leads to the discovery of new chemical disciplines, such as combinatory chemistry. Chemists conduct both basic research and applied research. In basic research, there is no specific goal beyond contributing to the field of knowledge about a topic. Applied research is conducted with a specific purpose in mind—perhaps a new therapeutic drug, a new fuel source, or a cheaper or more efficient product to solve an everyday problem.

Many chemists' jobs are found in materials chemistry, working for chemical manufacturing companies and the government. Materials chemists conduct research and development in areas such as paints, soaps, plastics, synthetic rubber and other polymers, as well as materials for computer circuitry. Much of their work results in improvements of daily-use items such as cosmetics, cars, and airplanes.

Other types of chemists perform tests and analysis of a wide variety of materials, including contaminated water and soil, pharmaceuticals, food products, blood drawn from humans and animals, as well as retail products such as soaps, shampoos, and clothing. Chemists also mix chemicals that compose some of the most common household products. Some chemists search for ways to save energy and reduce pollution.

The amount of time spent in the lab and the amount spent documenting lab results can vary. Sometimes chemists are on their feet working at lab benches eight hours a day; at other times, they are in front of the computer researching scientific literature or documenting their work. On most days, it is a combination of both.

Duties and Responsibilities

- Developing new formulas, processes, techniques and methods for solving scientific and technical problems
- Preparing and presenting findings
- Administering and managing programs in research and industrial production
- Conferring with fellow scientists and engineers

OCCUPATION SPECIALTIES

Analytical Chemists

Analytical Chemists analyze chemical compounds and mixtures to determine their composition. They also conduct research to develop or improve techniques, methods, procedures and the application of instruments to chemical analysis.

Organic Chemists

Organic Chemists study the chemistry of carbon compounds. Organic chemists conduct research into agricultural products and foods and have a responsibility in the development of many commercial products such as drugs, plastics and fertilizers.

Inorganic Chemists

Inorganic Chemists conduct experiments on substances which are free or relatively free of carbon. They may also conduct research in relation to metals, ores, gases, heavy chemicals and products such as glass.

Physical Chemists

Physical Chemists conduct research into the relationships between chemical and physical properties of organic and inorganic compounds. Their research often results in new and better sources of energy.

Biochemists

Biochemists study the chemical composition of living cells and organisms along with processes such as metabolism, reproduction, growth, and heredity.

WORK ENVIRONMENT

Physical Environment

Chemists work mostly in lab and office environments, standing up or sitting on stools at standard lab benches. In situations where chemicals should not be inhaled, chemists use fume hoods. Most labs contain various pressurized gases as well as special ion-free water. Chemists are required to wear personal protective equipment, such as safety glasses, gloves, and lab coats. In some cases, they may need to wear face shields, respirators, or even full-body suits with supplied air to guard against biohazards or exposure to other toxic materials.

Relevant Skills and Abilities

Communication Skills
- Speaking effectively
- Writing concisely

Organization & Management Skills
- Coordinating tasks
- Managing people/groups
- Paying attention to and handling details
- Performing duties which change frequently

Research & Planning Skills
- Analyzing information
- Creating ideas
- Developing evaluation strategies
- Using logical reasoning

Technical Skills
- Performing scientific, mathematical and technical work
- Working with data or numbers

Human Environment

Depending on the situation, chemists may interact with other scientists and engineers in a team or may work independently. Some sub-fields of chemistry are more interdisciplinary and involve the collaboration of biologists, chemists, and physicists. In these cases, it is essential to be able to communicate well in a team environment.

Technological Environment

Most chemists work with highly sophisticated technologies inside both the laboratory and the office. They work with advanced analytical equipment and access the Internet to read scientific papers on topics they may be researching. They spend hours at computers using data acquisition, analytical, and presentation software to obtain, analyze, and document their lab findings. Strong

computer skills and knowledge of a variety of software applications is
a necessity.

EDUCATION, TRAINING, AND ADVANCEMENT

High School/Secondary

High school students interested in becoming a chemist should pursue
a college preparatory course, with an emphasis on math and science.
They should be curious, enjoy investigating theories and testing
them through experimentation, and have a strong aptitude for
logical reasoning. Preparing for advanced-level studies in chemistry
requires maintaining good grades overall. Some chemical companies
make summer jobs or internships available to interested high school
students.

Suggested High School Subjects
- Algebra
- Biology
- Calculus
- Chemistry
- College Preparatory
- Computer Science
- English
- Geometry
- Physics
- Science
- Trigonometry

Famous First

The first fullerene to be identified was a sphere-like molecule discovered in 1985 by chemists at Rice University. Fullerenes, carbon molecules that take spherical or cylindrical form, may have applications in medicine, materials science, and nanotechnology. They are produced naturally as a result of lightning strikes but can also be generated in the laboratory by sending a large charge between two graphite electrodes.

College/Postsecondary

A bachelor's degree in chemistry is the minimum requirement for employment; however, most chemistry jobs require at least a master's degree. For those who desire career advancement in research and development or teaching, a doctorate is necessary. Postsecondary students interested in pursuing a career as a chemist will be immersed in math as well as in materials, inorganic, organic, and medical chemistry. They should also join university chemistry organizations, network with chemistry professors, and find internships where they can gain practical experience. Becoming a teacher's assistant can be an advantage when applying to graduate programs.

Related College Majors
- Chemistry, General
- Physics, General

Adult Job Seekers

Adults interested in a chemistry career may find some companies offer technician or support positions that do not require an advanced degree in the field. Many companies provide for tuition reimbursement for continuing education, and it is beneficial to take advantage of this to further one's career.

Through professional chemistry associations, there may be opportunities to learn more about the field, speak with career counselors, access job boards, and make useful contacts with colleagues.

Professional Certification and Licensure

For certification based on education, examination, and experience, chemists can join of the National Registry of Certified Chemists, which is recognized in the industry as setting the standard for professionalism.

Additional Requirements

Prospective chemists should be aware that while the career is mentally exciting and financially rewarding, many chemistry positions involve working with potentially hazardous chemicals. Chemists must be willing to work daily in an environment where there is exposure to acids, bases, toxic chemicals, biohazards, blood, pharmaceutical drugs, solvents, and diseases. Above all, they should be logical and analytical individuals who enjoy applying those skills to the systematic pursuit of new knowledge. As it takes many years of education to become a chemist, interested individuals should have a passion for learning and strong commitment to their goal.

Fun Fact

M. Waldman is the professor of chemistry who sparked Victor Frankenstein's interest in science which led, of course, to Frankenstein's monster.

Source: www.sparknotes.com/lit/frankenstein/characters.html

EARNINGS AND ADVANCEMENT

Earnings depend on the size and type of employer and employee's education, experience and nature of responsibilities. According to a survey by the National Association of Colleges and Employers, beginning salary offers for graduates with a bachelor's degree in chemistry were $43,597 in 2012. Mean annual earnings of chemists were $79,140 in 2014. The lowest ten percent earned less than $41,560, and the highest ten percent earned more than $126,220.

Chemists may receive paid vacations, holidays, and sick days; life and health insurance; and retirement benefits. These are usually paid by the employer.

Metropolitan Areas with the Highest Employment Level in this Occupation

Metropolitan area	Employment [1]	Employment per thousand jobs	Annual mean wage
Wilmington, DE-MD-NJ	3,370	9.98	$94,440
Philadelphia, PA	3,300	1.77	$88,540
Los Angeles-Long Beach-Glendale, CA	2,670	0.66	$69,700
Houston-Sugar Land-Baytown, TX	2,600	0.92	$75,400
Boston-Cambridge-Quincy, MA	2,270	1.26	$82,350
Edison-New Brunswick, NJ	2,220	2.22	$85,640
San Francisco-San Mateo-Redwood City, CA	2,180	2.01	$99,800
New York-White Plains-Wayne, NY-NJ	2,020	0.38	$82,550
Bethesda-Rockville-Frederick, MD	1,790	3.17	$117,220
San Diego-Carlsbad-San Marcos, CA	1,780	1.34	$90,050

[1]Does not include self-employed. Source: Bureau of Labor Statistics

EMPLOYMENT AND OUTLOOK

There were approximately 88,000 chemists employed nationally in 2012. Nearly half of all chemists were employed in manufacturing firms that produce plastics and synthetic materials, drugs, soaps and cleaners, paints, industrial organic chemicals and other chemical products. Employment of chemists is expected to grow slower than the average for all occupations through the year 2022, which means employment is projected to increase 3 percent to 9 percent. This is primarily the result of a decline in the chemical manufacturing industry tempered by growth in the areas of biotechnology, pharmaceuticals and environmental research. Some job openings will occur as a result of chemists retiring or transferring to other occupations. Job prospects are best for chemists with a Ph.D. who may find opportunities with pharmaceutical and biotechnology firms, in addition to teaching positions in colleges and universities.

Employment Trend, Projected 2012–22

Total, all occupations: 11%

Chemists: 6%

Materials scientists: 5%

Note: "All Occupations" includes all occupations in the U.S. Economy. Source: U.S. Bureau of Labor Statistics, Employment Projections Program

Related Occupations
- Chemical Engineer
- Environmental Engineer
- Hazardous Waste Manager
- Medical Scientist
- Petroleum Engineer
- Pharmacist

Related Occupations
- Chemist

Conversation With . . .
MELINDA (MINDY) KEEFE

Senior Research & Development Manager
The Dow Chemical Company, Collegeville PA
Chemist, 14 years

1. What was your individual career path in terms of education/training, entry-level job, or other significant opportunity?

I am an R&D manager at The Dow Chemical Company, where I lead a team of chemists and do my own research. My path has been an exciting ride, with a few key turning points. In high school I was very interested in both science and art, so I choose to attend Penn State because it offered strong programs in both areas. Ultimately, I decided to major in chemistry and used all of my electives for studio art. Working in the lab of Dr. Michael Natan all four years of my undergraduate schooling, I learned how to do laboratory research, prepare presentations and write manuscripts. These skills helped me gain admission to the excellent graduate program at Northwestern University, where I earned a Ph.D. in inorganic chemistry. Upon graduation in 2001, I joined Dow's R&D group in Michigan. My research at Dow focuses on the design and testing of paint formulations—which is not surprising, considering my love of art. In 2007, I further merged my two passions by leveraging my Dow experience and technical capabilities to aid research supporting the conservation and treat-ment of artwork. In 2015, I transitioned from working "at the bench" to leading a team of scientists in Dow's coating materials business.

In 2014, I was recognized by Fortune Magazine with a "Heroes of the 500 Award" for my work supporting the art conservation community. In 2015, I was received the Rising Star Award from the Women Chemists Committee of the American Chemical Society.

2. What are the most important skills and/or qualities for someone in your profession?

Chemists study substances at the atomic and molecular levels, and the ways in which substances react with each other. We use our knowledge to develop new and improved products and to test the quality of manufactured goods. Important skills for professional chemists are a strong foundation in chemistry and physics, coupled with an aptitude for laboratory work, a willingness to learn new areas of science, inquisitiveness and a capacity to communicate well with different types of people.

Successful careers today require the ability to work and thrive in a collaborative environment, as well as the flexibility to adapt and embrace change.

3. What do you wish you had known going into this profession?

I wish I had known more about how to navigate a large corporate environment—including how to network effectively in both school and professional settings. Much of the classical training in science and engineering is very focused on the technical components. Building softer skills in networking, time management, stakeholder management and collaborative leadership are all necessary. In my role as a leader, I also would have benefited from formal training in finance, public speaking, and marketing.

4. Are there many job opportunities in your profession?

Yes! There are opportunities for chemists in a broad range of jobs, including teaching, academic research, start-up companies and in the chemical industry at companies like Dow and DuPont. The United States has a strong commitment to education in STEM (science, technology, engineering, math) because these fields are critical for continued innovation, manufacturing and economic growth. Here at Dow, many scientists and engineers have stayed in technical roles throughout their entire careers, but many others have taken their technical skills and applied them in roles such as project management, sales or new business development. The bottom line is that students with a predisposition toward science and engineering will have many options available to them.

5. How do you see your profession changing in the next five years? What role will technology play in those changes, and what skills will be required?

Technology will continue to transform and enable scientific research. Advances in science and technology make experimental equipment more accurate, efficient and able to yield better results. For example, Dow utilizes high throughput research powered by robotics and advanced data analytics in many areas of product development. This allows researchers to yield superior solutions faster.

6. What do you enjoy most about your job?

I most enjoy mentoring people and helping them discover their strengths, development needs, and career direction. I also greatly enjoy being able to combine my two passions of science and art. Having the opportunity to lead the art conservation collaboration between industry and the art conservation community has been very rewarding both personally and professionally.

I least enjoy the many factors outside of R&D control that often slow down commercialization of new products.

7. **Can you suggest a valuable "try this" for students considering a career in your profession?**

I suggest building relationships with your science teachers in high school and college. Learn what "being a scientist" is for them based on their own schooling and professional activities. Extracurricular activities like science fairs and competitions, including Chemistry Olympiad, Science Olympiad, The Intel Science Talent Search, and FIRST Robotics Competition, are great exposure to scientific research and discussion. At the college level, undergraduate research (including the National Science Foundation's Research Experiences for Undergraduates REU program), co-ops, internships and participation in professional organizations like the American Chemical Society, allows students to try "being a scientist" before settling into a career.

SELECTED SCHOOLS

Most colleges and universities offer programs in chemistry. Some of the more prominent schools in this field are listed below.

California Institute of Technology
Division of Chemistry and Chemical Engineering
1200 E. California Boulevard
Pasadena, CA 91125
Phone: (626) 395-6110
http://www.caltech.edu

Columbia University
Department of Chemistry
344 Havemeyer Hall
New York, NY 10027
Phone: (212) 854-2433
http://www.columbia.edu

Harvard University
Department of Chemistry and Chemical Biology
12 Oxford Street
Cambridge, MA 02138
Phone: (617) 496-3208
http://www.harvard.edu

Massachusetts Institute of Technology
Department of Chemistry
77 Massachusetts Avenue
Cambridge, MA 02139-4307
Phone: (617) 253-1845
http://web.mit.edu

Northwestern University
Department of Chemistry
2145 Sheridan Road
Evanston, IL 60208-3113
http://www.northwestern.edu/

Scripps Research Institute
Kellogg School of Science and Technology
10550 N. Torrey Pines Road
La Jolla, CA 90237
Phone: (858) 784-2400
http://www.scripps.edu

Stanford University
Department of Chemistry
333 Campus Drive
Stanford, CA 94305-5080
Phone: (650) 723-1525
https://www.stanford.edu

University of California, Berkeley
College of Chemistry
Room 419 Larimer Hall
Berkeley, CA 94720-1460
Phone: (510) 642-5882
http://www.berkeley.edu

University of Illinois, Urbana, Champaign
Department of Chemistry
308 Noyes Lab, Box 57-1
Urbana, IL 61801
Phone: (800) 516-0276
http://illinois.edu

University of Wisconsin, Madison
Department of Chemistry
1101 University Avenue
Madison, WI 53706-1322
Phone: (888) 997-2436
http://www.wisc.edu

MORE INFORMATION

American Association for Clinical Chemistry
1850 K Street NW, Suite 625
Washington, DC 20006-2215
800.892.1400
www.aacc.org

American Chemical Society
Education Division
Career Education Program
1155 16th Street, NW
Washington, DC 20036
800.227.5558
www.chemistry.org

American Chemistry Council
700 Second Street, NE
Washington, DC 20002
202.249.7000
www.americanchemistry.com

American Institute of Chemists
315 Chestnut Street
Philadelphia, PA 19106
215.873.8224
www.theaic.org

Chemical Heritage Foundation
315 Chestnut Street
Philadelphia, PA 19106
215.925.2222
www.chemheritage.org

National Registry of Certified Chemists
927 S. Walter Reed Drive, #11
Arlington, VA 22204
703.979.9001
www.nrcc6.org

Susan Williams/Editor

Civil Engineer

Snapshot

Career Cluster: Building & Construction; Science, Technology, Engineering & Mathematics

Interests: Infrastructure, construction, solving problems

Earnings (Yearly Average): $87,130

Employment & Outlook: Faster Than Average Growth Expected

OVERVIEW

Sphere of Work

Civil engineers plan and oversee infrastructure construction projects such as bridges, dams, roads and highways, sewer systems, power plants, and buildings. They assess costs, durability of building materials, and the physical environments in which the project is being constructed. Civil engineers direct and help survey sites, analyze all blueprints, drawings, and photographs, test soil and other materials, and write and present important reports. They work for federal, state, and local governments as well as engineering and architectural firms. Most

civil engineers specialize in a subfield such as sanitation engineering, structural engineering, or transportation engineering.

Work Environment

Civil engineers work in government offices, architectural firms, engineering consultant groups, utility companies, and other office environments where meetings are conducted, plans are drafted, and reports are filed. Civil engineers also spend a great deal of time at project sites, which include building renovation and construction projects, active roadways and highways, along sewer and water lines, and other parts of a region's infrastructure. Many civil engineers spend the majority of their time on site. Although most civil engineers work a standard forty-hour workweek, they may work extra hours as deadlines approach or emergencies occur.

Profile

Working Conditions: Work both Indoors and Outdoors
Physical Strength: Light Work
Education Needs: Bachelor's Degree, Master's Degree, Doctoral Degree
Licensure/Certification: Required
Opportunities For Experience: Internship, Apprenticeship, Military Service, Part-Time Work
Holland Interest Score*: IRE

* See Appendix A

Occupation Interest

Civil engineering is essential to all developed communities—civil engineers help build roads, water and sewer systems, waste management units, and irrigation networks. As they are responsible for public safety, civil engineers must be attentive to detail, demonstrate sound judgment, work well under pressure, and adhere to a strict code of ethics. They also need to be innovative and have strong reasoning skills. The demand for civil engineers remains high, and the number of open jobs is expected to increase dramatically over the next decade. Civil engineering salaries are competitive, and civil engineers typically receive strong benefits.

A Day in the Life—Duties and Responsibilities

Civil engineers' daily responsibilities and duties vary based on their place of employment and specialty. A civil engineer employed by a city government may focus on only one or two major projects per year, while a civil engineer employed by a major architectural firm may be involved in a greater number of projects. Some civil engineers conduct thorough soil studies in addition to structural integrity and strength tests on building materials. Many civil engineers are also supervisors, overseeing construction crews and other engineers at work sites. Civil engineers occasionally act as consultants, providing technical advice and studies to the client as needed.

In general, civil engineers conduct studies and evaluations of existing engineering issues, such as traffic flow studies for roadway construction projects or flow rate analyses for water system upgrades. They prepare public reports, such as environmental impact assessments, bid proposals for contractors, and detailed descriptions of the proposed project site or sites. Civil engineers write feasibility studies in which they estimate the costs and quantities of building materials, equipment, and labor required for a given project. Using drafting tools and software, they create designs for new or improved infrastructure. During the construction phase, civil engineers visit and inspect work sites regularly, monitoring progress and ensuring compliance with government safety standards and the client's wishes. These inspections also entail testing the strength and integrity of the materials used as well as the environment in which they are being used.

Duties and Responsibilities

- Preparing plans and specifications
- Estimating costs and requirements of projects
- Testing materials to be used
- Determining solutions to problems
- Supervising construction and maintenance
- Inspecting existing or newly constructed projects and recommending repairs
- Performing technical research
- Determining the impact of construction on the environment

OCCUPATION SPECIALTIES

Transportation Engineers

Transportation Engineers design and prepare plans, estimates and specifications for the construction and operation of surface transportation projects. Transportation engineers may specialize in a particular phase of the work such as making surveys of roads, improving road signs or lighting, or directing and coordinating construction or maintenance activity.

Structural Engineers

Structural Engineers plan, design and oversee the erection of steel and other structural materials in buildings, bridges and other structures that require a stress analysis.

Hydraulic Engineers

Hydraulic Engineers design and direct the construction of power and other hydraulic engineering projects for the control and use of water.

Construction Engineers

Construction Engineers manage construction projects to ensure that they are built according to plan and completed on schedule.

Geotechnical Engineers

Geotechnical Engineers are concerned primarily with foundations and how structures interact with the earth (i.e., soil, rock).

Fun Fact

Civil engineers do more that build roads and bridges . . . a civil engineer created the slippery part of a water slide by designing a pumping system to circulate the proper amount of water to the flume, along with the proper design to hold the rider's weight, the water, and the wind force!

Source: www.nspe.org/resources/media/resources/ten-fun-and-exciting-facts-about-engineering#sthash.Q4ova3Js.dpuf

WORK ENVIRONMENT

Physical Environment

Civil engineers work in office environments, where they conduct meetings with clients and government officials, prepare public reports, design systems and structures, and organize all documentation pertaining to projects. They also spend a great deal of time at project sites, conducting inspections and overseeing personnel. Some civil engineers also teach at colleges and universities.

Relevant Skills and Abilities

Communication Skills
- Speaking effectively
- Writing concisely

Organization & Management Skills
- Coordinating tasks
- Demonstrating leadership
- Managing people/groups
- Paying attention to and handling details

Research & Planning Skills
- Analyzing information
- Solving problems

Technical Skills
- Performing scientific, mathematical and technical work

Human Environment

Depending on their areas of specialty, civil engineers interact and collaborate with government officials, architects, construction crews, materials and equipment suppliers, business executives, and other engineers. Civil engineering professors also work with students, other professors, and school administrators.

Technological Environment

Civil engineers work with a wide range of technologies and tools during the course of their work. In the office, they use computer-aided design (CAD) and other design software, cartography software, project management systems and databases, and other analytical and scientific programs. At a project site, they use soil collection equipment, electronic distance-measuring devices, levels, compasses, pressure gauges, and scales.

EDUCATION, TRAINING, AND ADVANCEMENT

High School/Secondary

High school students should study physics, chemistry, and biology. Mathematics, including algebra, geometry, trigonometry, and calculus, are also essential courses. Furthermore, high school students should take computer science courses and hone their writing and public speaking skills through English and communications classes. Courses that help students understand blueprints and architecture, such as drafting and industrial arts, are also highly useful.

Suggested High School Subjects
- Algebra
- Applied Communication
- Applied Math
- Applied Physics
- Biology
- Blueprint Reading
- Calculus
- Chemistry
- College Preparatory
- Composition
- Computer Science
- Drafting
- Economics
- English
- Geometry
- Mathematics
- Mechanical Drawing
- Physics
- Science
- Trigonometry

Famous First

The first bridge with piers sunk in the open sea, thus forming the foundation for its towers, was the Golden Gate Bridge in San Francisco, pictured. It was the first bridge to be built across the outer mouth of a major ocean harbor—in this case, San Francisco Bay, opening out to the Pacific Ocean. Construction took from 1933 to 1937.

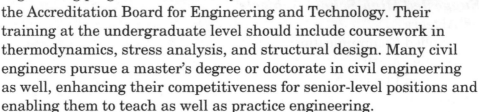

College/Postsecondary

Civil engineers must receive a bachelor's degree in civil engineering from an engineering program accredited by the Accreditation Board for Engineering and Technology. Their training at the undergraduate level should include coursework in thermodynamics, stress analysis, and structural design. Many civil engineers pursue a master's degree or doctorate in civil engineering as well, enhancing their competitiveness for senior-level positions and enabling them to teach as well as practice engineering.

Related College Majors
- Architectural Engineering
- Civil Engineering
- Civil Engineering/Civil Technology
- Engineering Design

Adult Job Seekers

Qualified civil engineers may apply directly to government agencies, architectural firms, and other employers with open positions. Many universities have placement programs that can help recent civil engineering graduates find work. Additionally, civil engineers may join and network through professional associations and societies, such as the American Society of Civil Engineers (ASCE).

Professional Certification and Licensure

Civil engineers who work with the public must be licensed as a Professional Engineer (PE) in the state or states in which they seek to practice. The licensure process includes a written examination, a specified amount of education, and at least four years of work experience. Continuing education is a common requirement for ongoing licensure.

Some professional civil engineering associations, like the American Society of Civil Engineers, the Academy of Geo-Professionals, and the American Academy of Water Resources Engineers, offer specialty certification programs as well. Leadership in Energy and Environmental Design (LEED) certification may be necessary for some projects.

Additional Requirements

Civil engineers must be able to analyze and comprehend complex systems. In addition to acquiring a strong understanding of the engineering field and their area of specialty, civil engineers must be excellent communicators, as they often work with others in a team environment or in a supervisory capacity. Successful completion of a civil service exam may be required for employment by a government agency.

EARNINGS AND ADVANCEMENT

Earnings depend on the size and geographic location of the employer and the employee's qualifications. In 2012, the average salary offer to college graduates with a bachelor's degree in civil engineering was $56,874 per year, according to the National Association of Colleges and Employers. Civil engineers with a master's degree were offered first year-salaries averaging $65,931, while those with a Ph.D. were offered $70,090 annually.

Mean annual earnings of civil engineers were $87,130 in 2014. The lowest ten percent earned less than $52,570, and the highest ten percent earned more than $128,110.

Civil engineers may receive paid vacations, holidays, and sick days; life and health insurance; and retirement benefits. These are usually paid by the employer.

Metropolitan Areas with the Highest
Employment Level in this Occupation

Metropolitan area	Employment [1]	Employment per thousand jobs	Annual mean wage
Houston-Sugar Land-Baytown, TX	10,850	3.81	$112,480
New York-White Plains-Wayne, NY-NJ	8,210	1.52	$97,680
Los Angeles-Long Beach-Glendale, CA	6,880	1.70	$97,980
Chicago-Joliet-Naperville, IL	6,640	1.77	$90,550
Seattle-Bellevue-Everett, WA	5,970	4.00	$86,100
Washington-Arlington-Alexandria, DC-VA-MD-WV	5,730	2.41	$93,710
Sacramento--Arden-Arcade--Roseville, CA	4,660	5.43	$97,870
Santa Ana-Anaheim-Irvine, CA	4,400	2.97	$97,410
Atlanta-Sandy Springs-Marietta, GA	4,320	1.81	$93,080
Oakland-Fremont-Hayward, CA	4,290	4.18	$107,990

[1]Does not include self-employed. Source: Bureau of Labor Statistics

EMPLOYMENT AND OUTLOOK

There were approximately 273,000 civil engineers employed nationally in 2012. Most were employed by firms providing architectural and engineering services, primarily developing designs for new construction projects. Employment of civil engineers is expected to grow faster than the average for all occupations through the year 2022, which means employment is projected to increase up to 20 percent or more.

As a result of growth in the population and an increased emphasis on security, more civil engineers will be needed to design and construct safe and higher capacity transportation, water supply and pollution control systems, in addition to large buildings and building complexes. They also will be needed to repair or replace existing roads, bridges and other public structures. Job openings will also result from the need to replace civil engineers who transfer to other occupations or leave the labor force

Employment Trend, Projected 2012–22

Civil engineers: 20%

Total, all occupations: 11%

Engineers (all): 9%

Note: "All Occupations" includes all occupations in the U.S. Economy. Source: U.S. Bureau of Labor Statistics, Employment Projections Program

Related Occupations
- Architect
- Construction & Building Inspector
- Energy Engineer
- Environmental Science Technician
- Mechanical Engineer
- Surveyor & Cartographer
- Urban & Regional Planner

- Water & Wastewater Engineer
- Wind Energy Engineer

Related Occupations
- Civil Engineer
- Environmental Health & Safety Officer
- Surveying & Mapping Manager

Conversation With . . .
JAMES W. BLAKE, P.E., P.L.S.

Owner, Blake Consulting Services, LLC
Civil Engineer, 35 years

1. What was your individual career path in terms of education/training, entry-level job, or other significant opportunity ?

My father was a civil engineer, and although I wasn't quite sure what I wanted to do, I knew if I had that degree, I'd have options. I earned a B.S. in civil engineering from the University of Maryland, and considered becoming a pilot. Unfortunately, my vision wasn't good enough. So I went to work as a civil/structural engineer, then went right back to school and earned a B.S. in business and accounting because I was interested in management and the business of engineering. My first job was a lot of sitting at a desk and crunching numbers and I wanted more variety, so I moved into transportation and general civil engineering, which allowed me to interact with clients, politicians and a greater variety of projects. I got into management about eight to 10 years out of college. My specialty is roadway design and construction management. A lot of what I do now is business development related and involves competing for and winning consulting contracts from federal, state, and local governmental agencies.

2. What are the most important skills and/or qualities for someone in your profession?

The ability to communicate technical ideas in plain language is critical. You also need to be organized, and to have the ability to analyze a complex problem quickly, break it down into its various parts and then come up with a practical and economical solution that serves the client's best interests.

3. What do you wish you had known going into this profession?

Construction and civil engineering can be cyclical, and it's very much tied to the economy. So that means my workload can be cyclical. The politics of winning work through public agencies is also more involved and complex than I'd imagined it to be. Someone who wants to win public sector work must be very visible and involved with a particular governmental agency and those who oversee it.

4

4. Are there many job opportunities in your profession? In what specific areas?

I'd say very many. Job opportunities are excellent in transportation, structural, civil, environmental and geotechnical engineering, as well as construction inspection. Civil engineering is a very broad and diverse field, and there are some great challenges and opportunities.

5. How do you see your profession changing in the next five years, what role will technology play in those changes, and what skills will be required?

Technical advances are being adapted to complete projects more efficiently and expeditiously. If you need to do a technical analysis of a building—for example, an unusually-shaped building or structure—software analysis and document production programs allow you to do a more elaborate analysis more quickly and cheaply. Aerial drones are being used for inspection work on tall buildings and bridges; you just fly your drone over the area you wish to observe and it takes video as well as pictures of the subject area. An engineer on the ground can then confirm that construction is in fact proceeding in accordance with the construction documents. GPS is relatively old news; it's being programmed into black boxes on earthwork machines so they automatically excavate and grade areas; the machine will then drive itself and make all the cuts and fills using GPS and lasers for elevations. Other construction-related uses for GPS have continued to become more common.

6. What do you enjoy most about your job? What do you enjoy least about your job?

I most enjoy the variety of projects and my ability to interact with various people who have different roles in the development and completion of a project. As with any industry, there are difficult people you have to deal with and that's probably the hardest part.

7. Can you suggest a valuable "try this" for students considering a career in your profession?

Find an engineering company and see if they sponsor a student mentor day. Some professional organizations do that, such as the American Society of Civil Engineers or the Society of American Military Engineers. You could also intern or work part-time. There are also many good books on the topic, as well as YouTube videos, of different types of construction projects.

SELECTED SCHOOLS

Most colleges and universities offer programs in engineering; a variety of them also have concentrations in civil engineering. Some of the more prominent schools in this field are listed below.

Carnegie Mellon University
5000 Forbes Ave
Pittsburgh, PA 15213
Phone: (412) 256-2000
http://www.cmu.edu

Cornell University
242 Carpenter Hall
Ithaca, NY 14850
Phone: (607) 254-4636
https://www.cornell.edu

Georgia Institute of Technology
225 North Avenue
Atlanta, GA 30332
Phone: (404) 894-2000
http://www.gatech.edu

Massachusetts Institute of Technology
77 Massachusetts Avenue
Room 1-206
Cambridge, MA 02139
Phone: (617) 253-1000
http://web.mit.edu

Purdue University, West Lafayette
701 W. Stadium Avenue
Suite 3000 ARMS
West Lafayette, IN 47907
Phone: (765) 494-4600
http://www.purdue.edu

Stanford University
Huang Engineering Center Suite 226
450 Serra Mall
Stanford, CA 94305-4121
Phone: (650) 723-2300
https://www.stanford.edu

University of California, Berkeley
320 McLaughlin Hall #1700
Berkeley, CA 94720-1700
Phone: (510) 642-6000
http://www.berkeley.edu/

University of Illinois, Urbana, Champaign
1398 West Green
Urbana, IL 061801
Phone: (217) 333-1000
http://illinois.edu

University of Michigan, Ann Arbor
Robert H. Lurie Engineering Center
Ann Arbor, MI 48109
Phone: (734) 764-1817
https://www.umich.edu

University of Texas, Austin (Cockrell)
301 E. Dean Keeton St.
Stop C2100
Austin, TX 78712
Phone: (512) 471-1166
http://www.engr.utexas.edu

MORE INFORMATION

Academy of Geo-Professionals
1801 Alexander Bell Drive
Reston, VA 20191
703.295.6314
www.geoprofessionals.org

**Accreditation Board for
Engineering and Technology**
111 Market Place, Suite 1050
Baltimore, MD 21202-4012
410.347.7700
www.abet.org

**American Academy of Water
Resources Engineers**
1801 Alexander Bell Drive
Reston, VA 20191
703.295.6414
www.aawre.org

**American Society of Civil
Engineers**
1801 Alexander Bell Drive
Reston, VA 21091-4400
800.548.2723
www.asce.org

**National Action Council for
Minorities in Engineering**
440 Hamilton Avenue, Suite 302
White Plains, NY 10601-1813
914.539.4010
www.nacme.org

**National Council of Structural
Engineers Associations**
645 North Michigan Avenue, Suite 540
Chicago, IL 60611
312.649.4600
www.ncsea.com

**National Society of Black
Engineers**
205 Daingerfield Road
Alexandria, VA 22314
703.549.2207
www.nsbe.org

**National Society of Professional
Engineers**
1420 King Street
Alexandria, VA 22314-2794
703.684.2800
www.nspe.org

**Society of Hispanic Professional
Engineers**
13181 Crossroads Parkway North,
Suite 450
City of Industry, CA 91746-3497
323.725.3970
www.shpe.org

Society of Women Engineers
203 N. La Salle Street, Suite 1675
Chicago, IL 60601
877.793.4636
www.swe.org

Technology Student Association
1914 Association Drive
Reston, VA 20191-1540
703.860.9000
www.tsaweb.org

Michael Auerbach/Editor

Computer Engineer

Snapshot

Career Cluster: Information Technology; Science, Technology, Engineering & Mathematics

Interests: Computer science, solving problems, collaborating with others

Earnings (Yearly Average): $110,650

Employment & Outlook: Average Growth Expected

OVERVIEW

Sphere of Work

Computer hardware engineers plan, design, and test computer components for use in a variety of industries. These components include computer chips, circuit boards, routers, and more. Computer engineers are involved in each stage of the development process, including designing blueprints, testing the components, and analyzing the results. They are also involved in the manufacturing process. Engineers sometimes work with computer software developers to make sure that the hardware and software components work together correctly.

Work Environment

Computer engineers typically work in research laboratories, where they build and test an assortment of computer models. The environments of these laboratories can vary; the majority of them are located in metropolitan areas. Manufacturing, design, or research-and-development firms commonly employ computer engineers. As communication technology improves, some engineers may be able to telecommute. While they typically work full time—forty hours per week—the work may require overtime on occasion.

Profile

Working Conditions: Work Indoors
Physical Strength: Light Work
Education Needs: Bachelor's Degree, Master's Degree
Licensure/Certification: Usually Not Required
Opportunities For Experience: Military Service, Part-time Work
Holland Interest Score*: IRE

* See Appendix A

Occupation Interest

The computer engineer profession tends to attract individuals with a strong background in computer science and hardware. Most have a degree in computer engineering from an Accreditation Board for Engineering and Technology (ABET)–accredited school. Computer engineers are problem solvers who enjoy figuring out the best solution to computer-related problems. They should also be able to communicate and collaborate with others in the field. Engineers should be interested in the latest technology and be willing to continue their education throughout their career.

A Day in the Life—Duties and Responsibilities

Computer engineers use their education and skills to design, develop, and test new computer hardware and components. These include computer systems, computer chips, and the physical parts of computers. Engineers are also involved in the design and development of new routers, printers, and keyboards. Their daily responsibilities vary depending on the project they are working on. Meetings may be held throughout the day with other engineers, technology vendors, and various other employees.

Computer engineers are normally involved in the entire process of product development and implementation. This includes the manufacturing process. Throughout the day, an engineer will provide technical support to other employees, including designers, the marketing department, and technology vendors. As computer technology is developed and created, engineers will perform tests and ensure that everything meets specifications and requirements. This testing process usually involves analyzing test data, product prototypes, or theoretical models. As new hardware is implemented, an engineer will monitor how it is functioning and make any modifications necessary so that it performs according to specifications. Engineers also make recommendations for additional hardware, such as keyboards, routers, and printers.

When new components are designed and manufactured, engineers have to make sure that the hardware is compatible with software developments. Because of this, hardware engineers collaborate closely with software developers throughout the process.

Duties and Responsibilities

- Designing new computer hardware and overseeing its manufacture
- Analyzing and testing computer hardware
- Modifying hardware to ensure its compatibility with new software and other technologies

WORK ENVIRONMENT

Physical Environment

Research laboratories predominate. At these laboratories, computer engineers design, develop, and build a broad range of computer models, both physical and theoretical. This is also where they test the models. These laboratories are often well lit, very clean, and well ventilated.

Relevant Skills and Abilities

Communication Skills
- Speaking effectively
- Writing concisely

Interpersonal/Social Skills
- Working as a member of a team

Research & Planning Skills
- Solving problems
- Using logical reasoning

Technical Skills
- Performing scientific, mathematical and technical work

Human Environment

Throughout the day, computer engineers will communicate and collaborate with a variety of other professionals in the field, including software developers, sales departments, technology vendors, manufacturers, and other engineers.

Technological Environment

Computer engineers work with a wide variety of computer-related technologies, including systems, hardware, and software. They also work with both physical and theoretical computer models. During the design and manufacturing process, blueprints and specifications are used. Servers that store massive amounts of data are also implemented

EDUCATION, TRAINING, AND ADVANCEMENT

High School/Secondary

Normally employers require applicants to have a high school diploma or an equivalent GED certificate. There are several basic and advanced high school courses that will greatly benefit a student interested in becoming a computer engineer. Courses in computer science, mathematics, and engineering will give a student a good background in the fundamentals of the profession. Extracurricular computer clubs are sometimes available; such a club would also benefit those interested in computer engineering.

Suggested High School Subjects
- Algebra
- Applied Communication
- Applied Math
- Applied Physics
- Calculus
- Computer Programming
- Computer Science
- English
- Geometry
- Mathematics
- Trigonometry

Famous First

The first commercially successful minicomputer was the Digital Equipment Corporation's PDP-8, introduced in 1965. Smaller and less expensive than a mainframe computer, but almost as powerful, the PDP-8 was priced at $18,000 and sold more than 50,000 units. Today, a specimen is on display at the Smithsonian's National Museum of American History in Washington, D.C.

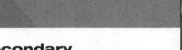

College/Postsecondary

Employers typically require a computer engineer to have at least a bachelor's degree in a related field. Some employers require that an engineer have a degree from an ABET-accredited school. The majority of entry-level professionals have a degree in computer engineering, but employers usually accept electrical-engineering degrees as well. Students should make sure they take the appropriate postsecondary courses that give them a strong background in math and science.

Some technical schools offer programs in computer and electronics technology, which typically include instruction in circuits, systems, and specialized techniques used in the field. Students are given formal classroom instruction as well as the opportunity for practical application in a laboratory setting. Many of these technical schools offer job-placement programs, and they are a great place to network with more experienced professionals.

Since computer engineers work closely with computer software systems, professionals need a solid background in computer programming as well. Most computer-engineering curricula include computer-science courses that can give a student experience with programming.

Specialized jobs in computer engineering and some large firms may require a master's degree. These degrees commonly take two years to complete. Many computer engineers take graduate courses after work, which allows them to acquire work experience while pursuing their master's degree

Related College Majors
- Computer Engineering
- Computer Engineering Technology
- Computer Maintenance Technology
- Computer Programming
- Computer Science
- Information Sciences & Systems

Adult Job Seekers

Because computer technology is always developing, it should be understood that computer engineers must continue their education throughout their careers. If an individual does not have any experience in computer engineering or related fields, he or she should enroll in a college or a technical school that offers a relevant program.

Professional Certification and Licensure

Although it is not normally required, the Institute of Electrical and Electronics Engineers (IEEE) Computer Society can certify computer engineers. Attaining certification helps engineers verify their skills and knowledge of the field's practices. Engineers who have completed a certification program are more likely to achieve higher-paying positions.

Additional Requirements

A computer engineer must possess great analytical skills in order to properly examine complex computer equipment. Problem-solving skills are needed to figure out the best way to improve upon computer hardware. Computer engineers need to be able to think critically in order to identify problems and determine solutions. They should also be willing to continue their education throughout their career in order to keep their knowledge up to date and relevant

Fun Fact

In 1947, computer engineers traced an error in the Mark II computer at Harvard Univer-sity to a moth trapped in a relay. They taped the insect to a log and wrote, "First actual case of bug being found." But Thomas Edison used the term "bug" in similar context decades earlier.

Source: http://americanhistory.si.edu/collections/search/object/nmah_334663

EARNINGS AND ADVANCEMENT

Computer engineers may be promoted after several years of experience. According to a salary survey by the National Association of Colleges and Employers, the starting salary offer for graduates with a bachelor's degree in computer engineering was $67,463 in 2012.

Mean annual earnings of computer hardware engineers were $110,650 in 2014. The lowest ten percent earned less than $66,070, and the highest ten percent earned more than $160,610.

Mean annual earnings of computer software developers were $106,050 in 2014. The lowest ten percent earned less than $63,250, and the highest ten percent earned more than $154,800.

Computer engineers may receive paid vacations, holidays, and sick days; life and health insurance; and retirement benefits. These are usually paid by the employer.

Metropolitan Areas with the Highest
Employment Level in this Occupation (Hardware)

Metropolitan area	Employment [1]	Employment per thousand jobs	Annual mean wage
San Jose-Sunnyvale-Santa Clara, CA	11,620	11.94	$136,220
San Diego-Carlsbad-San Mar-cos, CA	3,820	2.89	$99,050
Dallas-Plano-Irving, TX	3,110	1.39	$101,310
San Francisco-San Mateo-Redwood City, CA	2,630	2.42	$130,470
Austin-Round Rock-San Marcos, TX	2,610	2.95	$106,220
Washington-Arlington-Alexandria, DC-VA-MD-WV	2,550	1.07	$117,180
Santa Ana-Anaheim-Irvine, CA	2,510	1.69	$120,280
Baltimore-Towson, MD	2,260	1.75	$123,020
Los Angeles-Long Beach-Glendale, CA	2,060	0.51	$109,030
Boston-Cambridge-Quincy, MA NECTA Division	1,990	1.11	$115,660

[1]Does not include self-employed. Source: Bureau of Labor Statistics

Metropolitan Areas with the Highest Employment Level in this Occupation (Software)

Metropolitan area	Employment [1]	Employment per thousand jobs	Annual mean wage
San Jose-Sunnyvale-Santa Clara, CA	27,080	27.82	$138,410
Washington-Arlington-Alexandria, DC-VA-MD-WV	24,720	10.39	$110,780
Boston-Cambridge-Quincy, MA	18,600	10.36	$116,270
Dallas-Plano-Irving, TX	13,280	5.93	$99,060
San Francisco-San Mateo-Redwood City, CA	11,360	10.45	$120,400
Los Angeles-Long Beach-Glendale, CA	11,190	2.76	$120,690
New York-White Plains-Wayne, NY-NJ	11,140	2.07	$113,700
Houston-Sugar Land-Baytown, TX	10,670	3.75	$106,090
Atlanta-Sandy Springs-Marietta, GA	10,160	4.26	$96,320
Seattle-Bellevue-Everett, WA	8,730	5.85	$115,800

[1]Does not include self-employed. Source: Bureau of Labor Statistics

EMPLOYMENT AND OUTLOOK

Computer hardware engineers held about 83,300 jobs nationally in 2012. Employment is expected to grow about as fast as the average for all occupations through the year 2022, which means employment is projected to increase 5 percent to 9 percent. Although the use of information technology continues to expand rapidly, the manufacture of computer hardware is expected to be adversely affected by intense foreign competition.

Computer software developers held about 1,020,000 jobs nationally in 2012. Employment is expected to grow much faster than the average for all occupations through the year 2022, which means employment is projected to increase 20 percent or more. This is a result of businesses and other organizations adopting and integrating new technologies and seeking to maximize the efficiency of their computer systems. Mobile technology, the growing use of software applications in the healthcare industry and concerns over cybersecurity will all contribute to job demand.

Employment Trend, Projected 2012–22

Software developers: 27%

Total, all occupations: 11%

Engineers (all): 9%

Computer hardware engineers: 7%

Note: "All Occupations" includes all occupations in the U.S. Economy. Source: U.S. Bureau of Labor Statistics, Employment Projections Program

Related Occupations
- Computer & Information Systems Manager
- Computer Network Architect
- Computer Programmer
- Computer Support Specialist
- Computer Systems Analyst
- Database Administrator
- Information Security Analyst
- Information Technology Project Manager
- Network & Computer Systems Administrator
- Operations Research Analyst
- Software Developer
- Web Administrator
- Web Developer

Related Occupations
- Computer Systems Officer
- Computer Systems Specialist

Conversation With . . . *MARGARET LE*

Engineering Manager, Heroku, San Francisco, CA
Computer Engineer, 15 years

1. What was your individual career path in terms of education/training, entry-level job, or other significant opportunity?

In seventh grade, I took a computer programming class and learned to write programs using the programming language Turbo Basic. We learned how to give the computer instructions to make it do things like move a duck across a pond on the screen. In high school, I learned another programming language, Pascal. Back then, not every family had access to a personal computer. I was lucky to go to a school that provided a computer curriculum.

Because I've always been interested in cultures and languages, I majored in Linguistics in college, but continued to take computer science courses. Luckily for me, a lot of the theory behind natural language grammars and syntax can be easily applied to computer languages. In fact, there's an area of linguistics called Computational Linguistics that deals with the computational aspects of human language.

The Internet was just becoming popular when I was in college. I got my first computer-related job working part-time helping to develop a website for the Great Lakes Commission, which combined my interests in web development and in the environment and conservation.

After college, I worked for a company that created web sites for companies. I talked to customers about the requirements for their site and developed them using a computer programming language that is no longer used. I continued working as a software developer, learning new programming languages and systems. I eventually gained enough experience creating production software to lead the technical direction for teams on which I was a developer. Several years ago, I transitioned from being a software developer to being an engineering manager. As an engineering manager, I'm responsible for ensuring that my engineering team has all the tools they need to build software.

2. What are the most important skills and/or qualities for someone in your profession?

One of the most important skills is to enjoy solving problems. You should have an interest in figuring out how to fix or improve things, whether it's finding the quickest/most scenic/least trafficked route to your favorite store or adding extra pockets to a jacket.

Being adaptable also helps. Software and the technology that runs it are constantly changing, both in terms of new advances and in the ways we interact with them. In order to deftly navigate this rapidly changing landscape, you have to be willing to adjust to new conditions.

3. What do you wish you had known going into this profession?

I wish I had known earlier that part of continually learning and developing new skills is a willingness to fail.

4. Are there many job opportunities in your profession? In what specific areas?

Opportunities in developing software, running software, and building the infrastructure on which that software runs are plentiful, as are roles like mine, leading teams in software development.

Web pioneer Marc Andreessen said, "Software is eating the world." From booking flights to analyzing health information and creating focused preventative care plans, reliance on software and computers is pervasive. There are myriad opportunities to participate as a designer, developer, or engineer. The options are astounding and offer ways to be creative, scientific, and experimental.

5. How do you see your profession changing in the next five years? What role will technology play in those changes, and what skills will be required?

In the next five years, I envision this profession changing dramatically. How and where we apply computer technology will continue to grow. I can see people who specialize in other fields acquiring skills in computer engineering to help solve problems in their particular fields. This means that even in traditionally non-computer related fields, we'll see more and more people using technology and engineering skills in their day-to-day jobs. That said, the fundamental skills of curiosity, adaptability, and a passion for solving problems will allow a good engineer to succeed with these changes.

As networked and connected devices become ever more popular, we're seeing an inordinate amount of potentially invaluable data being passed around. Understanding this and opening our minds to the possibilities will be key for computer engineers.

6. What do you enjoy most about your job? What do you enjoy least about your job?

The thing I enjoy most is solving new problems. Every time I find a path toward a solution, I add new skills to my toolbox, whether it's new algorithms and technological frameworks to utilize myself or to teach to other developers.

The thing I enjoy least is sometimes being paged in the middle of the night to resolve an issue with software. This occurs infrequently, but does sometimes happen.

7. Can you suggest a valuable "try this" for students considering a career in your profession?

As a student, you can start by hopping online and trying out the wealth of coding tutorials. Code.org/learn is a great resource. You can also participate in competitions like Technovation Challenge, which is a technology entrepreneurship competition for girls, or Microsoft's Imagine Cup. Both are awesome introductions to computer engineering and great ways to use your creativity and technology skills to create things.

SELECTED SCHOOLS

Many colleges and universities offer programs in computer science; a variety of them also have concentrations in computer engineering. Some of the more prominent schools in this field are listed below..

Carnegie Mellon University
5000 Forbes Avenue
Pittsburgh, PA 15213-3891
Phone: (412) 268-8525
http://www.cs.cmu.edu

Cornell University
4130 Upson Hall
Ithaca, NY 14853-7501
Phone: (607) 255-7316
http://www.cs.cornell.edu/degreeprogs/grad/index.htm

Georgia Institute of Technology
801 Atlantic Drive
Atlanta, GA 30332-0280
Phone: (404) 894-4267
http://www.cc.gatech.edu

Massachusetts Institute of Technology
77 Massachusetts Avenue
Room 38-401
Cambridge, MA 02139-4307
http://www.eecs.mit.edu/index.html
Phone: (617) 253-4603

Purdue University, West Lafayette
701 W. Stadium Avenue, Suite 3000 ARMS
West Lafayette, IN 47907-2045
https://engineering.purdue.edu/Engr
Phone: (765) 494-5345

Stanford University
353 Serra Mall
Stanford, CA 94305-9025
Phone: (650) 723-2273
http://www.cs.stanford.edu

University of California, Berkeley
205 Cory Hall
Berkeley, CA 94720-1770
Phone: (510) 642-3068
http://www.eecs.berkeley.edu

University of Illinois, Urbana, Champaign
201 N. Goodwin Avenue
Urbana, IL 61801
Phone: (217) 333-3527
http://www.cs.uiuc.edu/graduate

University of Michigan, Ann Arbor
Robert H. Lurie Engineering Center
1221 Beal Avenue
Ann Arbor, MI 48109-2102
Phone (734) 647- 7000
http://www.engin.umich.edu/college

University of Texas, Austin
1 University Station C0500
Austin, TX 78712-1188
Phone: (512) 471-9503
http://www.cs.utexas.edu

MORE INFORMATION

Association for Computing Machinery
2 Penn Plaza, Suite 701
New York, NY 10121-0701
800.342.6626
www.acm.org

Computing Research Association
1828 L Street NW, Suite 800
Washington, DC 20036
202.234.2111
www.cra.org

Institute for the Certification of Computer Professionals
2400 East Devon Avenue, Suite 281
Des Plaines, IL 60018-4610
800.843.8227
www.iccp.org

Institute of Electrical and Electronics Engineers Computer Society
2001 L Street NW, Suite 700
Washington, DC 20036-4928
202.371.0101
www.computer.org

Patrick Cooper /Editor

Electrical & Electronics Engineer

Snapshot

Career Cluster: Manufacturing; Science, Technology, Engineering & Mathematics

Interests: Electronics, engineering, performing research, solving problems

Earnings (Yearly Average): $97,720

Employment & Outlook: Slower Than Average Growth Expected

OVERVIEW

Sphere of Work

Electrical and electronics engineers can work directly for companies in the manufacturing and utilities industries, for an engineering services firm, for the federal government (including the military), or for a university or other educational or research institution. Their work includes basic research and development of new electrical and electronic equipment, as well as the practical design, development, and testing of that equipment and supervision of its manufacture and operation. New electrical and electronic equipment ranges from consumer

electronics and electrical power tools to telecommunications satellites and space probes. Computer hardware engineering is considered a separate occupation.

Work Environment

Work is usually done in a laboratory or office setting, primarily using computers but also with practical testing of physical models of newly designed electrical and electronic equipment. Work can be at temporary locations for a specific project, such as designing and implementing the electrical and electronic infrastructure of a new airport. Some work is done outside, especially when testing newly installed major equipment.

Electrical and electronics engineers often work in teams with other engineers, scientists, and technicians. They also have to interact with customers and clients, many of whom do not have an engineering background.

Profile

Working Conditions: Work Indoors
Physical Strength: Light Work
Education Needs: Bachelor's Degree, Master's Degree, Doctoral Degree
Licensure/Certification: Usually Not Required
Opportunities For Experience: Internship, Apprenticeship, Military Service, Part-time Work
Holland Interest Score*: IRE

* See Appendix A

Occupation Interest

Aspiring electrical and electronics engineers should be interested in engineering work and willing to earn at least an undergraduate engineering degree. They should be interested in developing new equipment and finding solutions to a variety of engineering challenges. Since the field of electronics changes rapidly, they should be willing to engage in lifelong learning and training.

Some electrical and electronics engineers are employed in purely research-focused positions. Individuals interested in such positions would be employed by a university or research institute and should earn a Ph.D. in the field.

A Day in the Life—Duties and Responsibilities

Key tasks of electrical and electronics engineers are design and development of new products. New equipment is created for a large variety of industrial, commercial, consumer, military, and scientific applications. This means that a day's work is determined by both the nature of a new project and its development phase.

At the beginning of a project, electrical and electronics engineers must communicate with customers and the team of engineers, technicians, and scientists involved. They can fill the role of a team member or a project manager and may also contribute to the analysis of the systems requirements, cost, and capacity and set up a project development plan. This is generally collaborative work.
Design of new electrical and electronic equipment involves the preparation of technical drawings and engineering sketches, which are created with computer-aided design (CAD) software. It is a highly creative task built on solid engineering knowledge.

During the implementation phase, electrical and electronics engineers supervise the manufacture of models, prototypes, and final products. These are constantly tested to make sure they operate as planned and designed. For large, new equipment, electrical and electronics engineers may be responsible for supervising installation and inspection on-site.

In addition to developing new electrical and electronic equipment, some jobs, especially at universities, include pure research and some teaching, work with more managerial and administrative tasks as a person advances.

Duties and Responsibilities

- Designing test apparatus
- Devising evaluation procedures
- Developing new and improved products
- Recommending equipment design changes
- Writing equipment specifications
- Writing performance requirements
- Directing field operations
- Developing maintenance schedules
- Solving operational problems

OCCUPATION SPECIALTIES

Electrical Engineers

Electrical engineers design, develop, test, and supervise the manufacturing of electrical equipment, such as electric motors, radar and navigation systems, communications systems, or power generation equipment. Electrical engineers also design the electrical systems of automobiles and aircraft.

Electronics Engineers

Electronics engineers design and develop electronic equipment, such as broadcast and communications systems, from smart phones to global positioning systems (GPS). Many also work in areas closely related to computer hardware.

Electrical and Electronics Engineering Technicians

Electrical and Electronics Engineering Technicians, who usually work under the direction of engineering staff, apply technical skills to design, build, repair, calibrate, and modify electrical components, circuitry, controls, and machinery for subsequent evaluation and use by engineering staff.

WORK ENVIRONMENT

Physical Environment

Electrical and electronics engineers often work for an engineering firm. Others work for private companies, especially in the power, utilities, or manufacturing industries. The primary workplace of electrical and electronics engineers tends to be a laboratory, an office, or a classroom. There is some travel to customers' sites, where field work can include outdoor settings.

Relevant Skills and Abilities

Communication Skills
- Speaking effectively
- Writing concisely

Organization & Management Skills
- Coordinating tasks
- Making decisions
- Managing people/groups
- Paying attention to and handling details

Research & Planning Skills
- Analyzing information
- Solving problems
- Using logical reasoning

Technical Skills
- Performing scientific, mathematical and technical work
- Working with machines, tools or other objects

Human Environment

Teamwork is very common for electrical and electronics engineers who interact with colleagues, technicians, and customers. There is also some interaction with individuals from public authorities and the business community.

Technological Environment

Work is generally done in a state-of-the-art, high-technology environment. Electrical and electronics engineering involves cutting-edge technological research and development. Tools used include highly sophisticated CAD/CAM software.

EDUCATION, TRAINING, AND ADVANCEMENT

High School/Secondary

HHigh school students should focus on classes that prepare them for a degree in electrical and electronics engineering, such as advanced placement (AP)–level electricity and electronics, applied physics, drafting, and machining technology. All areas of mathematics should be studied, including algebra, calculus, geometry, trigonometry, and applied mathematics. Physics, chemistry, general science, and computer-science classes are all valuable. Shop classes can help determine if a person enjoys working with technical apparatuses. Communication and English classes should also be taken.

Students should join a high school science or field-related hobby club if one is available. Summer or part-time work, either with an electrical and electronics engineering company or in an electronics shop, can also be helpful.

Suggested High School Subjects
- Algebra
- Applied Communication
- Applied Math
- Applied Physics
- Calculus
- Chemistry
- College Preparatory
- Composition
- Drafting
- Electricity & Electronics
- English
- Geometry
- Humanities
- Machining Technology
- Mathematics
- Physics
- Science
- Trade/Industrial Education
- Trigonometry

Famous First

The first collegiate electrical engineering school was established in 1883 at Cornell University in Ithaca, N.Y., pictured. The school's four-year program included theoretical principles; construction and testing of telegraph lines, cables, and instruments; and operation of dynamo machines.

College/Postsecondary

An undergraduate degree is required. Some universities offer a combined five-year program that allows students to simultaneously attain their undergraduate and graduate degrees in engineering. College students should take science and practical engineering courses such as general electronics, electrical circuit theory, or digital systems design. A student may wish to specialize in either electrical or electronics engineering.

In addition to classroom courses, an engineering program includes laboratory work and field studies. Students can gain practical experience through internships, summer jobs, or cooperative programs that combine teaching with practical work experience.

After graduating with a bachelor's or master's degree in electrical and electronics engineering, a person entering the job force must be prepared for some on-the-job training. Professional advancement tends to depend on actual job performance. Individuals hoping to pursue research positions at the university level must obtain a PhD.

Related College Majors
- Electrical, Electronics & Communications Engineering
- Engineering Design

Adult Job Seekers

If an adult job seeker holds an electrical and electronics engineering degree, reentering the work force should not be difficult. This is true especially if the job seeker has kept up with professional developments in the field. Adult job seekers without a bachelor's degree should consider earning at least a related associate's degree and getting practical experience.

Professional Certification and Licensure

In the United States, professional engineering licenses are granted by the individual states. Few electrical and electronics engineers are required to obtain a professional engineer's license, especially if their work is focused on product design, though an engineer working in facilities design may need to be licensed. To obtain a license, applicants must have an engineering degree from an accredited institution. Accreditation is awarded through the Accreditation Board for Engineering and Technology (ABET). They must pass the Fundamentals of Engineering exam, which can be taken after graduation. After gaining professional experience, they must pass the Principles and Practice of Engineering exam.

Additional Requirements

Electrical and electronics engineers should enjoy engineering work and be ready to keep abreast of advancing knowledge in the field. Good organizational skills and leadership qualities can lead to managerial positions in the field. Alternatively, a university career is ideal for those with a passion for pure research and teaching.

EARNINGS AND ADVANCEMENT

Earnings depend on the type, size, and geographic location of the employer, and the employee's education, experience, capabilities and responsibilities. According to a salary survey by the National Association of Colleges and Employers, beginning electrical and electronics engineers with a bachelor's degree earned average starting annual salaries of $65,701 in 2012. Those with a master's degree had beginning annual salaries averaging $74,722, and those with a doctoral degree earned starting annual salaries averaging $85,518.

Mean annual earnings of electrical engineers were $95,780 in 2014. The lowest ten percent earned less than $59,140, and the highest ten percent earned more than $143,200.

Mean annual earnings of electronics engineers were $99,660 in 2014. The lowest ten percent earned less than $61,780, and the highest ten percent earned more than $147,580.

Electrical and electronics engineers may receive paid vacations, holidays, and sick days; life and health insurance; and retirement benefits. These are usually paid by the employer. Some employers may also provide educational reimbursements.

Metropolitan Areas with the Highest Employment Level in this Occupation (Electrical)

Metropolitan area	Employment [1]	Employment per thousand jobs	Annual mean wage
San Jose-Sunnyvale-Santa Clara, CA	5,940	6.10	$128,220
Boston-Cambridge-Quincy, MA	4,990	2.78	$104,480
Los Angeles-Long Beach-Glendale, CA	4,710	1.16	$110,990
Houston-Sugar Land-Baytown, TX	4,250	1.49	$108,210
San Diego-Carlsbad-San Marcos, CA	4,140	3.14	$111,180
Seattle-Bellevue-Everett, WA	4,130	2.76	$105,620
New York-White Plains-Wayne, NY-NJ	3,890	0.72	$98,370
Washington-Arlington-Alexandria, DC-VA-MD-WV	3,730	1.57	$108,900
Dallas-Plano-Irving, TX	3,680	1.64	$92,010
Warren-Troy-Farmington Hills, MI	3,590	3.14	$86,080

[1]Does not include self-employed. Source: Bureau of Labor Statistics

Metropolitan Areas with the Highest
Employment Level in this Occupation (Electronics)

Metropolitan area	Employment [1]	Employment per thousand jobs	Annual mean wage
San Jose-Sunnyvale-Santa Clara, CA	7,340	7.54	$130,570
Los Angeles-Long Beach-Glendale, CA	6,530	1.61	$106,770
Dallas-Plano-Irving, TX	4,770	2.13	$101,530
San Diego-Carlsbad-San Marcos, CA	4,390	3.32	$111,920
Washington-Arlington-Alexandria, DC-VA-MD-WV	3,600	1.51	$114,020
Santa Ana-Anaheim-Irvine, CA	3,590	2.42	$104,300
Atlanta-Sandy Springs-Marietta, GA	3,310	1.39	$90,820
Boston-Cambridge-Quincy, MA	3,120	1.74	$115,010
Denver-Aurora-Broomfield, CO	3,090	2.33	$96,270
Houston-Sugar Land-Baytown, TX	3,040	1.07	$99,890

[1]Does not include self-employed. Source: Bureau of Labor Statistics

EMPLOYMENT AND OUTLOOK

There were approximately 306,000 electrical and electronics engineers employed nationally in 2012, making up the largest branch of engineering. Employment is expected to grow slower than the average for all occupations through the year 2022, which means employment is projected to increase 3 percent to 9 percent. Although rising demand for electrical and electronic goods, including advanced communications equipment, defense-related electronic equipment and consumer electronics products should increase, foreign competition for electronic products and increasing use of engineering services performed in other countries will limit employment growth.

Continuing education is important for electrical and electronics engineers. Those who fail to keep up with the rapid changes in technology in some specialties risk becoming more susceptible to layoffs or, at a minimum, more likely to be passed over for advancement.

Employment Trend, Projected 2012–22

Total, all occupations: 11%

Electrical engineers: 5%

Electrical and electronics engineers: 4%

Electronics engineers (except computer): 3%

Note: "All Occupations" includes all occupations in the U.S. Economy. Source: U.S. Bureau of Labor Statistics, Employment Projections Program

Related Occupations
- Aerospace Engineer
- Broadcast Technician
- Electrician
- Energy Engineer
- Laser Technician
- Mechanical Engineer
- Robotics Technician
- Water & Wastewater Engineer
- Wind Energy Engineer

Related Military Occupations
- Civil Engineer
- Electrical & Electronics Engineer

Fun Fact

Electrical engineering is engineering's largest field. It includes large projects, such as power grids to light big cities to tiny projects, such as device smaller than a millimeter that tells a car's airbags when to inflate.

Source: www.engineeryourlife.org/cms/Careers/Descriptions/Electrical.aspx

Conversation With . . .
MIKE RUST

Electrical Engineer
Senior engineer/Co-owner, D2D Technologies
Jacksonville, FL
In the field, 35 years

1. What was your individual career path in terms of education/training, entry-level job, or other significant opportunity?

I knew I wanted a career in some type of science starting in high school. I like seeing things work, and I knew engineering had good-paying jobs, usually in high demand. I took a lot of math, physics, biology, and chemistry courses with this in mind. After high school, I started at the University of Maryland with a declared major of biology, but soon realized I really wanted to be an electrical engineer because it was a more financially lucrative field and there were more opportunities. I've always been practical like that. I earned a Bachelor of Science in electrical engineering and did all the coursework for my Master of Science in electrical engineering during the following two years. My first job was in avionics, designing circuit boards to allow systems on planes to communicate with each other. Over time, I moonlighted side jobs because I was always interested in having my own consulting business. When the company I worked for wanted to transfer me, I asked for a layoff because, at the time, they offered a good severance package. I took it and started my own business. I like consulting; I have more control over my time, am not tied to a commute, and can live where I want to. My specialty is PC (printed circuit) board design, which are the boards inside all of the electronics in your home and business. I also design field programmable gate arrays, which are used in broadcast facilities such as cable TV or satellite, as well as many other places.

2. What are the most important skills and/or qualities for someone in your profession?

When you're in school, math skills are needed and physics helps. Once you move into your professional life, the desire to make things work and work correctly all the time are key. You also need learn how to communicate technical subject matter to people who don't quite understand how something works.

3. What do you wish you had known going into this profession?

I wish I had known that it is difficult to remain a working engineer versus being pushed into management, but that is probably true with most professions. In engineering, about ten years into a career, people get moved into management. It's hard to find working engineers over 40 or 45; by then they've either washed out or moved into management. The technical stuff is the fun stuff even though it's harder; in management, you're dealing with people and deadlines.

4. Are there many job opportunities in your profession? In what specific areas?

Yes, there are many opportunities in my field as it is a key part of so many things in today's world – smartphones, computers, robotics, the Internet, social media, space exploration, biomedical, telecommunications, solar energy, the automotive industry…

5. How do you see your profession changing in the next five years, what role will technology play in those changes, and what skills will be required?

Since electrical engineering is at the forefront of a lot of technological change, you must always stay on top of many of the latest computer technologies. Most of the tools we use to design products are computer-based software programs. Significant portions of the electrical engineering field are very close to computer science; sometimes we have to write the software to put our tools together.

Also, computer languages are always evolving and you need to stay abreast of that as well. I don't think the field will change drastically over the next few years, but it is constantly evolving and people in the field must be very adaptable.

6. What do you enjoy most about your job? What do you enjoy least about your job?

I really enjoy seeing something I created work as I envisioned it during the design process. I don't enjoy all the documentation – sometimes pages and pages - that must be done to ensure that someone else can reproduce the design, but it is necessary so other people can carry on my work since I'm a consultant.

7. Can you suggest a valuable "try this" for students considering a career in your profession?

Getting involved in programming languages and Arduino board projects and making something that works while you're still in high school (or before) are inexpensive ways to determine if you like doing that type of thing. For instance, you could start building a robot with an Arduino board and a couple of stepper motors. You could also write an app for a smartphone. Most people don't realize how close electrical engineering is to computer science these days, but an electrical engineer has many more career choices than a computer scientist.

SELECTED SCHOOLS

Many colleges and universities offer programs in electrical and electronics engineering. Some of the more prominent schools in this field are listed below.

California Institute of Technology
1200 E. California Boulevard
Pasadena, CA 91125-4400
Phone (626) 395-6811
http://www.caltech.edu

Carnegie Mellon University
5000 Forbes Avenue
Pittsburgh, PA 15213
http://engineering.cmu.edu

Georgia Institute of Technology
225 North Avenue
Atlanta, GA 30332-0360
Phone (404) 894-2000
http://www.gatech.edu

Massachusetts Institute of Technology
77 Massachusetts Ave
Cambridge, MA 02139
Phone (617) 253-1000
http://web.mit.edu

Purdue University, West Lafayette
475 Northwestern Ave
West Lafayette, IN
Phone (765) 494-3540
https://engineering.purdue.edu/ECE

Stanford University, School of Engineering
475 Via Ortega
Stanford, CA 94305
Phone (650) 725-1575
https://engineering.stanford.edu

University of California, Berkeley
320 Mclaughlin Hall
Berkeley, CA
Phone (510) 642-5771
http://engineering.berkeley.edu

University of Illinois, Urbana, Champaign
1308 W Green St
Urbana, IL 61801
(217) 333-2151
http://engineering.illinois.edu

University of Michigan, Ann Arbor
1221 Beal Ave
Ann Arbor, MI 48109
(734) 647-7000
http://www.engin.umich.edu/college

University of Texas, Austin (Cockrell)
301 E Dean Keeton St
Austin, TX 78712
(512) 471-1166
http://www.engr.utexas.edu

MORE INFORMATION

Accreditation Board for Engineering and Technology
111 Market Place, Suite 1050
Baltimore, MD 21202
410.347.7700
www.abet.org

American Society for Engineering Education
1818 N Street NW, Suite 600
Washington, DC 20036
202.331.3500
www.asee.org

Institute of Electrical & Electronics Engineers
3 Park Avenue, 17th Floor
New York, NY 10016-5997
212.419.7900
www.ieee.org

National Action Council for Minorities in Engineering
440 Hamilton Avenue, Suite 302
White Plains, NY 10601-1813
914.539.4010
www.nacme.org

National Council of Examiners for Engineering and Surveying
280 Seneca Creek Road
Seneca, SC 29678
800.250.3196
www.ncees.org

National Society of Black Engineers
205 Daingerfield Road
Alexandria, VA 22314
703.549.2207
www.nsbe.org

National Society of Professional Engineers
1420 King Street
Alexandria, VA 22314
703.684.2800
www.nspe.org

Society of Hispanic Professional Engineers
13181 Crossroads Parkway North, Suite 450
City of Industry, CA 91746-3497
323.725.3970
www.shpe.org

Society of Women Engineers
203 N. La Salle Street, Suite 1675
Chicago, IL 60601
877.793.4636
www.swe.org

Technology Student Association
1914 Association Drive
Reston, VA 20191-1540
703.860.9000
www.tsaweb.org

R. C. Lutz/Editor

Geologist and Geophysicist

Snapshot

Career Cluster: Environment & Conservation; Natural Resources Development; Science & Technology

Interests: Seismology, hydrology, earth science

Earnings (Yearly Average): $108,420

Employment & Outlook: Faster Than Average Growth Expected

OVERVIEW

Sphere of Work

Geologists and geophysicists—also called geoscientists—study the composition, natural history, and other aspects of the earth. Geologists analyze rocks, plant and animal fossils, soil, minerals, and precious stones. They work for government agencies, oil and petroleum corporations, construction companies, universities, and museums. Geophysicists use physics, chemistry, mathematics, and geology to study the earth's magnetic fields, oceans, composition, seismic forces, and other elements. Most geologists and geophysicists

specialize in sub-fields such as mineralogy, hydrology, paleontology, seismology, and geochemistry. Geologists and geophysicists may be employed by organizations that intend to locate new oil deposits, predict earthquakes and volcano activity, or analyze environmental degradation.

Work Environment

Most geologists and geophysicists spend a significant portion of their time in the field conducting research. Fieldwork often involves traveling great distances into remote, rugged environments. Some geologists and geophysicists travel to foreign countries to pursue field research opportunities. Geologists and geophysicists must also work in all weather conditions. When performing field research, geologists and geophysicists typically work long and irregular hours. When not conducting fieldwork, geologists and geophysicists are at work in offices and laboratories, studying samples, writing papers, and analyzing and interpreting data.

Profile

Working Conditions: Work both Indoors and Outdoors
Physical Strength: Light Work, Medium Work
Education Needs: Master's Degree, Doctoral Degree
Licensure/Certification: Required
Physical Abilities Not Required: No Heavy Labor
Opportunities For Experience: Military Service, Part-Time Work
Holland Interest Score*: IRE, IRS

* See Appendix A

Occupation Interest

Geophysicists and geologists play an important role in protecting people from natural disasters – their work in seismology, hydrology, and other fields can help people avoid flood damage, prepare for seismic activity, or escape the impending eruption of a volcano. These geoscientists also help businesses, universities, and government agencies locate safe locations for construction, find dinosaur remains, and identify new areas in which to dig for oil, metals, or precious stones. The work performed by geophysicists and geologists changes frequently, and new research contributes to a growing body of knowledge about the history and characteristics of the earth. This occupation attracts inquisitive individuals with an interest in earth sciences and a desire to help others.

A Day in the Life—Duties and Responsibilities

The work performed by geologists and geophysicists varies based on their area of expertise. For example, some mineralogists prepare cross-sectional diagrams and geographic surveys of areas from which precious stones and metals may be located and extracted. Others set up and maintain seismic monitors in and around active volcanic areas. Some geophysicists and geologists spend a great deal of time in the laboratory, while others spend the vast majority of time in the field.

Most often, geologists and geophysicists plan and conduct geological surveys, field studies, and other technical analyses. They take small samples of stones, soil, and sediment, or use sensory equipment to sample magnetic waves, tremors, and subterranean water flows. Using these samples and data, geologists and geophysicists compile technical reports, academic papers, charts, maps, and policy recommendations. Geologists and geophysicists rely on computer modeling software, sensory data recorders, and other pieces of hardware and software to ensure that data is complete and organized. Scientists who study the compositions of rocks, minerals, and other resources must also conduct laboratory experiments using chemicals and other analytical tools.

Geologists and geophysicists employed by educational institutions may also need to write research proposals and grant applications in addition to performing their own research. Some geologists and geophysicists are also university professors, overseeing lectures and laboratory sections in addition to performing their own independent research.

Duties and Responsibilities

- Examining rocks, minerals, and fossil remains
- Determining and explaining the sequence of the earth's development
- Interpreting research data
- Recommending specific studies or actions
- Preparing reports and maps
- Managing and cleaning up toxic waste
- Exploring for natural resources (e.g., oil and natural gas)

OCCUPATION SPECIALTIES

Petroleum Geologists

Petroleum Geologists study the earth's surface and subsurface to locate gas and oil deposits and help develop extraction processes.

Mineralogists

Mineralogists examine, analyze and classify minerals, gems and precious stones and study their occurrence and chemistry.

Paleontologists

Paleontologists study the fossilized remains of plants and animals to determine the development of past life and history of the earth.

Hydrologists

Hydrologists study the distribution and development of water in land areas and evaluate findings in reference to such problems as flood and drought, soil and water conservation and inland irrigation.

Oceanographers

Oceanographers study the physical aspects of oceans such as currents and their interaction with the atmosphere. They also study the ocean floor and its properties.

Seismologists

Seismologists interpret data from seismographs and other instruments to locate earthquakes and earthquake faults. Stratigraphers   Stratigraphers study the distribution and arrangement of sedimentary rock layers by examining their contents.

WORK ENVIRONMENT

Physical Environment

Geologists and geophysicists spend much of their time in the field. Fieldwork is typically conducted in remote areas and may require long travel across rugged terrain to reach. These geoscientists must work outdoors in a wide range of climates and weather conditions. When not in the field, geologists and geophysicists work in offices and laboratories, which are clean, comfortable work environments.

Relevant Skills and Abilities

Analytical Skills
- Collecting and analyzing data

Communication Skills
- Editing written information
- Writing concisely

Interpersonal/Social Skills
- Cooperating with others
- Working as a member of a team

Organization & Management Skills
- Paying attention to and handling details

Research & Planning Skills
- Analyzing information
- Creating ideas
- Gathering information
- Solving problems

Technical Skills
- Applying the technology to a task
- Performing scientific, mathematical and technical work
- Working with machines, tools or other objects

Work Environment Skills
- Working outdoors

Human Environment

Depending on their area of specialty, geologists and geophysicists work with a number of different individuals. Among the people with whom they interact are engineers, other geoscientists, laboratory assistants, environmental scientists, oceanographers, chemists, geographers, business executives, and government officials.

Technological Environment

Geologists and geophysicists need to use a wide range of technology to complete their work. Geological compasses, electromagnetic instruments, water flow measurement instruments, soil core sampling tools, sonar, magnetic field measurement devices, geographic information systems software (GIS), global positioning systems (GPS), map creation systems, and scientific databases are only some of the tools and technologies used by individuals in this field.

EDUCATION, TRAINING, AND ADVANCEMENT

High School/Secondary

High school students should study chemistry, physics, environmental science, and other physical science courses. Math classes, such as algebra, geometry, and trigonometry, are essential in geology and geophysics. History, computer science, geography, English, foreign language, and photography courses can also be highly useful for future geologists and geophysicists.

Suggested High School Subjects
- Algebra
- Applied Math
- Chemistry
- College Preparatory
- Earth Science
- English
- Geography
- Geometry
- History
- Photography
- Physical Science
- Science
- Trigonometry

Famous First

The first woman geologist and the first woman to earn a PhD at Johns Hopkins University was Florence Bascom (1862-1945). She was appointed assistant geologist to the US Geological Survey in 1896. She founded the geology department at Bryn Mawr College in Pennsylvania and edited the magazine *American Geologist*.

College/Postsecondary

Geologists and geophysicists generally need a master's degree in geology, paleontology, mineralogy, or a related geosciences subject for entry-level jobs. Those who wish to pursue a senior-level research position or employment at an educational institution will need to obtain a doctorate.

Related College Majors
- Geography
- Geological Engineering
- Geophysical Engineering
- Geophysics & Seismology
- Ocean Engineering
- Oceanography

Adult Job Seekers

Qualified geologists and geophysicists may apply directly to postings by government agencies and private business organizations. University geology departments may also have access to entry-level openings. Geoscience journals frequently post openings in this field, and professional geology and geophysics societies and associations create opportunities for job searching and networking.

Professional Certification and Licensure

Some states require geologists and geophysicists who work for government agencies to obtain state licensure. An examination and proof of academic and professional experience are typically required for these licenses. Geologists and geophysicists may choose to pursue voluntary certification in specialized areas of expertise.

Additional Requirements

Geologists and geophysicists should be physically fit, as they frequently work in remote and rugged areas and sometimes carry heavy equipment and samples. They should also have familiarity with computer systems, GIS, GPS, and other technologies. Strong communication and interpersonal skills, writing abilities, and a sense of teamwork are important for geologists and geophysicists, as are an inquisitive nature and the desire to spend time working outdoors.

Fun Facts

Landslides occur in all of the 50 states. Washington, Oregon, and California's mountainous and coastal regions are the areas where most landslides occur. Eastern U.S. mountain and hill regions are also susceptible.
Source: http://geology.com/usgs/landslides

Expansive soils include minerals such as smectite clays that absorb water, then shrink when they dry out. The American Society of Civil Engineers estimates that one-fourth of all homes in the U.S. have some damage caused by expansive soils.
Source: http://geology.com/articles/expansive-soil.shtml

EARNINGS AND ADVANCEMENT

Earnings depend on the individual's particular position, occupational specialty, amount of experience and level of education. Although the petroleum, mineral, and mining industries offer higher salaries, changes in oil and gas prices result in less job security in this area. According to the National Association of Colleges and Employers, starting annual salaries for graduates with a bachelor's degree in geology and related sciences averaged $47,243 in 2012.

Mean annual earnings of geologists and geophysicists were $108,420 in 2013. The lowest ten percent earned less than $49,000, and the highest ten percent earned more than $175,000.

Geologists and geophysicists may receive paid vacations, holidays, and sick days; life and health insurance; and retirement benefits. These are usually paid by the employer.

Metropolitan Areas with the Highest Employment Level in This Occupation

Metropolitan area	Employment[1]	Employment per thousand jobs	Hourly mean wage
Houston-Sugar Land-Baytown, TX	7,070	2.57	$80.54
Denver-Aurora-Broomfield, CO	1,830	1.43	$55.31
Seattle-Bellevue-Everett, WA	800	0.55	$40.17
Los Angeles-Long Beach-Glendale, CA	790	0.20	$47.98
Santa Ana-Anaheim-Irvine, CA	710	0.49	$43.56
Dallas-Plano-Irving, TX	700	0.33	$68.12
Sacramento--Arden-Arcade--Roseville, CA	670	0.80	$44.78
Oklahoma City, OK	660	1.11	$65.30
San Francisco-San Mateo-Redwood City, CA	620	0.59	$53.07
San Diego-Carlsbad-San Marcos, CA	600	0.46	$39.80

[1] Does not include self-employed. Source: Bureau of Labor Statistics

EMPLOYMENT AND OUTLOOK

Geologists and geophysicists held about 38,000 jobs nationally in 2012. In addition, many more individuals held geoscience faculty positions in colleges and universities. About one-fourth were employed in architectural and engineering firms, and another one-fourth worked for oil and gas extraction companies. State agencies, such as state geological surveys and state departments of conservation, and the Federal Government, mostly within the U.S. Department of the Interior for the U.S. Geological Survey (USGS) and within the U.S. Department of Defense, also employed significant groups of these workers.

Employment of geologists and geophysicists is expected to grow faster than the average for all occupations through the year 2022, which means employment is projected to increase 15 percent to 20 percent.

In the past, employment of geologists and other geoscientists has been cyclical and largely affected by the price of oil and gas. In recent years, a growing worldwide demand for oil and gas and new exploration and recovery techniques have returned some stability to the petroleum industry, with a few companies increasing their hiring of geoscientists. Geoscientists who speak a foreign language and who are willing to work abroad should enjoy the best opportunities.

Employment Trend, Projected 2012–22

Geologists and Geophysicists: 16%

Total, All Occupations: 11%

Scientific Occupations (All): 10%

Note: "All Occupations" includes all occupations in the U.S. Economy. Source: U.S. Bureau of Labor Statistics, Employment Projections Program.

Related Occupations

- Geographer
- Metallurgical/Materials Engineer
- Mining & Geological Engineer
- Oceanographer
- Petroleum Engineer
- Surveyor & Cartographer

Related Military Occupations

- Oceanographer

Conversation With . . .
RON PYLES

Geotechnical Engineer
Principal Engineer, VP
Kim Engineering, Baltimore MD
In the field, 15 years

1. What was your individual career path in terms of education/training, entry-level job, or other significant opportunity?

I first was exposed to construction, and went to a junior college in Upstate New York for construction management. Then I decided to go on to a four-year school where I took civil engineering. While there, I found the geotechnical discipline, which offered more of a challenge, and took as many courses in that area as I could. I went on to work for three years to make sure I was interested in geotech, and then I earned a Master's in Civil Engineering specializing in geology.

Being a geotechnical engineer is not being a geologist per se. My field merges geology and engineering, and I mostly deal with foundations that a specific building requires, or pilings, groundwater problems, retaining walls, and that sort of thing.

Geotechnical engineering, in my opinion, is more creative than other engineering disciplines. When you think of the different formations associated with the massive earth movements that formed some of this geology, it takes a lot of force. You need to know geology. For example, if a region is limestone, which creates sinkholes, you need to know that and recommend specific techniques to build within and/or explore the karst terrain. If you're in an area where massive erosion occurred in past geologic times, and everything is consolidated because it's overburdened, then bearing capacities for foundations or walls can be much higher. Areas of Maryland, Washington, DC and Virginia, for example, have specific types of clays. These clays have specific characteristics, with high plasticity, and they may swell or shrink with moisture changes. You need to know that.

To specialize in geotechnical engineering, you should pursue advanced degrees. In geology that's not necessary, although it's always good to have an advanced degree.

2. What are the most important skills and/or qualities for someone in your profession?

Good writing skills are critical, because we produce reports that other engineers and developers read. You need good verbal communications skills with clients. It can be a high-risk business if you're not careful with your quality of work, so you need to be cognitive of legal aspects. Being organized is a plus. And, you need to be able to manage people if you are directing subordinates.

3. What do you wish you had known going into this profession?

In our work we deal with the substrate but once they build a foundation, they cover up the substrate. You can't stand there and appreciate your work.

4. Are there many job opportunities in your profession? In what specific areas?

There is very good demand relative to employment. Geotechical engineering is good, and geologists interfacing with the geotechical field have pretty good overall demand as well.

5. How do you see your profession changing in the next five years, what role will technology play in those changes, and what skills will be required?

Many of our theories have not changed a lot over the years. As technology has progressed we've obtained newer advanced equipment to assess the soils. An example would be the geophysical device that sends electrical waves to measure the resistance of those waves as they pass through the earth. We use that to find sinkholes and rock levels.

6. What do you enjoy most about your job? What do you enjoy least about your job?

Most enjoyable is exploring new areas from a geology viewpoint and soils aspect relative to proposed construction. Each site offers sort of a surprise because you don't know what's under the ground. You have the ability to assess and confirm the geology of the site, then look forward to the lab analysis.

This is a pretty demanding business, and there can be demanding turnaround. Unfortunately, sometimes clients can be hard to deal with.

7. Can you suggest a valuable "try this" for students considering a career in your profession?

Visit construction sites and field trips with a geologist or engineer. There are a lot of areas where you can get exposed to geologic formations; field trips are obviously an excellent way to get some exposure. Also, consider interning. Each summer my company has an intern program. We bring in 3-4 interns from colleges who are taking engineering and they can learn more about what we do.

SELECTED SCHOOLS

Most colleges and universities have bachelor's degree programs in geology or related subjects. The student may also gain an initial grounding in the field at an agricultural, technical, or community college. For advanced positions, a master's or doctoral degree is commonly obtained. Below are listed some of the more prominent graduate schools in this field.

California Institute of Technology
Division of Geological and Planetary Sciences
1200 East California Boulevard
Mail Code 170-25
Pasadena, CA 91125
(626) 395-6123
www.gps.caltech.edu

Massachusetts Institute of Technology
Earth, Atmospheric, and Planetary Sciences
77 Massachusetts Avenue
Cambridge, MA 02139
(617) 253-2127
eapsweb.mit.edu

Penn State University
Geosciences Department
503 Deike Building
University Park, PA 16802
(814) 867-4760
www.geosc.psu.edu

Stanford University
Geological and Environmental Sciences
450 Serra Mall, Building 320
Stanford, CA 94305
(650) 723-0847
pangea.stanford.edu/departments/ges

University of Arizona
Department of Geosciences
1040 E. 4th Street
Tucson, AZ 85721
(520) 621-6000
www.geo.arizona.edu

University of California, Berkeley
Earth and Planetary Science
307 McCone Hall
Berkeley, CA 94720
(510) 642-3993
eps.berkeley.edu

University of Colorado, Boulder
Department of Geological Sciences
UCB 359
Boulder, CO 80309
(303) 492-8141
www.colorado.edu/geolsci

University of Michigan, Ann Arbor
Earth and Environmental Sciences
2534 C.C. Little Building
1100 North University Avenue
Ann Arbor, MI 48109
(734) 763-1435
www.lsa.umich.edu/earth

University of Texas, Austin
Department of Geological Sciences
2275 Speedway Stop C9000
Austin, TX 78712
512.471.5172
www.jsg.utexas.edu/dgs

University of Wisconsin, Madison
Department of Geoscience
1215 West Dayton Street
Madison, WI 53706
608.262.8960
www.geoscience.wisc.edu

MORE INFORMATION

**American Association of
Petroleum Geologists**
P.O. Box 979
Tulsa, OK 74101-0979
800.364.2274
www.aapg.org

American Geosciences Institute
4220 King Street
Alexandria, VA 22302-1502
703.379.2480
www.americangeosciences.org

**Environmental and Engineering
Geophysical Society**
1720 South Bellaire, Suite 110
Denver, CO 80222-4303
303.531.7517
www.eegs.org

Geological Society of America
P.O. Box 9140
Boulder, CO 80301-9140
303.357.1000
www.geosociety.org

Paleontological Society
P.O. Box 9044
Boulder, CO 80301
855.357.1032
www.paleosoc.org

Seismological Society of America
201 Plaza Professional Building
El Cerrito, CA 94530
510.525.5474
www.seismosoc.org

**Society of Exploration
Geophysicists**
P.O. Box 702740
Tulsa, OK 74170-2740
918.497.5500
www.seg.org

United States Geological Survey
12201 Sunrise Valley Drive
Reston, VA 20192
703.648.5953
www.usgs.gov

Michael Auerbach/Editor

Industrial Engineer

Snapshot

Career Cluster: Manufacturing; Science, Technology, Engineering & Mathematics

Interests: Science, engineering, mathematics, developing solutions

Earnings (Yearly Average): $85,110

Employment & Outlook: Slower Than Average Growth Expected

OVERVIEW

Sphere of Work

Industrial engineering is essential to the successful performance of manufacturing processes and services. Industrial engineers design and refine manufacturing systems to improve their efficiency in order to reduce waste and achieve the desired product within budgetary constraints. They are often responsible for reviewing and streamlining work flows and other manufacturing procedures in order to expedite production processes. Some industrial engineers may specialize in one technological component or aspect of production systems.

Some industrial engineers work as consultants or hold nonmanufacturing positions in the communications or medical industries. These engineers are frequently responsible for projects associated with health and safety engineering.

Work Environment

Industrial engineers typically work in office settings as well as in factories or manufacturing plants where they may observe the machinery and procedures implemented in order to determine how effectively their solutions function and identify elements for further improvement. As industrial engineers collaborate with professionals from a variety of disciplines, they must have a knowledge of terminology relevant to related fields and be capable of communicating engineering concepts effectively.

Profile

Working Conditions: Work Indoors
Physical Strength: Light Work
Education Needs: Bachelor's Degree, Master's Degree, Doctoral Degree
Licensure/Certification: Required
Opportunities For Experience: Internship, Apprenticeship, Military Service, Part-time Work
Holland Interest Score*: EIR

* See Appendix A

Occupation Interest

Industrial engineering encompasses a variety of technical, scientific, and managerial tasks. Most industrial engineers enjoy addressing the complex issues associated with their projects and developing solutions to achieve efficiency while maintaining overall quality. People who are detail oriented, creative, and capable of thinking creatively to develop alternative solutions are particularly well suited to a career in industrial engineering.

A Day in the Life—Duties and Responsibilities

Industrial engineers often begin the day with meetings, discussing production and financial parameters in groups consisting of other engineers, scientists, manufacturers, business advisers, and managers, with whom they consult as needed while carrying out projects. These meetings help industrial engineers determine how best to allocate their time between offices, laboratories, factories, and testing sites. Industrial engineers aspire to achieve optimal manufacturing efficiency and quality and consistency in the production and distribution of products. They analyze the best methods for preventing waste during various stages of production, from the extraction of raw resources through the distribution of the completed products. Other engineers may work to improve services, simplifying processes such as the hospitalization of patients or the processing of bank transactions.

Industrial engineers work to minimize energy usage and toxic emissions, promoting sustainable practices. Some industrial engineers are supervisors or obtain managerial positions based on their qualifications. Industrial engineers are responsible for suggesting improvements to engineering standards and for establishing safety procedures. They may also serve as investigators when accidents occur in industrial settings, recording what happened and assessing whether regulations were violated before preparing statements for the management and authorities.

In academia, industrial engineers teach, advise students, and guide research projects. Inventive industrial engineers may need to protect their unique designs and methods with patents or seek out entrepreneurs interested in purchasing the rights to use their technologies and processes in other factories and businesses. Occasionally, industrial engineers serve as consultants for governmental groups, offering their expertise to aid politicians in developing policies and legislation relevant to the fields of engineering and technology.

Duties and Responsibilities

- Designing production planning and control systems to coordinate activities and control product quality
- Designing or improving systems for the actual distribution of goods and services
- Studying data to determine the functions and responsibilities of workers and work units
- Establishing work measurement programs and making observations to determine the best use of equipment and workers
- Developing programs to simplify work flow, work count, economy of worker motions and layout of units

OCCUPATION SPECIALTIES

Safety Engineers

Safety Engineers develop and implement safety programs to prevent or correct unsafe environmental working conditions, utilizing knowledge of industrial processes, mechanics, chemistry, psychology and industrial health and safety laws.

Manufacturing Engineers

Manufacturing Engineers plan, direct and coordinate manufacturing processes in industrial plants.

Quality-Control Engineers

Quality-Control Engineers plan and direct the development, application and maintenance of quality standards for processing materials into partially-finished or finished products.

WORK ENVIRONMENT

Physical Environment

Most industrial engineers alternate between working in office settings and traveling to laboratories, industrial sites, and test facilities, where they analyze the implementation and operation of manufacturing systems and services.

Plant Environment

Industrial engineers often travel to plants, testing sites, and factories. As they may encounter dangerous machinery and risk exposure to toxic substances used in manufacturing processes when visiting these locations, engineers must adhere to all safety procedures.

Relevant Skills and Abilities

Communication Skills
- Speaking effectively
- Writing concisely

Interpersonal/Social Skills
- Cooperating with others
- Working as a member of a team

Organization & Management Skills
- Coordinating tasks
- Managing people/groups
- Paying attention to and handling details
- Performing duties which change frequently

Research & Planning Skills
- Creating ideas
- Using logical reasoning

Technical Skills
- Performing scientific, mathematical and technical work
- Working with machines, tools or other objects

Human Environment

Industrial engineers collaborate with a diverse array of workers from a variety of disciplines. They must be able to interact effectively with other engineers and scientists, managers, business advisers, technical assistants, and consumers. Industrial engineers benefit from having clear communication skills, which will help them to understand the needs of their clients and implement their feedback.

Technological Environment

Industrial engineers rely on a variety of simple and complex technologies to perform their work, including advanced computer software and hardware used to model prototypes.

EDUCATION, TRAINING, AND ADVANCEMENT

High School/Secondary

High school students who are intrigued by industrial engineering should take courses in mathematics, physics, chemistry, biology, and computer science. Economics, political science, business, sociology, and English courses also help to provide students with the well-rounded education essential to success in the field. When available, students should take advanced-placement classes, especially mathematics, science, and business courses.

Workshops and camps hosted by universities and professional industrial engineering groups provide opportunities for students to explore the engineering profession. Students may also benefit from preparing projects for science and engineering contests and participating in mathematics, science, and technical clubs as well as Junior Achievement and Future Business Leaders of America programs. High school students are sometimes eligible for internships that will help them to meet and work with industrial engineers and experience the demands and opportunities associated with the field.

Suggested High School Subjects
- Algebra
- Applied Communication
- Applied Math
- Applied Physics
- Blueprint Reading
- Calculus
- Chemistry
- College Preparatory
- Composition
- Computer Science
- Drafting
- English
- Geometry
- Humanities
- Machining Technology
- Mathematics
- Mechanical Drawing
- Physical Science
- Physics
- Science
- Shop Mechanics
- Statistics
- Trigonometry

Famous First

The first use of quality control charts was in 1924, when Walter Shewhart of Western Electric Company created a diagram and a set of principles that allowed managers to distinguish between *assignable* causes and *chance* causes of variation. Today, the American Society for Quality (formerly the American Society for Quality Control) confers the prestigious Shewhart Medal annually for "outstanding technical leadership in the field of modern quality control."

College/Postsecondary

A number of accredited colleges and universities offer bachelor's degree programs in industrial engineering that provide students with the knowledge necessary to work in the field. Graduates of related engineering, science, or business programs may also pursue industrial engineering careers. Undergraduate industrial engineering students complete classes that emphasize engineering foundations, with courses focusing on information technology, manufacturing processes, quality control, and ergonomics. Students may also complete minors in management, economics, or systems theory to supplement their engineering knowledge and thereby increase their value to potential employers.

Graduate degrees enable industrial engineers to concentrate on specialized fields of study or related disciplines, such as marketing or finance, in order to extend their comprehension of various industrial engineering applications. Managerial positions in the field of industrial engineering often require candidates to hold advanced degrees.

Schools with accredited engineering programs and professional organizations such as the Institute of Industrial Engineers (IIE) often offer internships or other networking opportunities for students. In addition to attending academic courses, many students take cooperative education jobs, which enable them to gain work experience, income, and contacts that will help them secure jobs after graduation.

Related College Majors
- Engineering, General
- Engineering/Industrial Management
- Industrial/Manufacturing Engineering

Adult Job Seekers

Industrial engineers seeking to reenter the field can educate themselves about recent industrial engineering developments by taking courses at local community colleges, participating in training workshops, attending conferences, and consulting professional materials available from the IIE and other technical groups. Some industrial engineers take classes in allied fields to expand their expertise and employability.

Professional organizations and alumni groups provide returning industrial engineers with opportunities to network with people in their field and potential employers. Industrial engineers can benefit by accepting short-term research projects in order to acquire skills they can add to their resumes.

Professional Certification and Licensure

Most industrial engineers, particularly those working for businesses with government contracts, become licensed engineers in order to comply with professional standards. To become licensed engineers, individuals must pass the Fundamentals of Engineering exam, which assesses their comprehension of engineering knowledge, and be certified as engineers in training. After acquiring work experience under the supervision of licensed engineers, the engineers in training may take the Principles and Practice of Engineering exam, successful completion of which will certify them as professional engineers. Several states require industrial engineers to take continuing education courses to retain their licenses.

Additional Requirements

Competent industrial engineers benefit from continual professional development in order to stay abreast of new information, technologies, and methods. As such, aspiring industrial engineers should be willing to devote themselves to lifelong learning.

Fun Fact

Frank Gilbreth, one of the fathers of industrial engineering, conducted "motion studies" that resulted in improvements for all sorts of workers. For instance, the reason surgeons extend an open hand to a nurse who places an instrument there is so that the surgeon won't waste time looking for that instrument.
Source: www.protech-ie.com/trivia.htm

EARNINGS AND ADVANCEMENT

Earnings depend on the employer and the employee's experience and education. According to a salary survey by the National Association of Colleges and Employers, those with a bachelor's degree in industrial engineering earned an average starting salary of $63,769 in 2012.

Mean annual earnings of industrial engineers were $85,110 in 2014. The lowest ten percent earned less than $52,510, and the highest ten percent earned more than $123,400.

Industrial engineers may receive paid vacations, holidays, and sick days; life and health insurance; and retirement benefits. These are usually paid by the employer.

Metropolitan Areas with the Highest
Employment Level in this Occupation

Metropolitan area	Employment [1]	Employment per thousand jobs	Annual mean wage
Warren-Troy-Farmington Hills, MI	6,820	5.96	$84,270
Los Angeles-Long Beach-Glendale, CA	6,340	1.56	$101,680
Houston-Sugar Land-Baytown, TX	6,140	2.16	$113,270
Minneapolis-St. Paul-Bloomington, MN-WI	6,080	3.33	$86,870
Detroit-Livonia-Dearborn, MI	5,810	8.11	$88,090
Seattle-Bellevue-Everett, WA	5,590	3.74	n/a
Chicago-Joliet-Naperville, IL	5,080	1.35	$78,550
San Jose-Sunnyvale-Santa Clara, CA	4,710	4.84	$114,650
Phoenix-Mesa-Glendale, AZ	4,110	2.25	$91,980
Cincinnati-Middletown, OH-KY-IN	3,930	3.88	$84,620

[1]Does not include self-employed. Source: Bureau of Labor Statistics

EMPLOYMENT AND OUTLOOK

There were about 223,300 industrial engineers employed nationally in 2012. Employment is expected to grow slower than the average for all occupations through the year 2022, which means employment is projected to increase 3 percent to 8 percent. Jobs will be created as companies look to industrial engineers to develop efficient processes in an effort to reduce costs, delays and waste and increase productivity.

Employment Trend, Projected 2012–22

Total, all occupations: 11%

Engineers (all): 9%

Industrial engineers: 5%

Note: "All Occupations" includes all occupations in the U.S. Economy. Source: U.S. Bureau of Labor Statistics, Employment Projections Program

Related Occupations
- Cost Estimator
- Energy Conservation & Use Technician
- Industrial Hygienist
- Marine Engineer & Naval Architect
- Mechanical Engineer
- Operations Research Analyst

Related Military Occupations
- Environmental Health & Safety Officer
- Industrial Engineer

Conversation With...
ERIN GATELY

Director of Alliance Development &
Manager of Epeat Conformity Assurance
Green Electronics Council, Portland, OR
Industrial Engineer, 24 years

1. **What was your individual career path in terms of education/training, entry-level job, or other significant opportunity?**

   I have an industrial engineering bachelor's from the University of Miami. I started working for Hewlett-Packard Company (HP) in 1991. Eventually, I moved into the marketing department, but it was for an engineering job that happened to be in that department. Industrial engineering deals with increasing efficiency and logistics.

   I was working in marketing for a giant company trying to sell more things to more people, and that was very much at odds with my personal values. I had been taking classes in living simply with the Northwest Earth Institute. I took a leave of absence from HP and thought about how I could align my job with my values. I approached one of the institute's founders and said, "Hey, I took all these classes with you and now you need to help me figure out what to do for a living." When I told her I worked for Hewlett-Packard, she said, "Well you need to stay there because we need more people like you in big companies."

   So I returned to HP and got a job as an Environmental Product Steward. It was my dream job. It was using my engineering skills, it was trying to build more environmentally friendly products - but I was terrible at it. I was like an evangelist. I'm sure the people I was in meetings with were rolling their eyes. I realized I didn't have the language to speak to business people, so I got an M.B.A. in 2004. My language totally changed. It wasn't "the right thing to do," it was "return on investment." Eventually I got a promotion and didn't like that job, so I left.

   Now I'm like an investigator. I work with companies to make sure they're telling the truth. It's technical, but it's not pure engineering. But I do have to understand the technical specifications, so I need that engineering background.

2. **What are the most important skills and/or qualities for someone in your profession?**

   Being willing to see new ways of doing things. Being really curious about "Is there a different way to do this? An environmentally friendly way?" You also have to have a commitment to lifelong education. I didn't stop at an engineering degree. I recently got a certificate in green chemistry, just for fun. Whatever engineering field you're working in, stay current with the exciting things that are happening in that discipline.

3. What do you wish you had known going into this profession?

I think the most important thing is something a manager said to me, which is that I am the driver of my own career. If you don't believe that, you'll be pushed along with the currents. You really have to stick up for yourself, especially as a woman, in all aspects of your career, whether that's speaking up in a meeting or making sure you're getting paid what you're worth. I'm generalizing, but often women are too nice. Again I'm generalizing, but a man wouldn't hesitate to say, "Hey, I did a great job on that. Can I get a raise?"

4. Are there many job opportunities in your profession? In what specific areas?

A lot of industrial engineering jobs are in manufacturing, of which there's not a ton in the U.S. I think it would be easier to find a job in industrial design.

5. How do you see your profession changing in the next five years? What role will technology play in those changes, and what skills will be required?

The Director of Alliance Development part of my job is all about looking for new, greener technologies. Companies are taking used toner and turning it into oil to run the machines in their factories. Toshiba is figuring out how to de-ink their paper so they can re-use the paper. Green products are here to stay.

6. What do you enjoy most about your job? What do you enjoy least about your job?

The thing that I like most is that it's like a puzzle. I'm always trying to figure out the most efficient ways to do things. What I like least is when it becomes rote. I said before the Environmental Product Stewardship job was my dream job–and it really was for about seven years. Then I was just doing the same thing over and over again.

7. Can you suggest a valuable "try this" for students considering a career in your profession?

Take something you do routinely and break it down into its component parts and see if there's any way you can make it more efficient. It can be something as simple as making a sandwich. Do you go to the fridge and get the meat out and put it on the counter, then go back to the fridge and get the mustard? If you enjoy figuring out things like this, you'll enjoy industrial engineering.

SELECTED SCHOOLS

Many colleges and universities offer programs in industrial engineering. Some of the more prominent schools in this field are listed below.

Georgia Institute of Technology
225 North Avenue
Atlanta, GA 30332-0360
Phone (404) 894-2000
http://www.gatech.edu

Massachusetts Institute of Technology
77 Massachusetts Ave
Cambridge, MA 02139
Phone (617) 253-1000
http://web.mit.edu

Purdue University, West Lafayette
475 Northwestern Ave
West Lafayette, IN
Phone (765) 494-3540
https://engineering.purdue.edu/ECE

Stanford University, School of Engineering
475 Via Ortega
Stanford, CA 94305
Phone (650) 725-1575
https://engineering.stanford.edu

University of California, Berkeley
320 Mclaughlin Hall
Berkeley, CA
Phone (510) 642-5771
http://engineering.berkeley.edu

University of Illinois, Urbana, Champaign
1308 W Green St
Urbana, IL 61801
(217) 333-2151
http://engineering.illinois.edu

University of Michigan, Ann Arbor
1221 Beal Ave
Ann Arbor, MI 48109
(734) 647-7000
http://www.engin.umich.edu/college

University of Southern California (Viterbi)
Los Angeles, CA 90089
(213) 740-2502
Viterbi.usc.edu

University of Texas, Austin (Cockrell)
301 E Dean Keeton St
Austin, TX 78712
(512) 471-1166
http://www.engr.utexas.edu

MORE INFORMATION

**American Society for Engineering
Management**
MST-223 Engineering Management
Building
600 W 14th Street
Rolla, MO 65409
573.341.6228
www.asem.org

American Society for Quality
P.O. Box 3005
Milwaukee, WI 53201-3005
800.248.1946
www.asq.org

**American Society of Safety
Engineers**
Educational Department
1800 East Oakton Street
Des Plaines, IL 60018
847.699.2929
www.asse.org

**Association for the Advancement
of Cost Engineering International**
1265 Suncrest Towne Centre Drive
Morgantown, WV 26505-1876
304.296.8444
www.aacei.org

**Association of Technology,
Management, and Applied
Engineering**
1390 Eisenhower Place
Ann Arbor, MI 48108
734.677.0720
www.atmae.org

**Human Factors and Ergonomics
Society**
P.O. Box 1369
Santa Monica, CA 90406-1369
310.394.1811
www.hfes.org

**Institute for Operations Research
and the Management Sciences**
7240 Parkway Drive, Suite 300
Hanover, MD 21076
443.757.3500
www.informs.org

Institute of Industrial Engineers
3577 Parkway Lane, Suite 200
Norcross, GA 30092
800.494.0460
www.iienet.org

Elizabeth D. Schafer/Editor

Marine Engineer and Naval Architect

Snapshot

Career Cluster: Manufacturing; Science, Technology, Engineering & Math

Interests: Mechanical Engineering, Design, Hydrodynamics, Physics, Shipbuilding, Marine Transport

Earnings (Yearly Average): $99,160

Employment & Outlook: Average Growth Expected

OVERVIEW

Sphere of Work

Marine engineers and naval architects design ship structures, power plants, propulsion systems, compartments, hulls, and many other ship systems. They also collaborate with other engineers and personnel on the construction and maintenance of those components to ensure plans are being followed and meet the client's specifications and budget. Most marine engineers and naval architects work for private shipbuilding companies, some of which do contract work for the US Navy

and Coast Guard, cruise lines, and other entities. Marine or naval architects are responsible for the overall design of ships, while marine engineers are focused specifically on designing marine propulsion systems.

Work Environment

Most marine engineers and naval architects work in office environments, where the majority of design and modeling operations are conducted. Marine engineers and naval architects are often called upon to travel to client offices, shipyards, and other production sites to follow up on construction. In such environments, they may be exposed to some physical risks, such as falling debris or leaking toxic substances. Marine engineers and naval architects typically work regular hours, although when faced with deadlines or setbacks in the work performed, they often work longer hours with greater degrees of pressure.

Profile

Working Conditions: Work both Indoors and Outdoors
Physical Strength: Light Work
Education Needs: Bachelor's Degree, Master's Degree, Doctoral Degree
Licensure/Certification: Required
Opportunities For Experience: Internship, Military Service, Part-time Work
Holland Interest Score*: IRE

* See Appendix A

Occupation Interest

Marine engineers and naval architects design ships and their systems. They are responsible for the latest in naval warships, Coast Guard watercraft, oil tankers, cargo freighters, cruise ships, recreational boats, and other vessels. Marine engineers and naval architects are often subject to rigid deadlines and time constraints, which can create a dynamic and energetic workplace. Additionally, marine engineers and naval architects often travel to shipyards around the country and the world to watch and contribute to the construction, repair, and maintenance of large watercraft.

A Day in the Life—Duties and Responsibilities

Marine engineers and naval architects utilize and build upon an extensive knowledge of shipbuilding processes, trends, and concepts. They attend conferences and seminars as well as conduct independent research on the latest in shipbuilding technologies and designs. They are focused on the most efficient, cost-effective, and safe concepts and approaches in the field. They also keep up to date on the various government regulations that apply to shipbuilding.

Using this knowledge, marine engineers and naval architects work with the client to establish a project's budget and timeline. Based on the client's needs, marine engineers and naval architects create a comprehensive plan for the vessel or system being constructed, using detailed modeling and computer-aided design (CAD) software. Additionally, these professionals select and purchase building materials, coordinate with construction crews and suppliers, and maintain consistent contact with the client throughout the project's lifespan. Marine engineers and naval architects frequently travel to the construction site to monitor progress and conduct stress tests. When the ship is put to sea for trials, the architect and/or engineer will be on board, observing the new system or design's effectiveness and ensuring that it conforms to the client's specifications as well as national and international maritime standards.

Most marine engineers and naval architects are part of larger private shipbuilding companies. Some are self-employed consultants and may have other responsibilities in addition to the shipbuilding field, including business development and administrative management.

Duties and Responsibilities

- Studying design proposals and specifications
- Overseeing construction and testing of models
- Designing structures, machinery and equipment according to specifications and data
- Overseeing and evaluating operation of craft equipment and machinery
- Determining extent of needed repairs, preparing recommendations and initiating materials procurement
- Maintaining cost records for repairs, supplies and personnel
- Cooperating with regulatory bodies to insure that requirements are met

OCCUPATION SPECIALTIES

Marine Engineers

Marine Engineers design, build, and maintain ships ranging from aircraft carriers to submarines, from sailboats to tankers. Marine engineers work on the mechanical systems, such as propulsion and steering.

Naval Architects

Naval Architects design and build ships of all types. They work on the basic design, including the form and stability of hulls.

WORK ENVIRONMENT

Physical Environment

Most of the work performed by marine engineers and naval architects is done in an office setting, where modeling and designs are drafted. Meetings with clients are also typically conducted in office environments. Marine engineers and naval architects frequently travel to shipyards and production facilities. Although safety standards at such sites are strong, they can pose some physical risks.

Human Environment

Marine engineers and naval architects coordinate with clients as well as construction crews, suppliers, and regulatory officials during the course of a project. If marine engineers and naval architects are working on a specific compartment of a ship under construction, they often interact and coordinate with other engineers and naval architects working on other areas of the ship. When a project is completed and the ship is put to sea for trials, marine engineers and naval architects also interact with the ship's officers and crew.

Relevant Skills and Abilities

Communication Skills
- Speaking effectively
- Writing concisely

Organization & Management Skills
- Coordinating tasks
- Managing groups/people

Organization & Management Skills
- Paying attention to and handling details
- Performing duties which change frequently

Research & Planning Skills
- Analyzing information
- Creating ideas
- Developing evaluation strategies

Technical Skills
- Performing scientific, mathematical and technical work

Technological Environment

Marine engineers and naval architects must be familiar with a wide range of technologies and equipment. In design phases, they utilize CAD and other modeling software, scientific databases, and office and management programs. On site, they also work with systems that gauge speed, stability, and stress on the ship and its new components.

EDUCATION, TRAINING, AND ADVANCEMENT

High School/Secondary

High school students are encouraged to take courses such as physics, computer science, drafting, and electronics. They should also take relevant math courses such as geometry, algebra, and calculus. Students should also study subjects that build communication skills.

Suggested High School Subjects
- Applied Communication
- Applied Math
- Applied Physics

- Blueprint Reading
- College Preparatory
- Computer Science
- Drafting
- Electricity & Electronics
- English
- Machining Technology

Famous First

The first Navy ship designed to be an aircraft carrier was the *USS Ranger* (CV-4), pictured, whose keel was laid in 1931 and whose launch occurred in 1934. The ship operated in the Atlantic during World War II. It was decommissioned in 1946 and sold for scrap in 1947.

College/Postsecondary

Marine engineers and naval architects should have a bachelor's degree in engineering. Graduate degrees in marine engineering, naval architecture, and similar fields bolster a job candidate's appeal to employers. Many individuals obtain additional training in the field by joining the US Navy, Coast Guard, or Merchant Marine after high school.

Related College Majors
- Engineering, General
- Marine Science/Merchant Marine Officer
- Naval Architecture & Marine Engineering
- Ocean Engineering

Adult Job Seekers

Many recent graduates of naval engineering or architecture postsecondary programs have opportunities for apprenticeships and internships with shipbuilders and other employers. Such positions can lead to full-time job opportunities. As with many occupations and industries, networking is often critical; engineers and naval architects may consider joining relevant professional organizations, such as the Society of Naval architects and Marine Engineers, as a means of professional networking.

Professional Certification and Licensure

All states require that engineers obtain professional engineer (PE) licenses, which require an engineering degree, four years of related work experience, and passage of a state examination. Marine naval architects and engineers who want to work directly for the US government must also take a civil service examination.

Additional Requirements

Marine engineers and naval architects must have a strong understanding of the materials, technology, and equipment involved in shipbuilding and ship operation. They should also have exceptional computer skills. Furthermore, they should be detail-oriented, able to analyze complex systems, and able to communicate clearly.

Fun Fact

Robert Fulton and Robert R. Livingstone met up in 1801, and went on to create the first commercial steamboat in 1807.

Source: www.thefamouspeople.com/profiles/robert-fulton-3376.php

EARNINGS AND ADVANCEMENT

Earnings of marine engineers and naval architects depend on the employee's experience, capability, job responsibility and education, as well as the type, size and geographic location of the employer.

Marine engineers and naval architects had mean annual earnings of $99,160 in 2014. The lowest ten percent earned less than $59,110, and the highest ten percent earned more than $146,840.

Marine engineers and naval architects may receive paid vacations, holidays, and sick days; life and health insurance; and retirement benefits. These are usually paid by the employer

Metropolitan Areas with the Highest Employment Level in This Occupation

Metropolitan area	Employment[1]	Employment per thousand jobs	Hourly mean wage
Houston-Sugar Land-Baytown, TX	1,620	0.57	$116,010
Virginia Beach-Norfolk-Newport News, VA-NC	800	1.09	$92,910
Washington-Arlington-Alexandria, DC-VA-MD-WV	600	0.25	$112,670
Seattle-Bellevue-Everett, WA	470	0.31	$93,990
Norwich-New London, CT-RI	240	1.86	n/a
Fort Lauderdale-Pompano Beach-Deerfield Beach, FL	220	0.29	$78,230
Baltimore-Towson, MD	200	0.16	$87,330
Pascagoula, MS	130	2.35	$85,180
Mobile, AL	120	0.72	$57,770
Honolulu, HI	110	0.24	$86,260

[1] Does not include self-employed. Source: Bureau of Labor Statistics

EMPLOYMENT AND OUTLOOK

Marine engineers and naval architects held about 7,300 jobs nationally in 2013. Employment of marine engineers and naval architects is expected to grow about as fast as the average for all occupations through the year 2022, which means employment is projected to increase 8 percent to 12 percent. The limited number of students choosing this career will contribute to demand, in addition to the need to replace those workers who leave the occupation or retire.

Employment Trend, Projected 2012–22

Total, all occupations: 11%

Marine engineers and naval architects: 10%

Engineers (all): 9%

Note: "All Occupations" includes all occupations in the U.S. Economy. Source: U.S. Bureau of Labor Statistics, Employment Projections Program.

Related Occupations

- Architect
- Industrial Engineer
- Mechanical Engineer

Related Military Occupations

- Marine Engineer

Conversation With . . .
MATTHEW TOMPKINS

COO, TC Defense, Arlington, VA
Marine Engineer, 10 years

1. What was your individual career path in terms of education/training, entry-level job, or other significant opportunity?

I originally came from Indiana, where there's no ocean or maritime-related work, but when I decided to attend the U.S. Merchant Marine Academy in Kings Point, NY, on Long Island, I was more interested in the military aspect. I earned a B.S. in Marine Engineering and Shipyard Management.The academy requires a lot of hands-on, co-op experience, including spending 360 days at sea on a commercial merchant ship. I went to 16 different countries while still in college, which opened my eyes to different opportunities. There's also a four-week internship requirement, which showed me what the commercial marine industry has to offer. I interned with a small Indiana company that made small vessels for inland waterways.

My first job was working for BAE Systems as a contractor to Naval Sea Systems Command designing and building ships. The Navy would have a portfolio of systems, and $20 to $30 million worth of equipment that had to be installed in a specific time period. So I managed those efforts onsite, reviewed design drawings, walked the project, ensured proper installation and inspected for quality control.

I went on to work for some large defense companies and I've done project management. T.C. Defense is a family business I co-founded, and I'm now working on a Ph.D. in systems engineering from George Washington University. I'm trying to achieve more senior levels of technical consulting within the defense market. I'm also a Naval Reservist in the Military Sealift Command, which has a cadre of licensed marine engineers.

One of the great things about being a licensed marine engineer is that you get a handle on everything mechanical or electrical-related on a ship. A traditional maritime engineer is a mariner who operates a ship, but I haven't done that since I graduated.

2. What are the most important skills and/or qualities for someone in your profession?

Being capable of dealing with people at all levels, from skilled laborers to senior executives. You have to be adaptable, persistent, persuasive and patient.

3. What do you wish you had known going into this profession?

There's a big knowledge gap for me with certain detail design characteristics, and I wish I had known that gap was there. In addition, it was a huge shock to encounter beauracracy-related waste, especially in government work. In addition, this is an age-dominated industry. There's not a lot of innovation and oftentimes I think there's too much value put on the number of years of experience a person has. That applies to both marine engineering and government. I've had to learn to work around that.

4. Are there many job opportunities in your profession? In what specific areas?

Yes. There's a shortage of licensed marine engineers in both the commercial and naval marine engineering markets. With a marine engineering license, you can operate commercial propulsion plants onboard ships or work shoreside in engineering fields, such as aerospace or defense engineering. Many of the systems and components you find on a ship are the same components found on other types of products, like airplanes.

5. How do you see your profession changing in the next five years, what role will technology play in those changes, and what skills will be required?

The biggest technological changes will be in how ships are fueled and powered. Commercial ships are seeking to lower fuel costs by using liquified natural gas instead of diesel, and Navy ships are seeking to have more power for advanced warfighting capabilities.

6. What do you enjoy most about your job? What do you enjoy least about your job?

I get to choose whether I want to "geek out" on technical projects or stay on the project management side of things. There's a shortage of engineers and technical folks out there, so if somebody's willing to step up and do the technical work, organizations are willing to let you do that.

I least enjoy dealing with difficult people. When I went through engineering school, I was told that 90 percent of engineering is dealing with people and 10 percent is technical, and that's pretty much how it turned out.

7. Can you suggest a valuable "try this" for students considering a career in your profession?

Many of the nation's maritime universities have special days where they invite high school students to visit, get exposure to the curriculum and actually board a training ship. Take advantage of those opportunities!

SELECTED SCHOOLS

Many colleges and universities offer programs in engineering and/or architecture; a number of them also have concentrations in marine engineering and naval architecture. Some of the more prominent schools in this field are listed below.

California Institute of Technology
1200 E. California Boulevard
Pasadena, CA 91125-4400
Phone (626) 395-6811
http://www.caltech.edu

Carnegie Mellon University
5000 Forbes Avenue
Pittsburgh, PA 15213
http://engineering.cmu.edu

Georgia Institute of Technology
225 North Avenue
Atlanta, GA 30332-0360
Phone (404) 894-2000
http://www.gatech.edu

Massachusetts Institute of Technology
77 Massachusetts Ave
Cambridge, MA 02139
Phone (617) 253-1000
http://web.mit.edu

Purdue University, West Lafayette
475 Northwestern Ave
West Lafayette, IN
Phone (765) 494-3540
https://engineering.purdue.edu/ECE

Stanford University, School of Engineering
475 Via Ortega
Stanford, CA 94305
Phone (650) 725-1575
https://engineering.stanford.edu

University of California, Berkeley
320 Mclaughlin Hall
Berkeley, CA
Phone (510) 642-5771
http://engineering.berkeley.edu

University of Illinois, Urbana, Champaign
1308 W Green St
Urbana, IL 61801
(217) 333-2151
http://engineering.illinois.edu

University of Michigan, Ann Arbor
1221 Beal Ave
Ann Arbor, MI 48109
(734) 647-7000
http://www.engin.umich.edu/college

University of Texas, Austin
301 E Dean Keeton St
Austin, TX 78712
(512) 471-1166
http://www.engr.utexas.edu

MORE INFORMATION

American Institute of Naval architects
1735 New York Avenue, NW
Washington, DC 20006-5292
800.242.3837
www.aia.org

American Society of Naval Engineers
1452 Duke Street
Alexandria, VA 22314
703.836.6727
www.navalengineers.org

Association of Collegiate Schools of Architecture
1735 New York Avenue, NW
Washington, DC 20006
202.785.2324
www.asca-arch.org

Coast Guard, Licensing and Evaluation Branch
Merchant Vessel and Personnel
Division
2300 Wilson Boulevard, Suite 500
Arlington, VA 20598
www.uscg.mil/stcw/index.htm

Junior Engineering Technical Society
JETS Guidance
1420 King Street, Suite 405
Alexandria, VA 22314-2794
703.548.5387
www.jets.org

Marine Technology Society
5565 Sterrett Place, #108
Columbia, MD 21044
410.884.5330
www.mtsociety.org

National Action Council for Minorities in Engineering
440 Hamilton Avenue, Suite 302
White Plains, NY 10601-1813
914.539.4010
www.nacme.org

National Marine Educators Association
P.O. Box 1470
Ocean Springs, MS 39566-1470
228.896.9182
www.marine-ed.org

National Society of Black Engineers
1454 Duke Street
Alexandria, VA 22314
703.549.2207
www.nsbe.org

Naval Sea Systems Command
1333 Isaac Hull Avenue SE
Washington Naval Yard
Washington, DC 20376
202.781.0000
www.navsea.navy.mil

Society of American Registered Naval architects
14 E. 38th Street
New York, NY 10016
888.385.7272
www.sara-national.org

Society of Marine Port Engineers
P.O. Box 369
Eatontown, NJ 07724
732.389.2009
dmoore@smpe.org
www.smpe.org

Society of Naval architects and Marine Engineers
601 Pavonia Avenue
Jersey City, NJ 07306
800.798.2188
www.snmae.org

Society of Women Engineers
120 S. LaSalle Street, Suite 1515
Chicago, IL 60611-3265
877.793.4636
www.swe.org

University of Michigan Naval Architecture and Marine Engineering
NAME Building, 2600 Draper Drive
Ann Arbor, MI 48109-2145
734.764.6470
name.engin.umich.edu

Michael Auerbach/Editor

Materials Engineer

Snapshot

Career Cluster: Manufacturing; Science, Technology, Engineering & Mathematics

Interests: Mathematics, physics, construction, solving problems

Earnings (Yearly Average): $91,150

Employment & Outlook: Slower Than Average Growth Expected

OVERVIEW

Sphere of Work

Materials engineers develop and test materials used to make a wide variety of products. Materials development is used in a variety of fields; the technology and computer science industries, for instance, employ materials engineers to develop materials used in the construction of computer chips and other parts, while the aerospace and transportation industries employ materials scientists to develop aircraft wings, automotive bodies, and a variety of other objects.

Materials engineers, particularly metallurgical engineers, need to know how to use a variety of specialized equipment used to heat and blend

metals. These processes are important parts of developing new alloys, which are liquid or solid mixtures of two or more types of metal. Metallurgical engineers also develop methods used to process metal ore into purified metals. Most materials engineers sometimes work with metal but may also work with synthetic materials such as plastic and silicon. They work to develop methods for manufacturing and working with various materials, as well as testing methods to evaluate the mechanical characteristics of various materials, including tensile strength, flexibility, and durability.

Work Environment

Materials engineers generally work full time and tend to work in laboratory or research office settings. Materials engineers who focus on the design aspects of the field typically work at a computer. Others spend most their time in a laboratory setting, either working on the formulation of new materials or running various tests on experimental materials.

Most materials engineers work during regular weekday hours, and most positions are salaried rather than for hourly wages. Overtime and evening work is generally not required but may be necessary in certain cases, such as when a project is approaching a deadline. Some engineers may serve in supervisory roles, helping to manage teams of engineers or research assistants working on various design, testing, or manufacturing processes.

Profile

Working Conditions: Work Indoors
Physical Strength: Light Work
Education Needs: Bachelor's Degree, Master's Degree, Doctoral Degree
Licensure/Certification: Required
Opportunities For Experience: Internship, Apprenticeship, Part-time Work
Holland Interest Score*: RIS

* See Appendix A

Occupation Interest

Those pursuing a career in material engineering should have a strong interest in mathematics, physics, and practical construction. Materials engineers must be highly detail oriented and comfortable with complex challenges. Engineers benefit from broad training in mathematics and science before specializing in one or more engineering fields, as many activities specific to engineering utilize these skills.

A Day in the Life—Duties and Responsibilities

The typical day for a materials engineer will vary according to specific subfields or specializations. While some engineers focus on materials design, others focus on the physical creation of new materials in laboratory settings. Some materials engineers divide their time between design and production activities.

In most cases, materials engineers work to produce materials that meet the specifications created by teams of individuals who work on other aspects of the design process; for instance, a materials engineer might work with a mechanical engineer to address requirements such as the density, flexibility, and mechanical strength of a specific material. Materials engineers also spend part of their time testing the characteristics of materials to determine how useful they will be for the manufacture of various objects. Materials engineers subject materials to a variety of highly specialized tests as part of the development process. In the aerospace field, for instance, materials used in the construction of aircraft wings must undergo wind testing to determine how well the materials hold up when subjected to conditions similar to those at high altitudes and speeds.

In many cases, engineers must prepare and conduct a variety of evaluations as they complete various aspects of their jobs. An engineer producing a new type of metal, for instance, must often produce reports on a variety of economic and budgetary factors, including labor and materials-sourcing costs and the estimated cost of producing materials given a variety of different design and component options. Engineers who work in a managerial capacity must also supervise and evaluate the performance of subordinate staff working on different aspects of the production or testing process.

Duties and Responsibilities

- Conducting research and development
- Testing metals, alloys and synthetic materials
- Developing processing methods plans
- Supervising production processes
- Consulting with other engineers and officials
- Selling and servicing metal products

OCCUPATION SPECIALTIES

Metallurgical Engineers

Metallurgical Engineers specialize in metals, such as steel and aluminum, usually in alloyed form with additions of other elements to provide specific properties.

Ceramic Engineers

Ceramic Engineers develop ceramic materials and the processes for making them into useful products, from high-temperature rocket nozzles to glass for LCD flat-panel displays.

Semiconductor Processing Engineers

Semiconductor Processing Engineers apply materials science and engineering principles to develop new microelectronic materials for computing, sensing, and related applications.

Composite Engineers

Composite Engineers work in developing materials with special, engineered properties for applications in aircraft, automobiles, and related products.

Plastics Engineers

Plastics Engineers work in developing and testing new plastics, known as polymers, for new applications

WORK ENVIRONMENT

Physical Environment

Materials engineers typically work in office or laboratory environments. Those involved primarily in the design and planning process are more likely to do most of their work in an office environment, utilizing computer design software to create schematic diagrams of devices and materials. Those involved in the physical production or testing of materials are more likely to work in laboratory environments and generally work with highly specialized equipment and technology. Many of the techniques and processes used in materials engineering can present physical dangers, so laboratories where development occurs must be outfitted with safety equipment and systems.

Relevant Skills and Abilities

Organization & Management Skills
- Coordinating tasks
- Following instructions
- Managing people/groups

Organization & Management Skills
- Paying attention to and handling details

Research & Planning Skills
- Creating ideas
- Using logical reasoning

Technical Skills
- Performing scientific, mathematical and technical work

Plant Environment

Production plants are common in the materials-engineering field, as many of the products developed and produced by engineers in these fields require large-scale production. Metallurgical plants require a number of specialized machines to produce or test metals; these often involve furnaces used to melt and heat metals. In addition, metallurgical machine shops often have specialized machines used to cut, carve, and bend metal for different applications. Materials engineers working in shops that do not produce metals may have a different host of equipment at their disposal. Engineers working with plastics may use specialized ovens to melt and heat plastics, as well as machines designed to carve and stamp plastic pieces. In both metallurgical and materials-engineering plants, computer-aided machines are used for various tests; some of these machines are large and complex enough that they must be housed individually in separate premises from the rest of the shop.

Human Environment

Materials engineers tend to work as part of an overall research-and-development team, along with other engineers, chemists, research technicians, machinists, computer specialists, and designers. In addition, engineers may work closely with individuals from other branches of a company, including executive managers, supervisors, and acquisition or purchasing specialists who obtain raw materials and equipment used in the development process.

Technological Environment

Engineering laboratories often use highly specialized equipment that has been manufactured specifically for certain types of tests or engineering procedures. Engineers must frequently engage in continuing education to learn about new software and equipment in their field, and many companies may pay employees to attend seminars and symposiums to meet this requirement of the job.

Those working on the design component of the job often work with computer-aided design (CAD) programs, as well as other programs that enable the creation of specialized three-dimensional models that can be manipulated as part of the testing and development process. The technology used by engineers to create and test materials includes both simple mechanical devices, such as saws, hammers, and other hand tools, and highly specialized computer-aided measurement and manufacturing equipment

EDUCATION, TRAINING, AND ADVANCEMENT

High School/Secondary

High school students hoping to work in the engineering field should take classes in mathematics, physics, chemistry, and basic engineering. Mathematics classes, including algebra, calculus, and trigonometry, are important to all engineering fields, but they are especially useful to mechanical and materials engineers involved in industrial design and manufacturing. In addition, training in computer operation, drafting, and design, if available, is useful to those hoping to train for careers in metallurgical or materials engineering. Some high schools offer metalworking and shop classes that can also prove beneficial. Metalworking classes may introduce students to welding, machining, and other processes that are part of manufacturing machined parts.

Suggested High School Subjects

- Algebra
- Applied Communication
- Applied Math
- Applied Physics
- Calculus
- Chemistry
- College Preparatory
- Computer Science
- Earth Science
- English
- Geometry
- Machining Technology
- Mathematics
- Metals Technology
- Physical Science
- Physics
- Science
- Shop Math
- Trigonometry
- Welding

Famous First

The first polycarbonate products were manufactured in 1958. Polycarbonate is a hard, semitransparent, impact-resistant plastic made from a polymer originally discovered in 1898 by German scientist Alfred Einhorn. In 1953, Hermann Schnell at Bayer in Germany and Daniel Fox at General Electric in the United States independently succeeded in synthesizing it for potential commercial applications. Patents were registered in 1955, and three years later the fully developed finished product was released. Bayer called it Makrolon, and GE called it Lexan.

College/Postsecondary

Most entry-level engineering jobs require at least a bachelor's degree in engineering, mathematics, or a related field. Many colleges and universities offer bachelor's degree programs in engineering, while some offer programs tailored to specific fields. Bachelor's degree programs in the engineering field are typically four-year programs that include both classroom and laboratory work to prepare students for careers in the field.

In addition to academic training, many universities and colleges offer programs that allow students to spend time working in professional engineering environments to earn credits toward their degree. Some colleges and universities offer five-year combined bachelor's/master's programs in which students train in a professional environment and take extra classes to earn a master's degree after graduation

Related College Majors
- Materials Engineering
- Materials Science
- Metallurgical Engineering
- Metallurgy

Adult Job Seekers

Adults with a background in mathematics, chemistry, and electrical manufacturing may be able to take additional courses or participate in continuing-education programs to transition into the professional engineering field. Companies hiring individuals to work as engineers generally prefer four- or five-year specific degree programs, though some might find opportunities by transitioning into materials engineering from a related field or a separate branch of engineering.

Professional Certification and Licensure

Engineering licenses in the United States are awarded by individual states, and prospective engineers should research the requirements in their particular state. In most cases, engineering students must take two exams to qualify as a professional engineer. The Fundamentals of Engineering (FE) exam may be taken immediately after graduation and demonstrates a student's basic grasp of engineering principles. After passing the FE exam, the student can become a professional intern at an engineering company while he or she learns the practical information that will be required to work as an independent professional. The second exam is the Professional Engineering (PE) exam, which demonstrates knowledge of advanced engineering principles. Organizations like the National Council of Examiners for Engineers and Surveyors (NCEES) offer classes and examinations for the FE and PE exams.

Additional Requirements

Engineers typically work as part of a larger design and production team, so interpersonal communication skills are important. Engineers also need to be detail oriented and have the ability to multitask effectively without sacrificing attention or focus. Engineers hoping to move into management or supervisory positions will also benefit from problem-solving and managerial skills

EARNINGS AND ADVANCEMENT

Earnings depend on the employer and the employee's education, experience and specialty. According to a salary survey by the National Association of Colleges and Employers, those with a bachelor's degree in materials engineering earned starting salaries averaging $62,666 in 2012. Mean annual earnings of materials engineers were $91,150 in 2014. The lowest ten percent earned less than $53,290, and the highest ten percent earned more than $138,450.

Materials engineers may receive paid vacations, holidays, and sick days; life and health insurance; and retirement benefits. These are usually paid by the employer.

Metropolitan Areas with the Highest Employment Level in this Occupation

Metropolitan area	Employment [1]	Employment per thousand jobs	Annual mean wage
Boston-Cambridge-Quincy, MA	910	0.50	$87,040
Houston-Sugar Land-Baytown, TX	660	0.23	$105,170
Los Angeles-Long Beach-Glendale, CA	610	0.15	$103,870
New York-White Plains-Wayne, NY-NJ	610	0.11	$89,580
Warren-Troy-Farmington Hills, MI	600	0.53	$85,550
Philadelphia, PA	510	0.28	$93,670
Dallas-Plano-Irving, TX	480	0.22	$92,500
Phoenix-Mesa-Glendale, AZ	440	0.24	n/a
San Jose-Sunnyvale-Santa Clara, CA	440	0.45	$127,190
Gary, IN	400	1.49	$70,870

[1]Does not include self-employed. Source: Bureau of Labor Statistics

EMPLOYMENT AND OUTLOOK

There were approximately 23,200 materials engineers employed nationally in 2012. Employment is expected to grow slower than the average for all occupations through the year 2022, which means employment is projected to increase only 1 percent, or so. More materials engineers will be needed to develop new materials using biotechnology and nanotechnology research. Job openings will also result from the need to replace materials engineers who transfer to other occupations or retire. At the same time, older manufacturing technologies will likely experience declines.

Related Occupations
- Ceramic Engineer
- Geographer
- Geologist & Geophysicist
- Mining & Geological Engineer
- Petroleum Engineer

Fun Fact

The discovery of new materials often are the basis for other engineering feats. For instance, the 1962 development of semiconductor lasers and LEDs are the basis of many inventions, including DVD players, laser printers, and barcode readers.

Source: www.sciencedirect.com/science/article/pii/S1369702107703516

Conversation With . . .
KIM K. de GROH

Senior Materials Research Engineer
NASA Glenn Research Center, Cleveland, OH
Materials Engineer, 27 years

1. What was your individual career path in terms of education, entry-level job, or other significant opportunity?

I became interested in the space program as a little girl when my father, a bio-medical engineer, shared his interest with me. During the Apollo 11 mission, my family watched together as Neil Armstrong took the first step onto the moon.

At Michigan State University (MSU), I decided to pursue a bachelor's in materials science because it encompassed various fields of interest to me: math, chemistry, atomic physics and art. My first technical job, a summer internship, taught me basic metallography skills and I realized I enjoyed research. I got my master's in materials science with an emphasis on electron microscopy—which I love. I trained in scanning, analytical and transmission electron microscopy, which helped me obtain my job at NASA.

As a grad student, I got an internship at NASA Glenn Research Center in Ohio. That summer, I met my future husband, Henry de Groh III, a NASA materials research engineer who was flying fascinating microgravity experiments on the shuttle. This confirmed my dream of someday flying materials experiments in space.

After earning my master's in 1987, I got a job as a contractor at NASA Glenn. One year later, NASA hired me as a materials research engineer.

I've had numerous materials experiments flown in space on the shuttle and the Russian space station Mir. As a senior materials research engineer in the Space Environment and Experiments Branch, I assess how space affects external spacecraft materials. I'm the principal investigator for 13 experiments flown on the exterior of the International Space Station (ISS) as part of the Materials International Space Station Experiment. I had a direct impact on the insulation chosen for replacement solar arrays placed on the Hubble Space Telescope during the first servicing mission and have analyzed insulation retrieved from Hubble during each of the five servicing missions.

2. **What are the most important skills and/or qualities for someone in your profession?**

    Analytical, math and problem-solving skills, along with the ability to speak and write well are all important.

3. **What do you wish you had known going into this profession?**

    I could have benefited from courses in statistics, error analyses and electrical engineering.

4. **Are there many job opportunities in your profession? In what specific areas?**

    Many materials engineers work in metal production and processing, but also in the manufacture of electronic components, transportation equipment, and industrial equipment, as well as in research and testing services. Others work for federal and state agencies, such as NASA. The Bureau of Labor Statistics says materials engineers are in demand in biomedicine, working, for instance, on new materials for medical implants.

5. **How do you see your profession changing in the next five years? What role will technology play in those changes, and what skills will be required?**

    Technology has led to drastic changes in the way I conduct and report research. Early in my career, we took Polaroid photos of microscope images and made our own viewgraph transparencies for presentations. Interaction with other researchers usually was limited to face-to-face meetings. Now I can operate a scanning electron microscope in one building and access the images from my office. I carry my presentations around on a flash drive. And e-mail has become a critical communication tool. I collaborate with researchers at NASA centers across the country and with space experts from around the world, such as at the European Space Agency and Japan Aerospace Exploration Agency. In the future, we'll likely see new materials discoveries, particularly in nanotechnology, composites, polymers and biomedicine.

6. **What do you enjoy most about your job? What do you enjoy least about your job?**

    It's exciting to have my experiments taken into space, and even placed outside the International Space Station by an astronaut during a spacewalk. After a certain amount of space exposure, the experiments are brought back to Earth and I get to test how well the samples survived in the space environment. I write about the results and my data is used by spacecraft designers to build more durable spacecraft!

I have enjoyed presenting my results at conferences and traveling throughout the United States and to Canada, Europe and Japan to attend space conferences. But I think the best part of my job is the people I have met: bright and energetic students, fellow researchers, and astronauts who have helped with my projects.

What I enjoy least are the non-technical tasks: paperwork, conference participation approvals, etc.

7. Can you suggest a valuable "try this" for students considering a career in your profession?

Job shadowing provides great exposure to daily work. Internships can help you determine if you truly enjoy the work and whether you prefer lab work or something else, such as numerical modeling. Internships also allow you to showcase your abilities.

I recommend taking a course such as "Introduction to Careers in Engineering." My husband and I both took one. It helped me settle upon materials science.

SELECTED SCHOOLS

Most colleges and universities offer programs in engineering; a variety of them also have concentrations in materials engineering. Some of the more prominent schools in this field are listed below.

California Institute of Technology
1200 E. California Boulevard
Pasadena, CA 91125-4400
Phone (626) 395-6811
http://www.caltech.edu

Carnegie Mellon University
5000 Forbes Avenue
Pittsburgh, PA 15213
http://engineering.cmu.edu

Georgia Institute of Technology
225 North Avenue
Atlanta, GA 30332-0360
Phone (404) 894-2000
http://www.gatech.edu

Massachusetts Institute of Technology
77 Massachusetts Ave
Cambridge, MA 02139
Phone (617) 253-1000
http://web.mit.edu

Purdue University, West Lafayette
475 Northwestern Ave
West Lafayette, IN
Phone (765) 494-3540
https://engineering.purdue.edu/ECE

Stanford University, School of Engineering
475 Via Ortega
Stanford, CA 94305
Phone (650) 725-1575
https://engineering.stanford.edu

University of California, Berkeley
320 Mclaughlin Hall
Berkeley, CA
Phone (510) 642-5771
http://engineering.berkeley.edu

University of Illinois, Urbana, Champaign
1308 W Green St
Urbana, IL 61801
(217) 333-2151
http://engineering.illinois.edu

University of Michigan, Ann Arbor
1221 Beal Ave
Ann Arbor, MI 48109
(734) 647-7000
http://www.engin.umich.edu/college

University of Texas, Austin (Cockrell)
301 E Dean Keeton St
Austin, TX 78712
(512) 471-1166
http://www.engr.utexas.edu

MORE INFORMATION

Accreditation Board for Engineering and Technology
111 Market Place, Suite 1050
Baltimore, MD 21202-4012
410.347.7700
www.abet.org

American Society for Engineering Education
1818 N Street NW, Suite 600
Washington, DC 20036
202.331.3500
www.asee.org

ASM International
9639 Kinsman Road
Materials Park, Ohio 44073-0002
440.338.5151
www.asminternational.org

Minerals, Metals & Materials Society
184 Thorn Hill Road
Warrendale, PA 15086-7514
800.759.4867
www.tms.org

National Action Council for Minorities in Engineering
440 Hamilton Avenue, Suite 302
White Plains, NY 10601-1813
914.539.4010
www.nacme.org

National Council of Examiners for Engineering and Surveying
P.O. Box 1686
Clemson, SC 29633
800.250.3196
www.ncees.org

National Society of Black Engineers
205 Daingerfield Road
Alexandria, VA 22314
703.549.2207
www.nsbe.org

Society for Mining, Metallurgy & Exploration
Career Information
12999 E. Adam Aircraft Circle
Englewood, CO 80112
800.763.3132
www.smenet.org

Society of Hispanic Professional Engineers
13181 Crossroads Parkway North
Suite 450
City of Industry, CA 91746-3497
323.725.3970
www.shpe.org

Society of Women Engineers
203 N. La Salle Street, Suite 1675
Chicago, IL 60601
877.793.4636
www.swe.org

Micah Issitt /Editor

Mathematician

Snapshot

Career Cluster: Science, Technology, Engineering & Mathematics

Interests: Solving problems, analyzing data, communicating with others

Earnings (Yearly Average): $104,350

Employment & Outlook: Faster Than Average Growth Expected

OVERVIEW

Sphere of Work

Mathematicians apply high-level mathematics to real-world problems and develop new mathematical principles to expand human understanding of the world. They work in government, business, science, engineering, and academia. Applied mathematicians work in computers, economics, and other industries, while theoretical mathematicians work to understand the philosophy and principles of mathematics. The work of mathematicians is often multidisciplinary. For example, mathematicians at NASA work closely with physicists and engineers.

Work Environment

A large number of mathematicians work for the government and in scientific research. Many work in teams with engineers and scientists related to their field. Theoretical mathematicians work through complex mathematical proofs, a process that requires hours of painstaking independent work. Mathematicians who work in academia also spend their time outside of the classroom at research facilities.

Profile

Working Conditions: Work Indoors
Physical Strength: Light Work
Education Needs: Bachelor's Degree, Master's Degree, Doctoral Degree
Licensure/Certification: Usually Not Required
Opportunities For Experience: Military Service, Volunteer Work, Part-time Work
Holland Interest Score*: IER

* See Appendix A

Occupational Interest

Mathematicians spend years studying for their chosen career. To become a mathematician, it helps to be a patient problem solver and a diligent worker. Mathematicians must be adept at both abstract and technical thinking. They are generally very intelligent people who enjoy working with complex ideas and are able to communicate these ideas to others.

A Day in the Life—Duties and Responsibilities

Mathematicians work as economists, statisticians, and engineers. They apply their knowledge to a diverse number of fields, including physics, chemistry, and computers. There are two types of mathematicians applied and theoretical. Both types deal with complex problems on a daily basis. To solve these problems, mathematicians run tests and computer applications. They may also work on problems using chalkboards, dry-erase boards, or pencil and paper. Mathematicians analyze data and prepare it for presentation. They regularly communicate analyses to team members or colleagues.

Applied mathematicians tackle practical problems related to engineering, science, and economics. These problems are tangible, specific, and immediate. For example, a mathematician might tweak the aerodynamics of a space-shuttle design or compile data to provide an economic analysis of a particular policy issue.

Theoretical mathematicians working in an academic or research environment spend a lot of time reading professional journals and communicating with other mathematicians. They regularly attend mathematics conferences. As teachers, they spend much their time in the classroom with students. Theoretical mathematicians also spend time working independently on mathematical problems, sharing their progress with colleagues and graduate students. Unlike an applied mathematician, a theoretical mathematician might labor for years on a single problem. Their work is rooted in the theory, philosophy, and art of mathematics.

Duties and Responsibilities

- Testing hypotheses and alternative theories
- Conceiving and developing ideas for the application of mathematics to a wide variety of areas
- Performing computations and applying methods of numerical analysis
- Operating or directing the operation of mechanical and electronic equipment in support of mathematical, scientific or industrial research

OCCUPATION SPECIALTIES

Statisticians

Statisticians conduct research into the mathematical theories and proofs that form the basis of the science of statistics and develop statistics and statistical methodology. Statisticians also investigate, evaluate and prepare reports on applicability, efficiency and accuracy of statistical methods used by physical and social scientists and other researchers.

Actuaries

Actuaries apply knowledge of mathematics, probability, statistics, and the principles of finance and business to problems in life, health, social, and casualty insurance, annuities and pensions.

Cryptanalysts

Cryptanalysts analyze secret coding systems and decode messages for military, political, or law enforcement agencies or organizations.

WORK ENVIRONMENT

Physical Environment

Theoretical mathematicians work in an academic or research setting. Applied mathematicians can work in a variety of environments, including offices, medical laboratories, and computer facilities.

Relevant Skills and Abilities

Communication Skills
- Expressing thoughts and ideas
- Speaking effectively

Organization & Management Skills
- Coordinating tasks
- Managing people/groups

Research & Planning Skills
- Analyzing information
- Creating ideas
- Using logical reasoning

Technical Skills
- Performing scientific, mathematical and technical work
- Working with machines, tools or other objects

Human Environment

Mathematicians work with others to solve problems. Theoretical mathematicians work regularly with graduate students and doctoral candidates, while applied mathematicians may work with specialists in other fields, such as physicists and engineers.

Technological Environment

Mathematicians regularly use computers in their work. Using specially designed computers and computer software, they build models, decipher and design code, make predictions, and compute large numbers to find patterns.

EDUCATION, TRAINING, AND ADVANCEMENT

High School/Secondary

Aspiring mathematicians should take as many high school math courses as possible. Where possible, they should study calculus and seek advanced-placement classes in science and math. Extracurricular activities involving technology or mathematics are also encouraged. Most high schools have math clubs. In the United States, there is a high school and two-year college mathematics honor society called Mu Alpha Theta that holds conventions and competitions for students. Students interested in becoming mathematicians should seek a wide base of understanding of the subject before enrolling in a college or university.

Suggested High School Subjects
- Algebra
- Applied Math
- Calculus
- Chemistry
- College Preparatory
- Computer Science
- Economics
- English
- Geometry
- Mathematics
- Physics
- Science
- Statistics
- Trigonometry

Famous First

The first patent on a number was granted in 1995 to a 150-digit sequence developed by mathematician Roger Schlafly of Real Software, Soquel, Cal. The number was used in expediting calculations performed within a public data encryption/decryption system known as the Diffie-Hellman key exchange.

College/Postsecondary

Many entry-level mathematics jobs require only a bachelor's degree in mathematics, but this is an exception in the field. Most mathematicians will continue to build upon their knowledge by majoring in the subject as an undergraduate and then pursuing a specialty or specific field in graduate school. Many colleges and universities require students to take courses in computer science, engineering, physical science, and economics as well. Undergraduate students majoring in mathematics can expect to take courses in calculus, differential equations, statistics, mathematical logic, and discrete mathematics.

Many employers seek mathematicians with a Ph.D., though there are opportunities available to mathematicians with lesser graduate degrees. Students can earn their master's and doctoral degrees in either theoretical or applied mathematics.

Related College Majors
- Applied Mathematics
- Mathematical Statistics
- Mathematics
- Physics, General

Adult Job Seekers

It is unusual for individuals to pursue a career in mathematics later in life. Many adults who studied mathematics as undergraduates later return to school for a master's or doctoral degree. It is particularly important for aspiring graduate students to score well on the Graduate Record Examinations (GRE) test, which is required by most graduate programs. Once enrolled, graduate students should network and meet as many people working in the field as possible.

Professional Certification and Licensure

There is no formal certificate or license that a mathematician receives upon graduating from a master's or doctoral program. However, some of the fields that employ mathematicians require special certification. For example, teachers and actuaries (individuals who work with insurance policies, pensions, and annuities) require separate training and licensure.

Additional Requirements

Mathematicians receive valuable training in the field. Some learn to apply their knowledge of probabilities to the study of nature or medicine. Others will apply calculus to a model of the known universe. All mathematicians approach their work with the problem-solving skills they learned during their years of education. As a discipline, mathematics requires diligence and patience. Often, mathematicians must derive pleasure from curiosity, the process of problem solving, and the pursuit of knowledge over immediate gratification.

Fun Fact

Consider yourself a math whiz? Think you know division inside and out? Then what's the name of the symbol inside the following parentheses (÷)? It's called an "obelus." You're welcome.

Source: https://mathemagicalsite.wordpress.com/2015/02/15/01-mathematical-trivia/

EARNINGS AND ADVANCEMENT

Mean annual earnings of mathematicians were $104,350 in 2014. The lowest ten percent earned less than $54,830, and the highest ten percent earned more than $157,090.

Mathematicians may receive paid vacations, holidays, and sick days; life and health insurance; and retirement benefits. These are usually paid by the employer.

Metropolitan Areas with the Highest Employment Level in this Occupation

Metropolitan area	Employment [1]	Employment per thousand jobs	Annual mean wage
Chicago-Joliet-Naperville, IL	320	0.09	n/a
Washington-Arlington-Alexandria, DC-VA-MD-WV	300	0.13	$134,150
Los Angeles-Long Beach-Glendale, CA	140	0.03	$105,980
San Diego-Carlsbad-San Marcos, CA	110	0.08	$96,240
Bethesda-Rockville-Frederick, MD	100	0.17	$128,760
Baltimore-Towson, MD	60	0.05	$97,200
Providence-Fall River-Warwick, RI-MA	40	0.06	n/a

[1]Does not include self-employed. Source: Bureau of Labor Statistics

EMPLOYMENT AND OUTLOOK

Mathematicians held about 3,500 jobs nationally in 2012. In addition, about 60,000 persons held mathematics faculty positions in colleges and universities in 2012. Most non-faculty mathematicians held jobs in federal and state government, working mostly for the Department of Defense and the National Aeronautics and Space Administration (NASA). Employment of mathematicians is expected to grow faster than the average for all occupations through the year 2020, which means employment is projected to increase 20 percent or more. Competition is expected to remain strong for the limited number of jobs. Master's degree and Ph.D. degree holders with a strong background in mathematics and a related discipline, such as engineering or computer science, should have the best opportunities.

Advancements in technology usually lead to expanding applications of mathematics, and more workers with knowledge of mathematics will be required in the future. However, jobs in industry and government often require advanced knowledge of related scientific disciplines in addition to mathematics. The most common fields in which mathematicians study and find work are computer science and software development, physics, engineering and operations research. More mathematicians also are becoming involved in financial analysis. Mathematicians must compete for jobs, however, with people who have degrees in these other disciplines. The most successful jobseekers will be able to apply mathematical theory to real-world problems and possess good communication, teamwork and computer skills.

Employment Trend, Projected 2012–22

Mathematical science occupations: 26%

Mathematicians: 23%

Total, all occupations: 11%

Note: "All Occupations" includes all occupations in the U.S. Economy. Source: U.S. Bureau of Labor Statistics, Employment Projections Program

Related Occupations
- Actuary
- Computer Programmer
- Computer Systems Analyst
- Economist
- Operations Research Analyst
- Social Scientist
- Statistician
- Surveyor & Cartographer

Related Military Occupations
- Industrial Engineer
- Intelligence Officer
- Intelligence Specialist

Conversation With . . .
KRISTIN LAUTER

Principal Researcher & Research Manager
Microsoft Research, Cryptography Group, Redmond WA
Mathematician, 25 years

1. What was your individual career path in terms of education/training, entry-level job, or other significant opportunity?

I graduated from high school when I was 15 and started college at the University of Chicago. I did my undergraduate degree in Mathematics and continued there until I earned my Ph.D. in Mathematics in 1996. The University of Chicago is a very theoretical place and doesn't even have an engineering school, so it wasn't obvious that I would end up in industry. My first job was as an Assistant Professor of Mathematics at the University of Michigan. I taught number theory and coding theory and was fascinated by my engineering graduate students and their experiences in industry. After three years, curiosity got the better of me and I accepted a job with Microsoft Research in cryptography and coding theory. Cryptography is the science of keeping secrets and forms the foundation for secure Internet commerce. Coding theory is the theory of error correcting codes, which protects digital information to make it resistant to error. So, for instance, if a CD gets a scratch, it can still be played. I've been at Microsoft for 16 years, managing the Cryptography Research team for eight.

I currently serve as president of the Association for Women in Mathematics, an organization devoted to advancing women and girls in mathematics.

2. What are the most important skills and/or qualities for someone in your profession?

Love of mathematics is the number one thing. Problem-solving skills are important. Mathematics helps you hone your thinking skills and that goes both ways—being a good thinker helps you with mathematics. You also have to be able to communicate, verbally and in writing, the importance of mathematics and the importance of your work. An important skill for mathematicians that gets overlooked is the ability to write code.

3. What do you wish you had known going into this profession?

I had not realized how few women there would be at the top levels of the profession. As a woman, it's important to encourage other young women and girls in the profession.

4. Are there many job opportunities in your profession? In what specific areas?

The thinking skills that you get as a mathematician allow you to do many jobs. If you have a bachelor's in mathematics, you have a lot of options—being an accountant, doing actuarial science in the insurance industry, business administration or going into engineering of many different types. If you're interested in pursuing a career in research, when you get your Ph.D., you can certainly be a professor. Teaching mathematics at any level is so important for society. It's a really great profession. In the pharmaceutical industry and in the biomedical field in general, mathematical modeling is very important. I have colleagues and friends working with physicians on using mathematics to understand disease and treatments. There are jobs in my area, which is security and privacy, information theory and information technology; in the high-tech industry, both in communications and in research about the design of large data centers; and in energy. An emerging area is called Big Data, or data analytics, which is helping companies understand their data so they can provide useful services to their customers and determine things like how much inventory they need at a given time, how many people to employ, how much cloud storage they need. Another great career path for mathematicians is working for the National Security Agency (NSA), which is the largest employer of mathematicians in the country. It's all about national security … protecting information and discovering information.

5. How do you see your profession changing in the next five years? What role will technology play in those changes, and what skills will be required?

I think there will be increased recognition of the importance of mathematics training in the industries I just mentioned. I see an expansion of opportunities for students with mathematics training, but that will be accompanied by the need for them to be fluent in computer languages.

6. What do you enjoy most about your job? What do you enjoy least about your job?

I enjoy talking to people about mathematics and I enjoy learning new problems that mathematics can be used to solve. For example, today I spoke with the head of the bioinformatics and genomics center at Stanford University about how they can get access to patient data to work on cures. The work I do helps protect the privacy of information through encryption while still allowing you to perform computations on that data.

I now have a lot of management and administrative responsibilities. That's not my favorite part of the job.

7. Can you suggest a valuable "try this" for students considering a career in your profession?

Try solving puzzles. If you get a puzzle book and find you enjoy it, mathematics will be a good fit. Try writing computer programs, either by taking a class or using online resources. Writing a computer program is like writing an algorithm to solve a problem, so it's a good proxy for what a mathematician does.

SELECTED SCHOOLS

Most colleges and universities offer programs in mathematics. Some of the more prominent schools in this field are listed below.

California Institute of Technology
1200 E California Blvd, Pasadena
CA 91125
(626) 395-6811
http://www.caltech.edu

Columbia University
Room 509 MC 4406, New York
NY 10027
(212) 854-4112
http://www.math.columbia.edu

Harvard University
Cambridge, MA 02138
Phone (617) 495-2171
http://www.math.harvard.edu

Massachusetts Institute of Technology
77 Massachusetts Ave
Cambridge, MA 02139
Phone(617) 253-1000
http://web.mit.edu

New York University
New York, NY
(212) 998-1212
http://www.nyu.edu

Princeton University
Princeton, NJ 08544
Phone (609) 258-3000
http://www.princeton.edu/main

Stanford University
450 Serra Mall
Stanford, CA 94305
Phone (650) 723-2300
https://www.stanford.edu

University of California, Berkeley
Berkeley, CA
(510) 642-6000
http://www.berkeley.edu

University of California, Los Angeles
Los Angeles, CA 90095
(310) 825-4321
http://www.ucla.edu

University of Chicago
5801 S Ellis Ave, Chicago, IL 60637
(773) 702-1234
http://www.uchicago.edu

MORE INFORMATION

American Institute of Mathematics
360 Portage Avenue
Palo Alto, CA 94306
650.845.2071
www.aimath.org

American Mathematical Society
201 Charles Street
Providence, RI 02904-6248
800.321.4267
www.ams.org

American Statistical Association
732 N. Washington Street
Alexandria, VA 22314-1943
888.231.3473
www.amstat.org

Association for Women in Mathematics
11240 Waples Mill Road, Suite 200
Fairfax, VA 22030
703.934.0163
www.awm-math.org

Conference Board of the Mathematical Sciences
1529 18th Street, NW
Washington, DC 20036
202.293.1170
www.cbmsweb.org

Institute of Mathematical Statistics
Business Office
P.O. Box 22718
Beachwood, OH 44122
877.557.4674
www.imstat.org

Mathematical Association of America
1529 18th Street, NW
Washington, DC 20036-1385
800.741.9415
www.maa.org

National Council of Teachers of Mathematics
1906 Association Drive
Reston, VA 20191-1502
703.620.9840
www.nctm.org

Society for Industrial and Applied Mathematics
3600 Market Street, 6th Floor
Philadelphia, PA 19104-2688
215.382.9800
www.siam.org

Molly Hagan/Editor

Mechanical Engineer

Snapshot

Career Cluster: Architecture & Construction; Manufacturing; Science, Technology, Engineering & Mathematics

Interests: Mechanics, science, design, technology

Earnings (Yearly Average): $87,140

Employment & Outlook: Slower Than Average Growth Expected

OVERVIEW

Sphere of Work

Mechanical engineers are responsible for designing, developing, testing, and maintaining mechanical equipment such as engines and machines, taking into account the ways in which temperature, energy expenditure, and other forces will affect the product materials while a device is in operation. These engineers are often involved in the development of automated systems using robotic technology and the production of transportation vehicles, heating and cooling devices, and other complex mechanical systems. Mechanical engineers work with physicists, chemists, and engineers in other fields  to meet design and performance needs for diverse consumer products.

They apply their expertise to meet evolving needs and develop better materials in order to refine mechanical technology and achieve optimum efficiency.

Work Environment

Depending on the specific projects they are assigned, mechanical engineers may interact with engineers and scientists from a wide range of disciplines. Each person involved in product design and development might specialize in a particular type of machinery, such as a specific component of automobiles or ventilation equipment, to which they devote time in laboratories, factories, and test facilities in order to improve the design and performance.

Mechanical engineers rely on effective communication, both verbal and written, to coordinate their unique ideas and strategies with colleagues, managers, and technicians. They also consider consumer input regarding needs and proposed uses for products created as well as accessibility and ease of operation.

Profile

Working Conditions: Work Indoors
Physical Strength: Light Work
Education Needs: Bachelor's Degree, Master's Degree, Doctoral Degree
Licensure/Certification: Required
Opportunities For Experience: Internship, Apprenticeship, Military Service, Part-time Work
Holland Interest Score*: RIS

* See Appendix A

Occupation Interest

Mechanical engineers are innovative individuals who are competent in scientific and technical fields and consider technological challenges appealing. They typically enjoy finding solutions to meet the various demands posed by industrial employers and consumers, creating the best designs in order to perform specific functions successfully, safely, affordably, and efficiently.

Schools and other educational institutions can prepare students to enter the field of mechanical engineering by developing curricula that emphasize basic technical proficiency and that offer engineering and science electives, which enhance the skills and insights of aspiring engineers.

A Day in the Life—Duties and Responsibilities

Mechanical engineers perform diverse tasks, including designing, programming, and project managing, depending on their credentials and the employers who need their services. These engineers apply their ingenuity in such areas as structural analysis, mechanical design, and systems manufacturing for corporations such as Boeing and government agencies such as the National Aeronautics and Space Administration (NASA).

Specific project goals determine how mechanical engineers conduct their daily tasks, whether in office buildings, factories, or other sites. Many devote part of their time to meeting with managers, colleagues, and clients to establish how a project should proceed. Mechanical engineers are often responsible for determining the budgets for specific projects. Sometimes these engineers are tasked with evaluating how their innovations might affect the environment and implementing measures to limit emissions and energy consumption. They consult with colleagues, both mechanical engineers and representatives of other specialties, when necessary. Mechanical engineers may also create computer software to aid them in assessing their manufacturing systems. Many mechanical engineers work to improve the safety and quality standards for new technology set by the American Society of Mechanical Engineers (ASME).

Mechanical engineers working for universities are responsible for preparing engineering-specific curricula and guiding students in their course choices and research projects. Engineers who patent devices or processes may spend time seeking investors to fund their research and help them manufacture and sell their products. Some mechanical engineers assist government officials, including members of the US Congress and the White House Office of Science and Technology, by advising leaders regarding mechanical engineering issues that affect federal policies addressing safety, environmental, or economic concerns.

Duties and Responsibilities

- Designing products or systems
- Planning and directing engineering personnel in the fabrication of test control apparatus and equipment
- Developing methods and procedures for testing products
- Directing and coordinating construction and installation activities
- Coordinating operation, maintenance and repair activities to obtain the best use of the machines and systems
- Evaluating field installations and recommending design changes to eliminate malfunctions
- Researching and analyzing data to determine if a design is feasible

OCCUPATION SPECIALTIES

Automotive Engineers

Automotive Engineers develop new or improved designs for automobile structural parts, engines, transmissions, suspension systems and associated equipment. They may also direct the building, modification and testing of vehicles.

Plant Engineers

Plant Engineers direct and coordinate activities relating to the design, construction and maintenance of equipment and machinery in an industrial plant.

Mechanical Engineering Technicians

Mechanical Engineering Technicians, who usually work under a Mechanical Engineer or other senior staff person, help design, test, and manufacture mechanical devices, including tools, engines, and machines.

WORK ENVIRONMENT

Physical Environment

Mechanical engineers may work in a variety of facilities, including factories, colleges and universities, laboratories, and corporate or government offices. Many mechanical engineers use laboratories equipped with advanced computerized systems to aid them in designing and analyzing prototypes. Test sites enable mechanical engineers to evaluate and adjust products in appropriate settings, such as paved tracks for vehicle assessments.

Relevant Skills and Abilities

Organization & Management Skills
- Coordinating tasks
- Managing people/groups

Organization & Management Skills
- Paying attention to and handling details

Research & Planning Skills
- Analyzing information
- Creating ideas
- Developing evaluation strategies
- Using logical reasoning

Technical Skills
- Performing scientific, mathematical and technical work
- Working with machines, tools or other objects

Human Environment

Lower-level mechanical engineers typically work under the supervision of their more experienced counterparts, while experienced engineers often perform managerial roles, overseeing multiple projects and employees at a site. Engineers often collaborate in teams with scientific and engineering colleagues, technicians, and interns. Mechanical engineers may also meet with business advisers.

Technological Environment

Mechanical engineers use diverse technologies, ranging from basic communications technology to advanced computer software and hardware that are essential to performing their tasks. They may also use handheld tools when testing or maintaining mechanical equipment.

EDUCATION, TRAINING, AND ADVANCEMENT

High School/Secondary

While attending high school, students interested in pursuing careers in mechanical engineering should enroll in available science, technology, engineering, and mathematics (STEM) classes to learn fundamental scientific and technical concepts and to improve computer proficiency. Students also can acquire practical engineering experience by joining clubs in their schools or communities, such as the Boy and Girl Scouts and 4-H, to earn robotics merit badges, participate in science and engineering programs, and enter competitions such as the FIRST (For the Inspiration and Recognition of Science and Technology) Robotics Competition.

Science fairs, camps, extension courses, and internships offer students access to mechanical engineering professionals and experiences, which can provide them with the opportunity to explore various aspects of mechanical engineering research. Engineers Week activities, often hosted by universities, help teenagers gain awareness of professional opportunities.

Suggested High School Subjects
- Algebra
- Applied Communication
- Applied Math
- Applied Physics
- Blueprint Reading
- Calculus
- Chemistry
- College Preparatory
- Computer Science
- Drafting
- Electricity & Electronics
- English
- Geometry
- Humanities
- Machining Technology

- Mathematics
- Mechanical Drawing
- Metals Technology
- Physical Science
- Physics
- Science
- Trigonometry

Famous First

The first laboratory for research in mechanical engineering was founded at the Stevens Institute of Technology, Hoboken, N.J., in 1874. The lab, pictured, was established by Robert Henry Thurston, professor of mechanical engineering and its effects were seen in the pupils he trained and in the advance of applied engineering as a discipline.

College/Postsecondary

A bachelor's degree from an accredited program is required for employment as a mechanical engineer. Such programs typically teach basic engineering courses in addition to thermodynamics, hydraulics, heat transfer, fluid mechanics, and robotics. Many mechanical engineers also pursue advanced degrees, such as master's or doctoral degrees in mechanical engineering. Engineering students investigate in-depth subjects relevant to specific aspects of mechanical engineering, such as the role of vibrations and heat transfer, that they intend to pursue professionally.

Students may also pursue internships or cooperative education jobs, which enable them to experience professional situations and meet potential employers. Many students participate in mechanical engineering competitions at their universities or at contests sponsored by state and national engineering organizations.

Related College Majors
- Construction/Building Technology
- Engineering, General
- Mechanical Drafting
- Mechanical Engineering

Adult Job Seekers

People reentering the mechanical engineering profession after an absence may benefit from the resources offered by ASME, including technical publications, continuing education courses, and training sessions. Many colleges and universities offer professional-development classes on campus and online to mechanical engineers who want to learn about new and emerging techniques and materials in the field, in addition to aspects of other engineering and science specialties, in order to expand their expertise and value to employers.

Professional associations often offer grants to qualified applicants so they can acquire the necessary education to become competitive in the job market. Returning mechanical engineers may seek out internships and other temporary employment and research opportunities to gain experience with various technologies and procedures. Many professional groups maintain career information resources and networking contacts for adult job seekers. Mechanical engineers who are military veterans are eligible for government resources intended to help them to reenter the workforce.

Professional Certification and Licensure

Mechanical engineers who have attained several years of work experience can take a state examination to qualify for professional licensure, which enables them to provide their services directly to the public. These tests evaluate candidates' knowledge of specific mechanical engineering practices. A license enables mechanical engineers to propose designs for projects and work as consultants. Several states require mechanical engineers to complete a specific number of continuing education credits every two years. Some mechanical engineers attain certification for specific engineering skills, which may help them earn salary increases and promotions.

Additional Requirements

As the field of mechanical engineering is continuing to develop, engineers must continually acquire new skills and scientific knowledge, training, and experience. Strong communication skills are essential, as mechanical engineers often collaborate with team members or work as consultants.

Fun Fact

In 1901, the Spanish engineer Leonar do Torres-Quevedo took the first steps toward remote control, with a device he called Telekine, that could perform "mechanical movements at a distance."

Source: http://www.reliableplant.com/Read/17159/30-fun-facts-about-engineering,-science-technology

EARNINGS AND ADVANCEMENT

Earnings depend on the type, size and geographic location of the employer and the employee's education, experience, skill level and job responsibilities. According to a salary survey by the National Association of Colleges and Employers, graduates with a bachelor's degree in mechanical engineering earned average starting salaries of $64,215 in 2012.

Mean annual earnings of mechanical engineers were $87,140 in 2014. The lowest ten percent earned less than $53,210, and the highest ten percent earned more than $126,430.

Mechanical engineers may receive paid vacations, holidays, and sick days; life and health insurance; and retirement benefits. These are usually paid by the employer. Some employers also provide reimbursement for further education.

Metropolitan Areas with the Highest Employment Level in this Occupation

Metropolitan area	Employment [1]	Employment per thousand jobs	Annual mean wage
Warren-Troy-Farmington Hills, MI	19,130	16.72	$91,810
Detroit-Livonia-Dearborn, MI	11,250	15.68	$93,850
Houston-Sugar Land-Baytown, TX	9,260	3.26	$106,620
Los Angeles-Long Beach-Glendale, CA	6,450	1.59	$98,730
Chicago-Joliet-Naperville, IL	5,570	1.49	$83,700
Minneapolis-St. Paul-Bloomington, MN-WI	5,400	2.96	$83,920
Boston-Cambridge-Quincy, MA	5,290	2.94	$93,510
Washington-Arlington-Alexandria, DC-VA-MD-WV	4,420	1.86	$110,060
San Jose-Sunnyvale-Santa Clara, CA	4,400	4.52	$111,720
Denver-Aurora-Broomfield, CO	3,940	2.97	$88,910

[1]Does not include self-employed. Source: Bureau of Labor Statistics

EMPLOYMENT AND OUTLOOK

There were approximately 258,000 mechanical engineers employed nationally in 2012. Employment of mechanical engineers is expected to grow slower than the average for all occupations through the year 2022, which means employment is projected to increase 2 percent to 8 percent. Growth in the fields of biotechnology, materials science and nanotechnology will create new job opportunities for mechanical engineers.

Employment Trend, Projected 2012–22

Total, all occupations: 11%

Engineers (all): 9%

Mechanical engineers: 5%

Note: "All Occupations" includes all occupations in the U.S. Economy. Source: U.S. Bureau of Labor Statistics, Employment Projections Program

Related Occupations
- Aerospace Engineer
- Architect
- Ceramic Engineer
- Civil Engineer
- Electrical & Electronics Engineer
- Energy Engineer
- Industrial Engineer
- Marine Engineer & Naval Architect
- Water & Wastewater Engineer
- Wind Energy Engineer

Related Military Occupations
- Aerospace Engineer

Conversation With . . .
DAVID J. REESE

Practice Leader, Mechanical
KCI Technologies, Sparks, MD
Mechanical Engineer, 35 years

1. What was your individual career path in terms of education/training, entry-level job, or other significant opportunity?

I attended a technical high school that had an engineering curriculum that I enjoyed and excelled in, and I was good at math and enjoyed solving problems. Originally, I had intended to be an architect, but by the time I graduated from high school, I decided that engineering was a better fit for me.

In college, I did a work-study co-op program through Virginia Tech, where you get the practical experience of working for a company. I don't know that I learned a whole lot, technically, in the workplace, but I got a working knowledge of what being a consulting engineer entails. Going to college via that program meant it took five years to earn an undergraduate degree, but I also earned money to pay for school. After graduation, I went to work at the same company; they knew me and I knew them.

I was drawn to mechanical engineering because it was a little more challenging than some of the other disciplines. I took the exam that's the first step toward sitting for your Professional Engineering Exam and getting licensed when I was a college senior.

Early in my career, I became very good at designing chilled water piping and pumping systems. The industry has become quite dynamic in recent years for requiring sustainability and energy requirements. It's made us have to work harder and smarter, and it's definitely an improvement, from a technical standpoint, from what we were doing when I first started out.

I came in to my current employer as a senior mechanical engineer and have since been promoted to lead the mechanical engineering practice. This is the eighth company I've worked for during my career, and that's pretty typical for the industry with the exception of those who may stay in one company for a whole career.

2. What are the most important skills and/or qualities for someone in your profession?

Number one is good communication. You're dealing with people all the time.

3. What do you wish you had known going into this profession?

In school, they don't really teach you a practical knowledge of building codes. When I started out, every jurisdiction had its own code. They've been going toward a standardized code but all jurisdictions are still allowed to have their own requirements on top of standard codes. A better working knowledge of building codes would have been helpful.

4. Are there many job opportunities in your profession? In what specific areas?

There are many jobs available in the mechanical engineering profession such as consulting, as I'm doing, and also in sales, or even contracting and construction.

5. How do you see your profession changing in the next five years, what role will technology play in those changes, and what skills will be required?

Energy-efficient systems and their design has been a huge factor recently and it's going to have a major impact on the industry. I think more than anything, you will see this in the equipment manufacturing realm of this industry because we need to find equipment that's more efficient, and efficiency is being ramped up. A couple of recent examples include one, known as a variable refrigerant flow system (VRF) that's big in Asia; these systems are highly efficient. Another that is relatively new to industry is the Energy Wheel, where you pre-treat outdoor air using exhaust air from a building.

6. What do you enjoy most about your job? What do you enjoy least about your job?

What I most enjoy is the people in the industry. I enjoy working with people and teaching young people what I've learned throughout my career. I least enjoy bureacracy and paperwork.

7. Can you suggest a valuable "try this" for students considering a career in your profession?

I'm Chairman of the Baltimore chapter of ASHRAE, the American Society of Heating, Refrigerating and Air-Conditioning Engineers (www.ashrae.org), and our chapter has a student challenge every year for local high school students. It's a teamwork type of excercise where participants actually get to do some design work for an air conditioning system for a commercial application of one sort or another. See if you can find a challenge such as that; participating in it would give you a real good clue if this is for you.

SELECTED SCHOOLS

Most colleges and universities offer programs in engineering; many of them have concentrations in mechanical engineering. Some of the more prominent schools in this field are listed below.

California Institute of Technology
1200 E. California Boulevard
Pasadena, CA 91125
Phone: (626) 395-6811
www.caltech.edu/

Carnegie Mellon University
5000 Forbes Avenue
Pittsburgh, PA 15213
Phone: (412) 268-2000
www.cmu.edu

Cornell University
242 Carpenter Hall
Ithaca, NY 14850
Phone: (607) 254-4636
www.cornell.edu

Georgia Institute of Technology
225 North Avenue
Atlanta, GA 30332
Phone: (404) 894-2000
www.gatech.edu

Massachusetts Institute of Technology
77 Massachusetts Avenue
Room 1-206
Cambridge, MA 02139
Phone: (617) 253-1000
web.mit.edu

Purdue University, West Lafayette
701 W. Stadium Avenue
Suite 3000ARMS
West Lafayette, IN 47907
Phone: (765) 494-4600
www.purdue.edu

Stanford University
Huang Engineering Center, Suite 226
450 Serra Mall
Stanford, CA 94305
Phone: (605) 723-2300
www.stanford.edu

University of California, Berkeley
320 McLaughlin Hall #1700
Berkeley, CA 94720
Phone: (510) 642-6000
www.berkeley.edu

University of Illinois, Urbana Champaign
1308 W. Green
Urbana, IL 61801
Phone: (217) 333-1000
www.Illinois.edu

University of Michigan, Ann Arbor
Robert H. Lurie Engineering Center
500 S. State Street
Ann Arbor, MI 48109
Phone: (734) 764-1817
https://umich.edu

MORE INFORMATION

American Society of Heating, Refrigerating and Air-Conditioning Engineers
Education Department
1791 Tullie Circle, NE
Atlanta, GA 30329
800.527.4723
www.ashrae.org

ASME International
Three Park Avenue
New York, NY 10016-5990
800.843.2763
www.asme.org

FIRST (For the Inspiration and Recognition of Science and Technology)
200 Bedford Street
Manchester, NH 03101
800.871.8326
www.usfirst.org

National Action Council for Minorities in Engineering
440 Hamilton Avenue, Suite 302
White Plains, NY 10601-1813
914.539.4010
www.nacme.org

National Society of Black Engineers
205 Daingerfield Road
Alexandria, VA 22314
703.549.2207
www.nsbe.org

Society of Automotive Engineers International
400 Commonwealth Drive
Warrendale, PA 15086
877.606.7323
www.sae.org

Society of Engineering Science
405 N Mathews Avenue
Room 3361
Beckman Institute for Advanced
Science and Technology
University of Illinois at Urbana-
Champaign
Urbana, IL 61801
703.845.9671
www.sesinc.org

Society of Hispanic Professional Engineers
13181 Crossroads Parkway North
Suite 450
City of Industry, CA 91746-3497
323.725.3970
www.shpe.org

Society of Women Engineers
203 N. La Salle Street, Suite 1675
Chicago, IL 60601
877.793.4636
www.swe.org

TryEngineering
445 Hoes Lane
Piscataway, NJ 08854-4141
www.tryengineering.org

Elizabeth D. Schafer/Editor

Medical Scientist

Snapshot

Career Cluster: Health Care; Science, Technology, Engineering & Mathematics

Interests: Science, medicine, chemistry, immunology, research and analysis, disease prevention and treatment

Earnings (Yearly Average): $90,160

Employment & Outlook: Average Growth Expected

OVERVIEW

Sphere of Work

Medical scientists, also referred to as laboratory scientists and medical researchers, perform research aimed at understanding and improving human health. They may study methods of disease prevention, treatment, and outbreak control, or work on developing new vaccines, medications, or diagnostic testing techniques. Medical scientists perform and oversee medical, chemical, biological, hematological, immunologic, microscopic, and bacteriological tests in the course of their research. They also supervise medical research and clinical laboratory staff.

Work Environment

Medical scientists may work in hospitals, government health agencies, medical technology businesses, educational facilities, pharmaceutical companies, or independent research laboratories. They generally work as many hours as needed to meet the demands of their research.

Profile

Working Conditions: Work Indoors
Physical Strength: Light Work
Education Needs: Doctoral Degree
Licensure/Certification: Required
Opportunities For Experience:
Military Service, Volunteer Work, Part-time Work
Holland Interest Score*: IRA

* See Appendix A

Occupation Interest

Individuals drawn to the profession of medical scientist tend to be analytical and detail oriented. A successful medical scientist should display initiative, focus, and good problem-solving and time-management skills. Medical scientists should be comfortable in laboratory settings and have a strong background in scientific research methods.

A Day in the Life—Duties and Responsibilities

The daily occupational duties and responsibilities of medical scientists will be determined by the individual's area of job specialization and work environment. For example, a medical scientist who specializes in disease treatment may formulate a hypothesis regarding a particular disease. After securing funding from private or public sources, the scientist would implement protocols to assess this hypothesis, such as a double-blind clinical trial of a new drug or treatment. He or she would then analyze the data, using qualitative and quantitative methods, and present the results in a professional peer-reviewed journal or at a conference.

Other aspects of a medical scientist's job may include analyzing human tissue sections and cell samples, developing and testing new vaccines and immunizations, or studying the life cycles of diseases and how they are transmitted. Medical scientists may travel to areas of disease outbreak to aid in disease control and containment efforts, or collaborate with government health agencies to implement public health initiatives. A senior scientist may be tasked with training laboratory technicians or overseeing students and research assistants. Medical scientists are also responsible for ensuring that their laboratories are in compliance with regulatory requirements.

Duties and Responsibilities

- Investigating the cause and spread of disease, methods of prevention and treatment options
- Performing research, analyzing data and explaining findings for the purposes of medical application
- Teaching physicians, residents and technicians about medical and laboratory principles and procedures
- Preparing and studying samples or organs, tissue and cells to identify toxins, bacteria or microorganisms
- Standardizing aspects of drug development, such as dosage levels, immunization methods and manufacturing procedures
- Handling toxic materials following precise safety procedures to avoid contamination
- Developing and overseeing the proper functioning of public health improvement programs and health safety standards
- Educating healthcare workers, patients and the public about the prevention and transmission of disease
- Communicating the results of research to health care practitioners, policy makers and the public
- Designing, managing and evaluating research procedures, such as questionnaire distribution, sample selection and analysis
- Monitoring and reporting infectious disease incidents to local and state health agencies

WORK ENVIRONMENT

Relevant Skills and Abilities

Communication Skills
- Speaking effectively
- Writing concisely
- Listening attentively
- Reading well
- Reporting information

Interpersonal/Social Skills
- Working as a member of a team
- Being able to work independently
- Cooperating with others

Organization & Management Skills
- Initiating new ideas
- Paying attention to and handling details
- Coordinating tasks
- Managing equipment/materials
- Making decisions
- Organizing information or materials
- Meeting goals and deadlines
- Performing duties which change frequently
- Handling challenging situations

Research & Planning Skills
- Identifying problems
- Identifying resources
- Gathering information
- Solving problems
- Setting goals and deadlines
- Analyzing information
- Developing evaluation strategies
- Using logical reasoning

Technical Skills
- Performing scientific, mathematical and technical work

Work Environment Skills
- Working in a medical setting

Physical Environment

Medical scientists spend their workdays in laboratories and research facilities, which should be clean and well ventilated. They are at risk for job-related injuries such as eyestrain, backache, and exposure to toxic and infectious substances.

Human Environment

Medical scientists should be comfortable interacting with research assistants, laboratory staff, pathologists, physicians, government health agents, and patients, as well as functioning in a supervisory and training role when required.

Technological Environment

Medical scientists use computers and laboratory instruments such as centrifuges, scales, automated analyzers, flasks, cell counters, and different types of microscopes. They should also be comfortable using databases, as well as software for scientific analysis, word processing, graphics imaging, and spreadsheets

EDUCATION, TRAINING, AND ADVANCEMENT

High School/Secondary

High school students interested in pursuing a career as a medical scientist should study biology, chemistry, anatomy, and mathematics. In addition, classes in communication will prepare students for writing grant proposals and reporting on their research.

Suggested High School Subjects
- Agricultural Education
- Algebra
- Applied Biology/Chemistry
- Applied Math
- Applied Physics
- Biology
- Calculus
- Chemistry
- College Preparatory
- English
- Geometry
- Health Science Technology
- Laboratory Technology
- Mathematics
- Physical Science
- Physics
- Physiology
- Science
- Statistics
- Trigonometry

Famous First

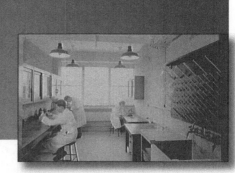

The first medical center devoted to teaching, treatment, and research was Columbia-Presbyterian Medical Center, New York, N.Y., which opened in 1928. It had a library of 100,000 books and was designed to serve 600 students.

College/Postsecondary

Postsecondary students interested in becoming medical scientists should work toward a doctoral degree in a biological science or a closely related field. Some senior medical scientist positions may also require a medical degree or a postdoctoral fellowship, and having both an MD and a PhD will greatly increase a job seeker's prospects; some medical colleges offer joint MD-PhD programs. Undergraduate studies should include courses in chemistry, anatomy, physiology, statistics, mathematics, and clinical laboratory practices, and may incorporate other sciences such as physics, engineering, and computer science. Students can also gain work experience and potential advantage in their future job searches by securing internships or part-time employment in laboratory and medical settings.

Related College Majors

- Anatomy
- Biochemistry
- Biology, General
- Biophysics
- Cell Biology
- Human & Animal Physiology
- Medicine (M.D.)
- Microbiology/Bacteriology
- Molecular Biology
- Toxicology

Adult Job Seekers

Adults seeking employment as medical scientists should have, at a minimum, a medical degree or a doctorate in a biological science. They will benefit from joining professional associations to help with networking and job searching. Professional medical science associations, such as the American Association of Pharmaceutical Scientists, the American Society for Microbiology, and the Association for Professionals in Infection Control and Epidemiology, may offer career workshops and inform members of available positions.

Professional Certification and Licensure

The certification and licensure requirements of medical scientists vary based on their research focus and scope of patient interaction. Medical scientists who focus on laboratory-based research may earn voluntary certification from the National Accrediting Agency for Clinical Laboratory Sciences as a Clinical Laboratory Scientist/Medical Technologist (CLS/MT) or a Clinical Laboratory Technician/Medical Laboratory Technician (CLT/MLT). Scientists who interact with patients in a medical capacity, such as administering drugs or vaccines or performing invasive procedures, must possess state medical licenses. Specific state-level physician certification and licensing requirement information should be sought directly from state departments of health.

Additional Requirements

High levels of integrity and professional ethics are required of medical scientists, as professionals in this role have access to private medical information. Membership in professional medical associations is encouraged.

Fun Fact

Government economists expect one of the fastest-growing careers through 2020 to be medical scientists, excluding epidemiologists.

Source: https://bigfuture.collegeboard.org/careers/science-medical-scientists

EARNINGS AND ADVANCEMENT

Mean annual earnings of medical scientists, except epidemiologists, were $90,160 in 2014. The lowest ten percent earned less than $43,150, and the highest ten percent earned more than $148,210.

Medical scientists may receive paid vacations, holidays and sick days; life and health insurance; and retirement benefits. These are usually paid by the employer.

Metropolitan Areas with the Highest Employment Level in this Occupation

Metropolitan area	Employment[1]	Employment per thousand jobs	Annual mean wage
Boston-Cambridge-Quincy, MA	8,710	4.85	$95,940
New York-White Plains-Wayne, NY-NJ	5,450	1.01	$87,160
Los Angeles-Long Beach-Glendale, CA	5,110	1.26	$94,700
San Francisco-San Mateo-Redwood City, CA	4,010	3.69	$122,800
Seattle-Bellevue-Everett, WA	3,730	2.50	$80,310
San Diego-Carlsbad-San Marcos, CA	3,490	2.64	$108,380
Philadelphia, PA	3,250	1.75	$102,470
Baltimore-Towson, MD	3,080	2.38	$77,630
Durham-Chapel Hill, NC	2,530	8.88	$96,180
Bethesda-Rockville-Frederick, MD	1,980	3.50	$106,970

[1]Does not include self-employed. Source: Bureau of Labor Statistics

EMPLOYMENT AND OUTLOOK

Medical scientists and epidemiologists held about 103,000 jobs nationally in 2012. About one-third worked in scientific research and development firms. Another one-fourth worked in educational services; while most of the remainder worked in pharmaceutical and medicine manufacturing and hospitals. Employment of medical scientists is expected to as fast as the average for all occupations through the year 2022, which means employment is expected to increase 10 percent to 15 percent. Employment growth should occur as a result of many factors, including the growth of biotechnology; the continuation of expanded research into the areas of AIDS, cancer, rare diseases, bioterrorism, and antibiotic resistance; and the study of environmental concerns such as overcrowding and the increase in international travel, and how those factors impact the creation and spread of disease.

Employment Trend, Projected 2012–22

Medical scientists (except epidemiologists): 13%

Total, all occupations: 11%

Life scientists (all): 9%

Note: "All Occupations" includes all occupations in the U.S. Economy. Source: U.S. Bureau of Labor Statistics, Employment Projections Program

Related Occupations
- Agricultural Engineer
- Agricultural Scientist
- Allergist & Immunologist
- Anesthesiologist
- Biological Scientist
- Biomedical Engineer
- Cardiologist
- Chemical Engineer
- Chemist
- Clinical Laboratory Technologist
- Dentist
- Dietitian and Nutritionist

- Environmental Engineer
- Forester and Conservation Scientist
- Medical Technologist
- Microbiologist
- Neurologist
- Ophthalmologist
- Pediatrician
- Pharmacist
- Physician

- Physicist
- Podiatrist
- Radiologist
- Surgeon

Related Military Occupations
- Life Scientist
- Physician & Surgeon

Conversation With . . .
SALLY M. BAKER, BSPH, MSc

MD/PhD, Physician Scientist Program
Tulane University School of Medicine
Medical Scientist, 4 years

1. What was your individual career path in terms of education/training, entry-level job, or other significant opportunity?

I was in high school during the SARS (severe acute respiratory syndrome) epidemic, which was all over the media. I followed that closely and got interested in public health; I thought it was a great way to have an impact on many people. I literally logged on to the World Health Organization website, looked at jobs and thought, "OK, 40 years from now, what will I still want to do?" But as I went through my graduate schooling, I realized that medicine is the foundation of everything we do in health care.

I earned a Bachelor of Science in public health, with an additional major in French, from Tulane University and a Master of Science in control of infectious disease from the London School of Hygiene and Tropical Medicine. After my master's, I honed my research skills in the lab and in the field as a research assistant for a large international research consortium in London studying water, sanitation and hygiene in developing countries. During this time, I applied for M.D./Ph.D. programs. I am now a fifth year student in the dual degree physician/scientist program at Tulane, about half-way through.

2. What are the most important skills and/or qualities for someone in your profession?

As science becomes more and more interdisciplinary, the ability to work with others in a team setting is invaluable. Science isn't just sitting at the bench pipetting; you need to brainstorm and come up with new ideas and be creative. Biomedical science encompasses an incredibly vast field of knowledge and it is impossible to know everything. By working with others, you draw from a much larger knowledge base and have a greater chance of success. Medicine is also all about teamwork with other healthcare providers. And you must form bonds with your patients to ensure they have healthy outcomes!

3. What do you wish you had known going into this profession?

An M.D./Ph.D. takes an average of seven to eight years, and that's after earning a bachelor's. Most graduates go on to a residency, which is another three to five years, and even a subsequent fellowship of one to three years. That means that by the time you're fully qualified, you can be in your late 30s. Most of your friends will have jobs, salaries and families while you're still a student. These are difficult realities and can make things lonely at times.

4. Are there many job opportunities in your profession? In what specific areas?

Absolutely! The beauty of becoming a physician/scientist is that you can play multiple roles. You have the flexibility to work as a clinician, as a bench scientist or as a clinical researcher. The breadth of knowledge you learn as a medical student and physician inspire the research questions you ask as a scientist, and the research you perform can inform your medical decision making. Jobs are available in academia—about a third of NIH grants go to M.D./Ph.D.s, so you really have a leg up in the competitive funding arena. You can see patients and have a laboratory. Another option is to go into industry, where you may do such things as research and development for a pharmaceutical company.

5. How do you see your profession changing in the next five years, what role will technology play, and what skills will be required?

I think one of the most exciting and important advancements is using a person's genome to make decisions about his or her healthcare. This could mean better and faster diagnoses, more efficient drug therapies and customized treatment plans. As genomic sequencing becomes faster and less expensive and we become better informed about how to use that information, personalized medicine will grow.

6. What do you enjoy most about your job? What do you enjoy least about your job?

I love that I am able to use my brain, think creatively and pose solutions to problems. A physician/scientist can draw from the depths of his or her knowledge and from the scientific field to find answers that have a profound impact on an individual's health and on medicine as a whole. However, science can be frustrating. Many times, hypotheses do not hold true or ideas fail to come to fruition. For instance, I worked for a year on a Ph.D. project that I ended up abandoning; the assays didn't work and I wasn't getting the answers I needed. It's frustrating to have things fall apart. By persevering, it is possible to stay positive and be successful.

7. **Can you suggest a valuable "try this" for students considering a career in your profession?**

Expose yourself to as many professionals as you can. Try shadowing a physician in a clinic or in the operating room to determine if medicine is a good fit. Speak with biomedical scientists to decide if you truly want to work in science, and with M.D./Ph.D.s to learn about the career paths someone with these degrees can follow. Don't be afraid to simply email someone, even if you don't know the person. Most faculty love to help and mentor students!

SELECTED SCHOOLS

Many colleges and universities offer programs related to medical science. Some of the more prominent schools in this field are listed below.

Columbia University
630 W. 168th Street
New York, NY 10032
Phone: (212) 854-1754
www.columbia.edu

Duke University
DUMC 3710
Durham, NC 27708
Phone: (919) 684-8111
https://duke.edu

Harvard University
25 Shattuck Street
Cambridge, MA 02115
 Phone: (617) 495-1000
www.harvard.edu

John Hopkins University
733 N. Broadway
Baltimore, MD 21205
Phone: (410) 516-8000
www.jhu.edu

Stanford University
300 Pasteur Drive, Suite M121
Stanford, CA 94305
Phone: (650) 723-2300
www.stanford.edu

University of California, San Francisco
513 Parnassus Avenue
Room S224
San Francisco, CA 94143
Phone: (415) 476-9000
www.ucsf.edu

University of Chicago (Pritzker)
5841 S. Maryland Avenue, MC 1000
Chicago, IL 60637
Phone: (773) 702-1234
www.uchicago.edu

University of Pennsylvania (Perelman)
237 John Morgan Building
3620 Hamilton Walk
Philadelphia, PA 19104
Phone: (215) 898-5000
www.upenn.edu

Washington University in St. Louis
660 S. Euclid Avenue
St. Louis, MO 63110
Phone: (314) 935-5000
www.wustl.edu

Yale University
333 Cedar Street
PO Box 208055
New Haven, CT 06520
Phone: (203) 432-4771
www.yale.edu

MORE INFORMATION

American Association of Pharmaceutical Scientists
2107 Wilson Boulevard, Suite 700
Arlington, VA 22201-3042
703.243.2800
www.aapspharmaceutica.com

American Medical Association (AMA)
515 North State Street
Chicago, IL 60654
www.ama-assn.org

American Society for Microbiology
Education Department
1752 N Street, NW
Washington, DC 20036-2904
202.737.3600
www.asm.org

American Society for Pharmacology and Experimental Therapeutics (ASPET)
9650 Rockville Pike
Bethesda, MD 20814
www.aspet.org

Association for Professionals in Infection Control and Epidemiology
1275 K Street, NW, Suite 1000
Washington, DC 20005-4006
202.789.1890
www.apic.org

Infectious Diseases Society of America
1300 Wilson Boulevard, Suite 300
Arlington, VA 22209
703.299.0200
www.idsociety.org

Simone Isadora Flynn/Editor

Microbiologist

Snapshot

Career Cluster: Health Care; Science, Technology, Engineering & Mathematics

Interests: Science, research and analysis, observation, microbiology, microorganisms, biotechnology

Earnings (Yearly Average): $76,530

Employment & Outlook: Average Growth Expected

OVERVIEW

Sphere of Work

Microbiologists study organisms such as bacteria, fungi, algae, protozoa, and viruses, which are only visible with the aid of microscopes. They research and analyze the structure, development, and other characteristics of these organisms using sophisticated scientific technology and equipment. Microbiologists observe and record the ways in which microorganisms influence the lives of higher organisms like plants and animals. They identify microscopic organisms' responses to environmental stimuli and analyze reproductive and other physiological processes.

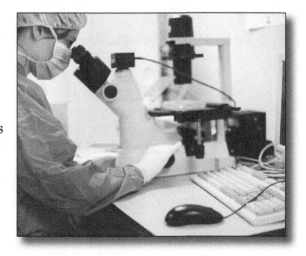

Work Environment

Microbiologists spend the majority of their time in the laboratory, conducting research using a wide array of microscopes and other analytical equipment. These environments are clean, bright, and well ventilated. Many microbiologists spend some working hours outdoors collecting samples from water sources, plant life, and other resources. Fieldwork may require travel to remote locations, hiking over rugged terrain, or working in difficult weather conditions. Microbiologists who hold positions at universities and colleges split their time between the classroom, the laboratory, and the office. Microbiologists usually work a regular forty-hour week, with extra hours typically required only when deadlines approach or an emergency occurs.

Profile

Working Conditions: Work Indoors
Physical Strength: Light Work
Education Needs: Doctoral Degree
Licensure/Certification: Usually Not
  Required
Opportunities For Experience:
  Internship
Holland Interest Score*: IRS

* See Appendix A

Occupation Interest

Microbiologists study the smallest organisms, an area of science that is currently evolving at a fast pace. New and exciting discoveries in the areas of clinical microbiology and biotechnology are common. Microbiologists are sometimes asked by government agencies or private companies and organizations to provide insight into the spread of germs and disease. Because the applications of microbiology span many areas, there is a wide range of subfields in which microbiologists may choose to specialize.

A Day in the Life—Duties and Responsibilities

Microbiologists work primarily in laboratories, using many different types of research and analytical equipment to formulate hypotheses and study different characteristics of particular microorganisms. They use advanced scientific technology to study algae, fungi, and bacteria or virus specimens. Conducting in-depth research into the structure, behavior, physiology, and environments of microorganisms, these scientists gather comprehensive data on their subject matter, information that is then entered into scientific databases. This work may include managing the activities of lab technicians, other scientists, and lab assistants.

Microbiologists write technical reports, academic papers, and books based on their findings and accumulated data. Some of these reports are submitted to government agencies to help formulate appropriate public policies and regulations or to assist medical researchers and doctors in isolating and delivering effective treatments for certain diseases. Research results and writings are shared with other biologists, regardless of publication. Even if the findings are not published in an academic journal, the microbiologists who conducted the research still communicate and share insights on how to direct future research. Some research results are published in scientific journals, allowing scientists throughout the world to share their thoughts on how the newly discovered information affects the overall body of knowledge on a subject.

When they are not in the laboratory, many microbiologists teach at colleges and universities. They provide classroom instruction to undergraduates and graduate students, conduct lectures, host lab sessions, and advise students on independent projects. Many microbiologists also present papers and theories at academic conferences and departmental meetings.

Duties and Responsibilities

- Growing organisms in liquid or solid media
- Injecting cultures or infected body fluids in lab animals
- Observing effects of new drugs or known disease-causing microorganisms
- Cultivating microorganisms that produce products such as alcohol or industrial solvents

WORK ENVIRONMENT

Physical Environment

Microbiologists work primarily in laboratories operated by the federal government, public and private universities, and private organizations and foundations. They may also conduct field research in remote locations and/or natural sources such as lakes and reservoirs.

Because a clean, sterile environment is necessary to ensure the validity of research results, laboratories have strict rules governing personal hygiene, surface cleanliness, clothing, and air quality. Despite these protocols, some microbiologists may experience a slight risk of exposure to dangerous chemicals or germs.

Relevant Skills and Abilities

Communication Skills
- Writing concisely

Interpersonal/Social Skills
- Being able to work independently
- Being patient
- Working as a member of a team

Organization & Management Skills
- Paying attention to and handling details

Research & Planning Skills
- Analyzing information

Technical Skills
- Performing scientific, mathematical and technical work

Human Environment

Depending on their areas of expertise, microbiologists interact and collaborate with a wide range of individuals. Among those with whom microbiologists work are laboratory technicians, lab assistants and interns, environmental scientists, medical doctors and researchers, government officials, and university students and professors.

Technological Environment

Microbiologists use a wide range of tools and technology to complete their work. Their equipment may include electron and light microscopes, sampling tools and equipment, centrifuges, infrared spectrometers, heating blocks, incubators, slides and test tubes, microbiology analyzers, and sterilization equipment. Additionally, they must use medical database systems, analytical software, and general office software (including presentation programs)

EDUCATION, TRAINING, AND ADVANCEMENT

High School/Secondary

High school students who wish to become microbiologists should take biology, chemistry, physics, physiology, and other natural sciences. Computer science training is also helpful, as are mathematics courses like algebra, calculus, and statistics. English and other classes that teach presentation and communication skills are highly useful.

Suggested High School Subjects
- Biology
- Chemistry
- English
- Physical Science
- Physiology
- Science

Famous First

The first genetically altered virus approved for use in a vaccine was in 1986 for veterinary use. The virus, *suid herpesvirus* 1 (SuHIV1), causes a disease in swine called Aujeszky's disease. A method known as gene deletion is used to alter the makeup of the virus, which is then introduced as a live virus vaccine to the animal. Research continues into other potential applications of genetically altered viruses.

College/Postsecondary

Some entry-level positions in applied research and product development only require a bachelor's degree, but in general, microbiologists should obtain a doctorate in their field. The doctoral degree qualifies them to teach at the college level and to obtain senior-level microbiology positions in research settings. Such educational training includes work in the classroom, the field, and the laboratory. Those who choose to pursue a subfield of microbiology may need additional or specialized training. For instance, some microbiologists complete medical school and obtain a doctor of medicine degree that focuses on clinical microbiology.

Related College Majors
- Biochemistry
- Cell Biology
- Epidemiology
- Medical Microbiology
- Microbiology/Bacteriology
- Virology
- Wildlife & Wildlands Management

Adult Job Seekers

Qualified microbiologists may apply directly to universities and colleges with openings. They may also find employment through university placement offices. Microbiologists who desire employment with state or federal government agencies may respond to postings on agency websites. Joining and networking through professional microbiology associations, such as the American Society for Microbiology, can be a useful job search strategy.

Professional Certification and Licensure

Some states have certification requirements for microbiologists working in laboratories. Interested individuals should consult the department of health in the state where they seek employment.

Additional Requirements

Microbiologists should demonstrate exceptional research and analytical skills and the ability to formulate theories and hypotheses based on a combination of smaller pieces of data. Strong knowledge of medical science is also useful, especially for microbiologists who work in virology, immunology, and similar subfields. Microbiologists must possess strong interpersonal and public speaking skills in order to collaborate on research and present research results to colleagues. They should be innately curious and find satisfaction in investigating microscopic life and broadening general understanding of it.

EARNINGS AND ADVANCEMENT

Earnings depend on the employer, geographic location and employee's education and level of responsibility. Mean annual earnings of microbiologists were $76,530 in 2014. The lowest ten percent earned less than $38,830, and the highest ten percent earned more than $125,000.

Microbiologists may receive paid vacations, holidays, and sick days; life and health insurance; and retirement benefits. These are usually paid by the employer

Metropolitan Areas with the Highest Employment Level in this Occupation

Metropolitan area	Employment [1]	Employment per thousand jobs	Annual mean wage
San Francisco-San Mateo-Redwood City, CA	1,450	1.33	$109,910
Boston-Cambridge-Quincy, MA	1,400	0.78	$68,290
Bethesda-Rockville-Frederick, MD	930	1.64	$110,700
San Diego-Carlsbad-San Marcos, CA	880	0.66	$96,210
Philadelphia, PA	690	0.37	$72,970
Atlanta-Sandy Springs-Marietta, GA	600	0.25	$87,810
Washington-Arlington-Alexandria, DC-VA-MD-WV	540	0.23	$84,600
Los Angeles-Long Beach-Glendale, CA	500	0.12	$86,080
New York-White Plains-Wayne, NY-NJ	420	0.08	$74,120
Nassau-Suffolk, NY	400	0.32	$73,540

[1]Does not include self-employed. Source: Bureau of Labor Statistics

EMPLOYMENT AND OUTLOOK

Microbiologists held about 20,000 jobs nationally in 2012. Employment is expected to grow nearly as fast as the average for all occupations through the year 2022, which means employment is projected to increase 5 percent to 9 percent. Contributing factors to this growth include environmental cleanup and preservation and research in health issues such as AIDS, cancer and Alzheimer's disease.

Employment Trend, Projected 2012–22

Total, all occupations: 11%

Life, physical, and social science occupations: 10%

Microbiologists: 7%

Note: "All Occupations" includes all occupations in the U.S. Economy. Source: U.S. Bureau of Labor Statistics, Employment Projections Program

Related Occupations
- Biological Scientist
- Botanist
- Medical Scientist
- Oceanographer
- Soil Scientist
- Veterinarian
- Wildlife Biologist
- Zoologist

Fun Fact

Ferdinand J. Cohn contributed to the founding of the science of bacteriology in 1875 when he published an early classification of bacteria using the genus name Bacillus for the first time.

Source: www.microbeworld.org/history-of-microbiology/1870s1880s

Conversation With . . .
HAILEY E. PETERSEN, PhD

Walter Reed Army Institute of Research
Silver Spring, MD
Microbiologist, 6 years

1. **What was your individual career path in terms of education/training, entry-level job, or other significant opportunity?**

    My AP biology teacher in high school took us into labs and assigned books like *The Hot Zone*. That really got me excited about science and, specifically, microbiology. Infectious disease is interesting, sexy and dangerous. I earned a B.S. in microbiology from Kansas State University, where I joined a laboratory as an undergraduate assistant. I gained a lot of practical experience and was exposed to lab culture. I also met my first significant mentor, a principal investigator who had other female students in her lab, which attracted me. With her help I decided to get my Ph.D. Together we navigated the process of asking for recommendations, applying to schools, and the interview process.

    During my grad school interviews, what struck me most was being told not to worry so much about what research I was doing but to find a school, a lab, and an advisor I was comfortable with. Don't get me wrong; grad school is intense. But some schools foster a community where students have time for a life of their own. When I visited Tulane University, I knew that was where I needed to be; the people were sincere and the students were hardworking but still happy.

    I worked on vaccine development with a bacteria that causes melidosis, which is like pneumonia. I was drawn to the project because pathogens are classified by how dangerous they are, and this was a level three out of four possible levels. So we wore full suits and worked in a contained, high-security lab.

    Entering the last year of my Ph.D. I started exploring my next step. I wanted to do a postdoc but didn't want to be an academic. My ultimate goal is to be head of a lab, but not necessarily at a university. I'm now doing a postdoc at Walter Reed Army Institute of Research, working on vaccine development for shigella, which is a diarrheal disease. The Army is interested because it's an expensive inconvenience for deployed troops and others in the field.

    I'm also doing a project management fellowship in the next year, which would be overseeing different projects in a science capacity. For instance, I might share new research that might be applicable to a particular project.

During my search for my postdoc, I did a lot of networking. It can be hard to approach people you don't know, but it was vital to finding my current position.

2. What are the most important skills and/or qualities for someone in your profession?

You must be persistent. A lot of doing science is failure. Experiments don't work the first time, or the second, or the 50th but you have to keep trying. You read more, you ask questions, you optimize and you try again. You also have to be persistent when it comes to getting funding and publishing. You will submit grants or manuscripts and get rejections and feedback and you need to be able to take that criticism, improve, and try again with a better product.

3. What do you wish you had known going into this profession?

I've been told that all grad students are miserable and that to really be successful you have to sacrifice personal time. But increasingly, I realize that you can accomplish your goals and do things in a way you are comfortable with if you plan for it.

4. Are there many job opportunities in your profession? In what specific areas?

Yes. Besides laboratory jobs in academia, industry or government, there are options like being a science writer, a consultant or a patent lawyer.

5. How do you see your profession changing in the next five years, what role will technology play in those changes, and what skills will be required?

Science is more collaborative than ever and a lot of that is because of technology. The speed of communication makes it easy to work with people all over the world. It has also boosted competition because you want to be the first to publish findings, and if you're not quick, someone may publish before you. You need to be able to build important collaborations with other scientists and communicate your ideas and discoveries clearly and quickly.

6. What do you enjoy most about your job? What do you enjoy least about your job?

The best part of being a scientist is that you are always on the edge of current knowledge. Every day, you and your colleagues are learning something no one has known before, and that's exciting. You get to tackle amazing questions. What I like least are the small things you must to do in order to get to the amazing experiments, such as paperwork, budgeting, and the bureaucracy involved in getting funding or managing a laboratory.

7. **Can you suggest a valuable "try this" for students considering a career in your profession?**

Summer internships, laboratory assistantships and lab tech positions are all good ways to get an idea of what it's like in a science lab and what grad school will be like. Most importantly, talk to Ph.D. students and postdocs about their experiences and find an advisor who can help you assess your strengths and weaknesses and help you make the jump to graduate student.

SELECTED SCHOOLS

Most colleges and universities offer programs in biology; many of them also have concentrations in microbiology. Some of the more prominent schools in this field are listed below.

Duke University
Durham, NC 27708
Phone: (919) 684-8111
https://duke.edu/

Harvard University
Cambridge, MA 02138
Phone: (617) 495-1000
www.harvard.edu

John Hopkins University
3400 N. Charles Street
Baltimore, MD 21218
Phone: (410) 516-8000
www.jhu.edu

Massachusetts Institute of Technology
77 Massachusetts Avenue
Cambridge, Massachusetts 02139
Phone: (617) 253-1000
www.mit.edu

Rockefeller University
1230 York Ave
New York, NY 10065
Phone: (212) 327-8000
www.rockefeller.edu

Stanford University
450 Serra Mall
Stanford, CA 94305
Phone: (650) 723-2300
www.stanford.edu

University of California, San Francisco
500 Parnassus Avenue
San Francisco, CA 94143
Phone: (415) 476-9000
www.ucsf.edu

University of Washington
Seattle, WA
(206) 543-21000
www.washington.edu

University of Wisconsin, Madison
500 Lincoln Drive
Madison, Wisconsin 53706
Phone: (608) 263-2400
www.wisc.edu

Washington University in St. Louis
1 Brookings Drive
St. Louis, MO 63130
Phone: (314) 935-5000
www.wustl.edu

MORE INFORMATION

American Society for Biochemistry and Molecular Biology
11200 Rockville Pike, Suite 302
Bethesda, MD 20852-3110
240.283.6600
www.asbmb.org

American Society for Microbiology
1752 N Street, NW
Washington, DC 20036-2904
202.737.3600
www.asm.org

Biotechnology Industry Organization
1201 Maryland Avenue, SW
Suite 900
Washington, DC 20024
202.962.9200
www.bio.org

Northeast Association for Clinical Microbiology and Infectious Disease
19 Sylvester Avenue
Chelsea, ME 04330
www.nacmid.unh.edu

Society for Industrial Microbiology
3929 Old Lee Highway, Suite 92A
Fairfax, VA 22030-2421
703.691.3357
www.simhq.org

Michael Auerbach /Editor

Mining and Geological Engineer

Snapshot

Career Cluster: Manufacturing; Science, Technology, Engineering & Mathematics

Interests: Geology, earth science, mining and infrastructure projects, mapping and computer simulation, math

Earnings (Yearly Average): $100,970

Employment & Outlook: Average Growth Expected

OVERVIEW

Sphere of Work

Mining and geological engineers use their problem-solving skills and advanced technical training to locate and extract natural resources such as coal, minerals, and metals for industrial use. They design and

oversee the construction of underground and open-pit mines and develop transportation systems by which coal, minerals, and metals are removed from the mines. They also ensure that mines are structurally sound and adhere to safety and environmental standards. Mining engineers often work as consultants to construction firms, advising on safe and environmentally sound methods for building dams and roads.

Work Environment

Mining and geological engineers do much of their work from offices in consulting firms, major energy corporations, construction companies, and government agencies. Such settings are comfortable, safe, and clean. Mining and geological engineers also spend many work hours in mines and at mining construction sites. These sites are frequently busy, with a great deal of heavy equipment in operation. Mines present dangers such as gas explosions and equipment-related injuries. Mining engineers also work in processing facilities where minerals are separated from soil and other materials. Mining and geological engineers typically work a standard forty-hour workweek, although as deadlines approach, they may be called upon to put in extra hours.

Profile

Working Conditions: Work both Indoors and Outdoors
Physical Strength: Light Work
Education Needs: Bachelor's Degree, Master's Degree, Doctoral Degree
Licensure/Certification: Required
Opportunities For Experience: Internship, Apprenticeship, Volunteer Work, Part-time Work
Holland Interest Score*: RIE

* See Appendix A

Occupation Interest

In spite of its inherent risks, the work of mining and geological engineers is complex and fascinating, especially when working on site. Mining and geological engineers are responsible for creating access to much-needed minerals, coal, gravel, and precious metals. They also play an important role in the sustainable development movement, designing important mining and infrastructure projects that have as little adverse impact on the natural environment as possible. Historically, there have been few schools with mine engineering programs; therefore, interested and qualified candidates should have excellent opportunities in finding both initial employment and experiencing further advancement.

A Day in the Life—Duties and Responsibilities

Mining and geological engineers select optimal sites for mining operations; plan, design, and develop the construction of mines; and oversee the safe extraction of metals or other materials. They use mapping systems and computer simulations to determine the most suitable sites for establishing open-pit and underground mines. Although they may be based in offices, mining engineers travel frequently to job sites in order to oversee and assess construction and operations.

They must also periodically analyze soil samples of deposit areas. Such activities help mining engineers locate new deposits, assess the viability of previously mapped deposits, and study the environmental impact of mining and development. Due to their expertise in this field, mining and geological engineers are often invited to participate in studies of air and water pollution. Mining and geological engineers also work on the development of new mining and construction equipment and more efficient material processing systems.

Duties and Responsibilities

- Working with scientists and other engineers to locate and evaluate deposits
- Determining the best method of entry, extraction and production by means of computer-simulation and other techniques
- Planning the location and development of underground and open pit mines
- Devising methods of storing excavated soil and returning the mine site to its natural state after the deposits have been exhausted

OCCUPATION SPECIALTIES

Geological Engineers

Geological Engineers use their knowledge of geology to search for mineral deposits and evaluate possible sites. Once a site is identified, they plan how the metals or minerals will be extracted in efficient and environmentally sound ways.

Mining Engineers

Mining Engineers often specialize in one particular mineral or metal, such as coal or gold. They typically design and develop mines and determine the best way to extract metal or minerals to get the most out of deposits.

Petroleum Engineers

Petroleum Engineers design and develop methods for extracting oil and gas from deposits below the earth's surface.

Geological and Petroleum Technicians

Geological and Petroleum Technicians provide support to scientists and engineers in exploring and extracting natural resources, such as minerals, oil, and natural gas.

WORK ENVIRONMENT

Physical Environment

Mining and geological engineers work in offices, but travel frequently to mines and other construction and/or industrial sites. Some of these sites are in remote locations. When working at mine construction sites or inside mines, engineers must be cognizant of physical risks, such as mine collapse, gas pocket explosion, toxic dust inhalation, or equipment-related incidents.

Relevant Skills and Abilities

Communication Skills
- Expressing thoughts and ideas
- Speaking effectively
- Writing concisely

Interpersonal/Social Skills
- Cooperating with others

Organization & Management Skills
- Making decisions
- Managing people/groups
- Paying attention to and handling details
- Performing duties which change frequently

Research & Planning Skills
- Creating ideas
- Developing evaluation strategies
- Using logical reasoning

Technical Skills
- Performing scientific, mathematical and technical work
- Working with machines, tools or other objects

Human Environment

Mining and geological engineers work with executives, business leaders, and government officials during the process of designing and studying mining and development sites. At project sites, they work with miners, construction crews, truck drivers, equipment technicians, and scientists such as geologists and mineralogists.

Technological Environment

Mining and geological engineers must use design and analytical software programs such as computer-aided design (CAD), mining database systems, and mapping programs. At mines and potential construction sites, they use sampling equipment, plotting systems, geographic information systems (GIS), global positioning systems (GPS), and geological compasses (which detect geological strata, or levels).

Fun Fact

The first metals man discovered were gold and copper, around 5000 BC.
Source: http://vcsmining.com/fun-facts.html

EDUCATION, TRAINING, AND ADVANCEMENT

High School/Secondary

High school students should take courses in mathematics, including advanced classes. Physics, chemistry, and other natural sciences classes are beneficial as well, while industrial arts courses help familiarize students with mechanical systems and schematics. High school students should also take computer science courses, because mining engineers must use many different types of engineering software on a daily basis.

Suggested High School Subjects
- Applied Communication
- Applied Math
- Applied Physics
- Blueprint Reading
- College Preparatory
- Computer Science
- English
- Machining Technology
- Mathematics
- Science

Famous First

Chemical elements tungsten and tellurium were first found in the United States in 1819 in a bismuth mine in Huntington, Conn. Tungsten, also called wolfram, was identified as one of the rare metals in the late 1700s in Europe. It was later used in the manufacture of filaments for incandescent light bulbs. Tellurium's primary use today is in the production of steel and copper alloys and in the manufacturing of semiconductors and solar panels.

College/Postsecondary

Mining and geological engineers should have a bachelor's degree in engineering, and some have additional training in natural sciences (such as geology or environmental science) or mathematics. Senior-level mining and geological engineers have doctoral degrees in such disciplines as soil science, geology, and other areas of relevance to mining and geological engineering.

Related College Majors
- Mining & Mineral Engineering
- Mining & Petroleum Technologies
- Petroleum Engineering

Adult Job Seekers

Qualified mining and geological engineers may apply directly to companies and consulting firms with open positions. The US Department of Energy and the US Geological Survey also post openings on their websites. Engineers can network for positions through professional trade organizations such as the Society for Mining, Metallurgy and Exploration.

Professional Certification and Licensure

All states require that an engineer must obtain a Professional Engineer certification, which may be obtained with a combination of education and experience and is also contingent upon passing an exam. Engineers seeking positions with federal government agencies may also be required to pass the civil service exam.

Additional Requirements

Mining and geological engineers must have a strong attention to detail and excellent analytical skills. They should have experience with relevant computer systems and software as well as an understanding of building materials and equipment. They tend to work as members of collaborative teams of engineers, and as such should have excellent communications skills. Because mining and geological engineers sometimes work in mines and at work sites, they must be physically fit and able to handle adverse weather and environmental conditions.

Prospective mining engineers should evaluate the risks involved in accessing mines and be willing to accept those risks as a necessary aspect of the job. Finally, they should find job satisfaction in using their knowledge and skills to protect the environment and the lives of the workers who extract profitable minerals from the mines.

EARNINGS AND ADVANCEMENT

Earnings depend on the type, size and geographic location of the employer, and the education, experience and level of responsibility of the employee. Mining and geological engineers employed in the coal industry, for example, usually earn higher salaries than those working for sand and gravel businesses.

According to the National Association of Colleges and Employers, starting annual salaries for those with a bachelor's degree in mining and mineral engineering were $70,376 in 2012. Mean annual earnings of mining and geological engineers were $100,970 in 2014. The lowest ten percent earned less than $52,780, and the highest ten percent earned more than $159,010.

Mining and geological engineers may receive paid vacations, holidays, and sick days; life and health insurance; and retirement benefits. These are usually paid by the employer. Some employers also pay expenses for additional education.

States with the Highest
Employment Level in this Occupation

State	Employment	Employment per thousand jobs	Annual mean wage
Texas	890	0.08	$143,370
Colorado	640	0.27	$127,130
Oklahoma	640	0.40	$108,590
Arizona	560	0.22	$82,290
California	560	0.04	$111,620

[1]Does not include self-employed. Source: Bureau of Labor Statistics

EMPLOYMENT AND OUTLOOK

Mining and geological engineers held about 8,000 jobs nationally in 2012. Employment is expected to grow about as fast as the average for all occupations through the year 2022, which means employment is projected to increase 10 percent to 15 percent. Excellent job opportunities are expected in this small occupation due to strong growth in demand for minerals and as a significant number of mining engineers currently employed are approaching retirement age. In addition, relatively few schools offer mining engineering programs, and the small number of yearly graduates is not expected to increase substantially. Favorable job opportunities may be available worldwide as mining operations around the world recruit graduates of U.S. mining engineering programs. As a result, some graduates may travel frequently or even live abroad.

Employment Trend, Projected 2012–22

Mining and geological engineers: 12%

Total, all occupations: 11%

Engineers (all): 9%

Note: "All Occupations" includes all occupations in the U.S. Economy. Source: U.S. Bureau of Labor Statistics, Employment Projections Program

Related Occupations
- Geographer
- Geologist & Geophysicist
- Metallurgical/Materials Engineer
- Petroleum Engineer
- Surveyor and Cartographer

Conversation With . . .
ANDREW P. SCHISSLER, PE

Principal, Schissler Engineering LLC
Adjunct Professor, Colorado School of Mines
Mining Engineer, SME PE Exam Coordinator
In the field, 42 years

1. What was your individual career path in terms of education/training, entry-level job, or other significant opportunity?

I always preferred technological and scientific subjects. I decided to go to the best science or technology university near my Colorado home, the Colorado School of Mines. I didn't have to declare a major until mid-sophomore year. I chose mining engineering because it combined elements of other engineering disciplines and had one of the highest starting salaries at that time.

After graduation, I worked for a large coal mining company in Falrmont, WV for two years and was in a management training program. Then, due to my aging parents, I moved back west, to Utah. My job as an engineer in a mine included mine design and related systems designs: water, power, haulage, mineral processing, and materials handling, as well as capital budget implementation.

I received my foreman certification during my second year of work. Well-grounded advancement comes from operations experience, and there's no better way to get it than as a first-line supervisor or by serving in a technical role at a mine.

I went on to move around and climb the ladder: as a chief engineer, superintendent of operations planning, mine manager, and manager of technical services. I worked for the fourth largest diversified mining company in the world from 1980 to 2000. Then I started and finished a Ph.D. that required a year on campus to focus and write my thesis. After graduation, I went to Penn State as an assistant professor. After three years, I decided to go back into industry as manager of engineering for a group of potash mines; potash is a critical agricultural fertilizer mineral. At that point, I was getting into my 50s and my wife's and my family is in Denver, so I made one more move—home, where I took an executive position. The 2008 financial crisis put my employer out of business so I went on to spend four years as a principal mining engineer for a major engineering company. Two years ago, I took on an operations manager role for another company, and then started my own consulting firm after that company had some restructuring a year ago.

In addition to being Principal Engineer of my own company, I am an adjunct professor at the Colorado School of Mines as well as the PE exam coordinator for the Society of Mining, Metallurgy and Exploration Inc.

One of my specialties has been rock mechanics. When dealing with rock, you need to know how strong it is. It's a science and practice of engineering but will always be challenging because rock is variable and not homogeneous.

2. What are the most important skills and/or qualities for someone in your profession?

You need the ability to listen and to show initiative.

3. What do you wish you had known going into this profession?

This industry is subject to economic cycles. During expansions, opportunity is high. During contractions, opportunity is low.

4. Are there many job opportunities in your profession? In what specific areas?

Overall, mining engineers will find a diverse range of opportunities. They may work at a mine, for a mining company, in mine construction or civil engineering, or in mining equipment manufacturing. You could also work as a technical service engineer, or in government with agencies like the Mine Safety Health Administration, the National Institute of Occupational Safety and Health, intelligence agencies analyzing underground (as in below the earth) foreign installations, or even as an officer in one of the armed forces. Mining Engineering is terrific pre-law or pre-med course of study as well.

5. How do you see your profession changing in the next five years, what role will technology play in those changes, and what skills will be required?

There's going to be continued re-definition of how engineering achieves the objective of extracting minerals. All disciplines of engineering are going to require additional training on the biological side and will need to consider societal interaction such as climate change. For example, all industrial and commercial enterprises incur what is called a carbon footprint. How do you calculate that? This will become the norm.

6. What do you enjoy most about your job? What do you enjoy least about your job?

I enjoy my diversity of assignments: this year, I've been to Australia, Spain and Peru as well as a few U.S. states. Each of my projects is different. I enjoy being my own boss, although—a small dislike—now I have to be my own accountant.

7. **Can you suggest a valuable "try this" for students considering a career in your profession?**

A Boy Scout can get a merit badge in mining. The mining industry is very supportive of this. In addition, many high school science departments bring in industry people to sponsor teams in science or engineering to perform an engineering project, which sometimes includes mining. Participating would be a good way to find an industry mentor. If you're already at a university, you might get a summer internship at a mining company.

SELECTED SCHOOLS

A variety of colleges and universities offer programs in mining and/or geological engineering. Some of the more prominent schools in this field are listed below.

California Institute of Technology
1200 E. California Boulevard
Pasadena, CA 91125
Phone: (626) 395-6123
www.gps.caltech.edu

Massachusetts Institute of Technology
77 Massachusetts Avenue
Cambridge, MA 02139
Phone: (617) 253-2127
www.mit.edu

Pennsylvania State University
507 Deike Building
University Park, PA 16803
Phone: (814) 865-7394
www.geosc.psu.edu

University of Arizona
1040 E. Fourth Street
Tucson, AZ 85721
Phone: (520) 621-6004
www.geo.arizona.edu

University of California, Berkeley
307 McCone Hall
Berkeley, CA 9720
Phone: (510) 642-5574
www.eps.berkeley.edu

University of California, Santa Barbara
1006 Webb Hall
Santa Barbara, CA 93106
Phone: (805) 893-3329
www.geol.ucab.edu

University of Colorado, Boulder
2200 Colorado Avenue
Boulder, CO 80309
Phone: (303) 492-8141
www.colorado.edu/geosci

University of Michigan, Ann Arbor
1100 N. University Avenue
Ann Arbor, MI 48109
Phone: (734) 764-1435
www.umich.edu/geo

University of Texas, Austin
2225 Speedway, Stop C1160
Austin, TX 78712
Phone: (512) 471-6098
www.utexas.edu

University of Wisconsin, Madison
236 Weeks Hall for Geological Sciences
Madison, WI 53706
Phone: (608) 262-9266
www.wisc.edu

MORE INFORMATION

American Geological Institute
4220 King Street
Alexandria, VA 22302-1502
703.379.2480
www.agiweb.org

**American Institute of Mining,
Metallurgical, and Petroleum
Engineers**
P.O. Box 270728
Littleton, CO 80127-0013
303.948.4255
www.aimehq.org

**Mining and Metallurgical Society
of America**
P.O. Box 810
Boulder, CO 80306-0810
303.444.6032
www.mmsa.net

**National Action Council for
Minorities in Engineering**
440 Hamilton Avenue, Suite 302
White Plains, NY 10601-1813
914.539.4010
www.nacme.org

National Mining Association
101 Constitution Avenue NW
Suite 500 East
Washington, DC 20001
202.463.2600
www.nma.org

**National Society of Black
Engineers**
205 Daingerfield Road
Alexandria, VA 22314
703.549.2207
www.nsbe.org

**Society for Mining, Metallurgy &
Exploration**
Career Information
12999 E. Adam Aircraft Circle
Englewood, CO 80112
800.763.3132
www.smenet.org

**Society of Hispanic Professional
Engineers**
13181 Crossroads Parkway North
Suite 450
City of Industry, CA 91746-3497
323.725.3970
www.shpe.org

Society of Women Engineers
203 N. La Salle Street, Suite 1675
Chicago, IL 60601
877.793.4636
www.swe.org

Technology Student Association
1914 Association Drive
Reston, VA 20191-1540
703.860.9000
www.tsaweb.org

Michael Auerbach/Editor

Nuclear Engineer

Snapshot

Career Cluster: Science, Technology, Engineering & Mathematics
Interests: Nuclear energy, radioactivity, mathematics, research, design and development, plant operation and maintenance systems
Earnings (Yearly Average): $104,630
Employment & Outlook: Average Growth Expected

OVERVIEW

Sphere of Work

Nuclear engineers research, analyze, and design systems and technologies related to nuclear energy, such as generators, reactors, and even entire power plants. Many are employed by the federal government, performing research and development activities pertaining to nuclear energy systems or weaponry. Others may be involved in the use of radioactive materials for medical, agricultural, scientific, and industrial purposes. Those nuclear engineers who work in the construction of nuclear power plants and the systems therein may spend a great deal of time on-site, supervising teams and coordinating with other site workers. Many nuclear

engineers work at nuclear power plants while they are in operation, monitoring radiation levels, supervising employees, and performing periodic maintenance and improvements to the systems on hand.

Work Environment

Nuclear engineers work in a wide range of professional environments. Some work for the US military or for federal government agencies such as the Department of Defense and the Nuclear Regulatory Commission. Others have jobs in the private sector at research and development laboratories, or are employed by the nuclear energy industry to provide ongoing management and oversight of operating systems. Many nuclear engineers use their knowledge of radioactive materials to provide solutions in fields beyond nuclear energy, such as health care and agriculture, among others. Nuclear engineers usually work standard forty-hour weeks in clean, well-organized environments that place great emphasis on safety and operational protocols. However, there is always a risk of exposure to radioactivity or nuclear waste, despite strict adherence to safety regulations and guidelines.

Profile

Working Conditions: Work Indoors
Physical Strength: Light Work
Education Needs: Bachelor's Degree, Master's Degree, Doctoral Degree
Licensure/Certification: Required
Opportunities For Experience: Internship, Apprenticeship, Military Service
Holland Interest Score*: IRE

* See Appendix A

Occupation Interest

Nuclear engineers have a wide range of career options, spanning many sectors. They may choose to design and maintain systems for nuclear power plants, helping to protect the environment by reducing society's reliance on fossil fuels. Alternatively, nuclear engineers may work on the construction of cutting-edge technology, including applications in naval architecture, space travel, medical treatment and research, and agricultural development. Nuclear engineers continue to be in demand in all of these industries.

A Day in the Life—Duties and Responsibilities

The daily responsibilities of nuclear engineers vary significantly based on the field or industry in which they work. For example, engineers employed at nuclear power plants track radiation, power output, and maintenance issues, while also supervising certain staff members.

Nuclear researchers may work longer hours than engineers who design and/or operate nuclear technologies.

Those engineers who work in a nuclear power plant direct the operation and maintenance of the facility's systems; implement protocols to address accidents when they occur as well as prevent future incidents; monitor output and radiation levels; write instructions governing handling nuclear waste and fuel materials; and design and improve equipment and systems such as reactor cores, containment devices, and radiation shielding. Nuclear engineers also design and operate emergency systems in order to facilitate worker safety and containment of any nuclear accident.

Outside of the power plant, many nuclear engineers design other nuclear-powered systems, such as submarines and naval vessels, weapons, medical devices, and space vehicle propulsion systems. When performing research or designing nuclear equipment, these engineers work in teams that include subordinates as well as superiors. Nuclear engineers prepare construction proposals and perform experiments that yield information about optimal waste storage, better fuel efficiency, and improved emergency practices. Many nuclear engineers are also university professors, teaching classes while conducting their own independent projects and research.

Duties and Responsibilities

- Conducting research into problems of nuclear energy
- Designing and developing nuclear equipment
- Monitoring the testing, operation and maintenance of nuclear reactors
- Planning and conducting research to test theories of nuclear energy
- Evaluating findings to develop new uses of radioactive processes
- Preparing technical reports

OCCUPATION SPECIALTIES

Nuclear Technicians

Nuclear Technicians assist physicists, engineers, and other professionals in nuclear research and nuclear production.

WORK ENVIRONMENT

Physical Environment

Nuclear engineers work at nuclear power plants and construction sites, government agencies, research and development laboratories, and universities. These environments are ideally very organized and well ventilated, with up-to-date safety and operational systems.

Relevant Skills and Abilities

Organization & Management Skills
- Paying attention to and handling details

Research & Planning Skills
- Analyzing information
- Developing evaluation strategies
- Using logical reasoning

Technical Skills
- Performing scientific, mathematical and technical work

Human Environment

Depending on the field in which they work, nuclear engineers interact with a wide range of individuals, including government officials, military officers, nuclear scientists, machine operators, electricians, emergency personnel, university administrators, and engineers with focuses in other areas.

Technological Environment

Nuclear engineers use technology such as reactor cores and frames, radioactivity sensors, and control rod systems, as well as safety equipment such as sprinklers and emergency ventilation systems. Nuclear engineers are also heavily reliant on computer systems and software, including computer-aided design (CAD) systems, related databases, analytical software, and office suites.

EDUCATION, TRAINING, AND ADVANCEMENT

High School/Secondary

High school students should study mathematics, including calculus, trigonometry, algebra, and geometry. Natural sciences such as chemistry and physics are also important, and computer science, drafting, and communications courses are extremely useful for nuclear engineering.

Suggested High School Subjects
- Algebra
- Applied Communication
- Applied Math
- Applied Physics
- Blueprint Reading
- Calculus
- Chemistry
- College Preparatory
- Composition
- Computer Science
- English
- Mathematics
- Physics
- Science

Famous First

The first commercial nuclear power plant was the Yankee Atomic Electric Company's plant in Rowe, Mass., which began distributing power in 1960. On the Deerfield River, the plant cost $57 million to build and generated 135,000 kilowatts of electricity. It was decommissioned in 1992 and permanently shut down in 1995.

College/Postsecondary

Nuclear engineers must have a bachelor's degree in engineering or a related field from an accredited four-year university, college, or engineering school. They should also pursue a graduate degree, such as a master's degree or a PhD, if they hope to attain senior-level research positions.

Related College Majors
- Engineering Design
- Nuclear Engineering
- Nuclear/Nuclear Power Technology

Adult Job Seekers

Nuclear engineers may obtain positions at nuclear facilities or other locations while still in college or graduate school through internships and work-study programs. Professional trade associations such as the American Society for Mechanical Engineers and the American Nuclear Society provide good resources and networking opportunities. Also, government agencies often post openings for nuclear engineers on their websites.

Professional Certification and Licensure

Nuclear engineers, like other engineers, must obtain a state Professional Engineer license in order to practice. Though the licensing process varies by state, it generally entails two separate

examinations, the Fundamentals of Engineering (FE) exam and
the Principles and Practice in Engineering (PE) exam, and up to
four years of work experience. Because federal nuclear activities
represent national security risks, engineers who seek to work for the
government must usually obtain appropriate clearance, which is given
after a thorough background check.

Additional Requirements

Nuclear engineers should demonstrate exceptional
analytical and problem-solving skills. They should be
calm under pressure, with an ability to communicate
effectively in any environment. Nuclear engineers
should also have a strong understanding of computers, software, and
other forms of technology. Additionally, they must be leaders, able
to organize and direct their respective groups, even when a major
incident or security risk occurs.

Fun Fact

Due to several high profile disasters, the thought of nuclear energy is scary to
many. But a switch from fossil fuels to nuclear energy would drastically reduce
greenhouse gas emissions, and Sweden and France are headed in that direction,
according to *Scientific American* magazine.

Source: http://www.scientificamerican.com/article/the-world-really-could-go-nuclear/

EARNINGS AND ADVANCEMENT

Earnings depend on the employer and the education, experience,
capabilities and job responsibilities of the employee. According to the
National Association of Colleges and Employers, nuclear engineers
with a bachelor's degree earned a starting salary of $67,323 in 2012.

Mean annual earnings of nuclear engineers were $104,630 in 2014. The lowest ten percent earned less than $66,890, and the highest ten percent earned more than $151,710.

Nuclear engineers may receive paid vacations, holidays, and sick days; life and health insurance; and retirement benefits. These are usually paid by the employer. Some employers may provide reimbursement for further education.

Metropolitan Areas with the Highest Employment Level in this Occupation

Metropolitan area	Employment	Employment per thousand jobs	Annual mean wage
Virginia Beach-Norfolk-Newport News, VA-NC	1,600	2.19	$80,550
Pittsburgh, PA	710	0.63	$89,320
Chicago-Joliet-Naperville, IL	520	0.14	$104,410
New York-White Plains-Wayne, NY-NJ	330	0.06	n/a
Portsmouth, NH-ME	280	4.84	$86,730
Knoxville, TN	250	0.75	$136,670
Augusta-Richmond County, GA-SC	210	1.03	$84,860
Omaha-Council Bluffs, NE-IA	170	0.37	$95,690
Florence, SC	120	1.51	$105,190
Bethesda-Rockville-Frederick, MD	120	0.20	n/a

Source: Bureau of Labor Statistics

EMPLOYMENT AND OUTLOOK

There were approximately 20,400 nuclear engineers employed nationally in 2012. Employment of nuclear engineers is expected to grow about as fast as the average for all occupations through the year 2022, which means employment is projected to increase 7 percent to 11 percent. Nuclear engineers will be needed for upgrading safety systems at power plants in operation and for helping to create and build nuclear power plants outside of the United States. In addition, nuclear engineers may be needed to research and develop future nuclear power sources, work in defense-related areas, develop nuclear medical technology and improve and enforce waste management and safety standards.

Employment Trend, Projected 2012–22

Total, all occupations: 11%

Engineers (all): 9%

Nuclear engineers: 9%

Note: "All Occupations" includes all occupations in the U.S. Economy. Source: U.S. Bureau of Labor Statistics, Employment Projections Program

Related Occupations
- Nuclear Quality Control Inspector

Related Military Occupations
- Nuclear Engineer

Conversation With . . .
SAM BRINTON

Senior Policy Analyst
Bipartisan Policy Center, Washington, D.C.
Nuclear engineer, 1 year

1. **What was your individual career path in terms of education/training, entry-level job, or other significant opportunity?**

   I was a missionary kid and traveled all the time. I got to live in the Amazon jungle, but I also lived in dirty cities that were essentially concrete jungles. The pollution affected my allergies and I realized that clean air was really important. I thought one way to improve air quality would be to improve nuclear energy as an engineer. My mom had grown up near the Three Mile Island nuclear accident, so my passion for nuclear engineering kind of confused my family! As an undergrad, I studied nuclear engineering as well as music at Kansas State University. I went to Massachusetts Institute of Technology (MIT) for graduate school because I could study both technology and policy there. After that, I did a fellowship at Third Way, which is a think tank here in DC.

   In my job as a Senior Policy Analyst, I'm kind of a translator, a technical translator. I'm not working in engineering, but because I have the technical background, I am respected.

   My involvement in two groups, Nuclear Pride (for nuclear engineers who are part of the LGBT community) and the American Nuclear Society were critical for developing a network. From them, I acquired "soft skills" and learned who to turn to when I don't have the best answer to a question asked by a congressman, for instance.

2. **What are the most important skills and/or qualities for someone in your profession?**

   A critical skill is a passion for systems. We do a massive amount of word problems based on how things work and are integrated with one another. Nuclear reactors run on physics, but you also need to know mechanical engineering, chemistry, math. The ability to wrap them all into one system is key. Even in my policy work, I need to bring together different parts of the system—this policy person, this business person, that senator—and integrate them to work together.

3. What do you wish you had known going into this profession?

I wish I had realized that science is always moving forward and the answers in your textbooks will change. Nuclear engineering involves fusion. It's on the very edge of what we know is possible in physics and engineering. You have to be able to go with the flow and not fight it.

Also, diversity might be a challenge. You won't always have professors or classmates who look like you or understand your perspective. I thought I was alone in this world, but Nuclear Pride made me realize I'm surrounded by members of the LGBT community.

4. Are there many job opportunities in your profession? In what specific areas?

There are growing opportunities in nuclear power, but it's a small industry. We're building four or five nuclear plants right now, each of which will be hiring nuclear engineers. There are dozens of nuclear startups. There's the entire field of nuclear waste. The joke is there's unlimited opportunity because the waste will be around for hundreds or thousands of years. You can also work in policy, as I do. The 20 to 30 nuclear engineering programs around the country offer the possibility of doing research or teaching at a university. You could also work for the Department of Energy or the Nuclear Regulatory Agency doing technology translation and helping people understand complicated topics.

5. How do you see your profession changing in the next five years? What role will technology play in those changes, and what skills will be required?

My hope is nuclear energy is going to be more compatible with the renewable community so that we're all working together. Nuclear has a very sordid and dirty history to some, but I think we can overcome that. Nuclear reactors are clean, safe and reliable. I think that with the next generation of reactors, we can be even better at safety and innovation.

6. What do you enjoy most about your job? What do you enjoy least about your job?

What I enjoy most is the flexibility and creativity. A nuclear engineer is not necessarily tackling the same problem over and over. I get to see new ideas and new conversations every week. And nuclear engineering is respectful of its next generation of engineers. Even a kid with a bright red mohawk like myself is listened to, because it's all about thinking outside the box and viewing a system from a variety of lenses.

What I like least is that you can't live everywhere you might want to. Working at a nuclear power plant, you'll probably be away from a city. If you're at a National Lab, you'll be even farther from any major metropolis.

7. Can you suggest a valuable "try this" for students considering a career in your profession?

Most nuclear power plants have a great tour where they tell you all about being a nuclear engineer. There are about 100 nuclear power plants across the country, so there may be one near you.

SELECTED SCHOOLS

Most colleges and universities offer programs in physics and engineering; a variety of them also have concentrations in nuclear engineering. Some of the more prominent schools in this field are listed below.

Georgia Institute of Technology
225 North Avenue NW
Atlanta, GA 30332
Phone: (404) 894-2000
www.gatech.edu

Pennsylvania State University, University Park
101 Hammond Building
University Park, PA 16802
Phone: (814) 865-4700
www.psu.edu

Massachusetts Institute of Technology
77 Massachusetts Avenue
Room 1-206
Cambridge, MA 02139
Phone: (617) 253-1000
www.mit.edu

North Carolina State University
PO Box 7901
Raleigh, NC 27695
Phone: (919) 515-2011
www.ncsu.edu

Texas A&M University, College Station
Jack K. Williams Building, Suite 312
401 Joe Routt Blvd
College Station, TX 77843
Phone: (979) 845-3211
www.tamu.edu

University of California, Berkeley
320 McLaughlin Hall #1700
Berkeley, CA
Phone: (510) 642-6000
berkeley.edu

University of Illinois, Urbana, Champaign
1308 W. Green
Urbana, IL 61801
Phone: (217) 333-1000
www.illinois.edu

University of Michigan, Ann Arbor
Robert H. Lurie Engineering Center
500 S. State St
An Arbor, MI 48109
Phone: (734) 764-1817
www.umich.edu

University of Tennessee, Knoxville
124 Perkins Hall
Knoxville, TN 37996
Phone: (865) 947-1000
www.utk.edu

University of Wisconsin, Madison
2610 Engineering Hall
Madison, WI 53706
Phone: (608) 263-2400
www.wisc.edu

MORE INFORMATION

American Nuclear Society
555 N. Kensington Avenue
La Grange Park, IL 60526
800.323.3044
www.new.ans.org

American Society for Mechanical Engineers, Nuclear Engineering Division
3 Park Avenue
New York, NY 10016
800.843.2763
www.asme.org

National Action Council for Minorities in Engineering
440 Hamilton Avenue, Suite 302
White Plains, NY 10601-1813
914.539.4010
www.nacme.org

National Council of Examiners for Engineering and Surveying
P.O. Box 1686
Clemson, SC 29633
800.250.3196
www.ncees.org

National Society of Black Engineers
205 Daingerfield Road
Alexandria, VA 22314
703.549.2207
www.nsbe.org

Society of Hispanic Professional Engineers
13181 Crossroads Parkway North
Suite 450
City of Industry, CA 91746-3497
323.725.3970
www.shpe.org

Society of Nuclear Medicine
1850 Samuel Morse Drive
Reston, VA 20190
703.708.9000
www.snm.org

Society of Women Engineers
203 N. LaSalle Street, Suite 1675
Chicago, IL 60601
877.793.4636
www.swe.org

Technology Student Association
1914 Association Drive
Reston, VA 20191-1540
703.860.9000
www.tsaweb.org

U.S. Nuclear Regulatory Commission
Washington, DC 20555
800.368.5642
www.nrc.gov

Michael Auerbach/Editor

Petroleum Engineer

Snapshot

Career Cluster: Manufacturing; Science, Technology, Engineering & Mathematics

Interests: Engineering, engineering and technology, geology, oil and gas production, manufacturing, science

Earnings (Yearly Average): $147,520

Employment & Outlook: Faster Than Average Growth Expected

OVERVIEW

Sphere of Work

Petroleum engineers develop and implement procedures for the extraction of petroleum and natural gas. They focus on increasing and optimizing oil and gas production, and to that end, they develop and modify tools and equipment, as well as overseeing the extraction of these resources. Petroleum engineers supervise the treatment, storage, and transport of oil and gas, adhering to best practices and government regulations to ensure the safety, profitability, and efficiency of operations.

Work Environment

Petroleum engineers who specialize in the design aspects of petroleum extraction and recovery generally spend their workdays in laboratory settings, while those specializing in the monitoring or overseeing of drilling, storage, treatment, or transportation operations spend their workdays in oil fields or on offshore drilling rigs. Engineers working in offices or laboratories typically work a forty-hour week. However, due to the remote locations of many oil fields, petroleum engineers working in the field frequently work seven days a week, often for extended periods. Petroleum engineers are at risk for injuries caused by equipment malfunctions and for exposure to harsh weather conditions.

Profile

Working Conditions: Work both Indoors and Outdoors
Physical Strength: Light Work
Education Needs: Bachelor's Degree, Master's Degree, Doctoral Degree
Licensure/Certification: Required
Opportunities For Experience: Internship, Apprenticeship, Part-time Work
Holland Interest Score*: RIE

* See Appendix A

Occupation Interest

Individuals drawn to the profession of petroleum engineer tend to be analytical and skilled at identifying and solving problems. Successful petroleum engineers are physically strong, enjoy working with machines, and work well in remote locations. Leadership, teamwork, and creativity are also desirable qualities in this profession.

A Day in the Life—Duties and Responsibilities

Petroleum engineers work to locate and extract oil and natural gas from underground deposits. To this end, they assist geologists in the exploration of oil sites and well testing, travel to and from remote oil fields or offshore oil rigs, and assess the potential production levels and economic value of subsurface oil and gas reservoirs. They review the geologic properties of proposed drilling areas to choose the most appropriate and efficient drilling methods, and they develop the procedures for extracting the resources. To aid in the extraction process, petroleum engineers design and modify tools and equipment such as drilling rigs, compressors, and valves. They also review and implement safety standards and develop plans for the treatment, storage, and transport of oil and gas.

When drilling operations are underway, petroleum engineers oversee the process, including the extraction of contaminants from the oil or gas. They maintain logs of flow rates, production or recovery amounts, safety checks, and well testing data. They review this data and perform further research focused on enhancing recovery and extraction methods in order to increase the efficiency and profitability of the extraction process.

Some petroleum engineers may choose to specialize in areas such as production oversight, equipment design and modification, safety inspection and enforcement, or treatment, storage, and transport. In addition, all petroleum engineers are responsible for satisfying environmental standards and preparing environmental impact statements as required.

Duties and Responsibilities

- Studying maps of subsurface oil and gas reservoirs
- Recommending processes to enhance the recovery of oil and gas
- Developing well drilling plans
- Monitoring the production rate of wells
- Designing pumping equipment, pipelines, and gas-oil separators

OCCUPATION SPECIALTIES

Reservoir Engineers

Reservoir Engineers estimate how much oil or gas can be recovered from underground deposits, known as reservoirs. They study a reservoir's characteristics and determine which methods will get the most oil or gas out of the reservoir. They also monitor operations to ensure that the optimal levels of these resources are being recovered.

Drilling Engineers

Drilling Engineers determine the best way to drill an oil or gas well, taking into account a number of factors, including cost. They also ensure that the drilling process is safe, efficient, and minimally disruptive to the environment.

Production Engineers

Production Engineers take over after a well is completed. They typically monitor the well's oil and gas production. If a well is not producing as much as it was expected to, production engineers figure out ways to increase the amount being extracted.

Petroleum Technicians

Petroleum Technicians provide support to scientists and engineers in exploring and extracting oil and natural gas.

WORK ENVIRONMENT

Physical Environment

The majority of petroleum engineers work in remote field locations, such as oil fields and offshore oil rigs, while those engaged in research or equipment design work in laboratories and offices. When necessary, they must observe safety procedures and wear protective clothing or hard hats.

Plant Environment

Petroleum engineers involved in oil and gas treatment may work or consult in a plant that removes contaminants from recently recovered oil and gas. Engineers working in a plant environment may experience physical risks resulting from fumes, noise, or equipment malfunctions.

Relevant Skills and Abilities

Communication Skills
- Speaking effectively
- Writing concisely

Interpersonal/Social Skills
- Cooperating with others
- Working as a member of a team

Organization & Management Skills
- Coordinating tasks
- Following instructions
- Making decisions
- Managing people/groups
- Paying attention to and handling details

Research & Planning Skills
- Creating ideas
- Developing evaluation strategies
- Using logical reasoning

Technical Skills
- Performing scientific, mathematical and technical work
- Working with machines, tools or other objects

Human Environment

Petroleum engineers tend to work in teams, whether in a laboratory or on an offshore rig. They should be comfortable interacting with a wide range of professionals, including geologists, petroleum technicians, office staff, laboratory technicians, oil rig workers, supervising engineers, and company owners and shareholders.

Technological Environment

To complete their work, petroleum engineers use a wide variety of tools and equipment, including drilling rigs, compressors, valves, flow monitors, acids, and wellheads. They also use computers, Internet communication tools, cameras, production logs, and geologic charts and surveys.

EDUCATION, TRAINING, AND ADVANCEMENT

High School/Secondary

High school students interested in pursuing a career as a petroleum engineer should study geology, mathematics, and chemistry. Students interested in this career path will benefit from seeking internships or part-time work in the field. They may also participate in related extracurricular programs.

Suggested High School Subjects
- Applied Communication
- Applied Math
- Applied Physics
- College Preparatory
- Computer Science
- English
- Mathematics
- Science

Famous First

The first offshore oil drilling rig was patented in 1869 by Thomas Rowland of Greenpoint, N.Y. for a "submarine drilling apparatus." The first true seagoing rig, however, was developed nearly a hundred years later, in 1955. Built by the Bethlehem Steel Company for C.G. Glasscock, the rig could operate in more than 100 feet of water, drive piles with a force of 827 tons, and pull with a force of 942 tons.

College/Postsecondary

Postsecondary students interested in becoming petroleum engineers should work toward a bachelor's degree in engineering or engineering technology from a school accredited by the Accreditation Board for Engineering and Technology (ABET). Coursework in mathematics, computer skills, and geology may also prove useful. Postsecondary students can gain work experience and potential advantage in their future job searches by securing internships or part-time employment in the field.

Related College Majors
- Mining & Petroleum Technologies
- Petroleum Engineering

Adult Job Seekers

Adults seeking employment as petroleum engineers should have, at a minimum, a bachelor's degree in engineering, engineering technology, or a related field from an ABET-accredited school. Some petroleum engineering jobs, particularly those involving research and supervisory responsibilities, require graduate degrees and extensive experience. Adult job seekers should educate themselves about the educational and professional license requirements of their home states and the organizations where they seek employment. Qualified job seekers should consider joining professional associations, such as the National Society of Professional Engineers (NSPE), the Society of Petroleum Engineers (SPE), and the Society for Mining, Metallurgy, and Exploration (SME), which may offer workshops, job postings, and networking opportunities.

Professional Certification and Licensure

All engineers whose work affects the public, including petroleum engineers, are required to hold a state license designating them as professional engineers (PEs). This license may be earned by completing an accredited engineering program, meeting work experience requirements, and passing an examination. In addition, voluntary certification is available from professional organizations such as SPE. Petroleum engineers interested in obtaining voluntary certification are advised to consult credible professional associations within the field and follow professional debate as to the relevancy and value of any certification program.

Additional Requirements

As professionals in this role make choices that affect the health and sustainability of the natural environment, they must possess a high level of integrity and professional ethics.

Fun Fact

At $7.71 a gallon, Norway had the highest gas prices in the world in 2015. Rather than subsidize fuel prices, the government—which owns most of the oil fields—uses the profit to offer free college education and pay for infrastructure improvements.

Source: http://www.bloomberg.com/visual-data/gas-prices/20152:Norway:USD:g; http://www.davemanuel.com/2009/09/08/the-norwegian-tax-system/

EARNINGS AND ADVANCEMENT

Earnings of petroleum engineers depend on their education, experience, and level of responsibility and the type, size and geographic location of the employer. Beginning graduates usually work under the supervision of experienced petroleum engineers. As they gain knowledge and experience, they are promoted to more difficult tasks with greater independence to develop designs, solve problems and make decisions. Some may become technical specialists, supervise team of engineers or become managers or administrators.

According to a salary survey by the National Association of Colleges and Employers, petroleum engineers with a bachelor's degree earned average starting salaries of $70,329 in 2012. Mean annual earnings of petroleum engineers were $147,520 in 2014. The lowest ten percent earned less than $73,990, and the highest twenty-five percent earned more than $185,200.

Petroleum engineers may receive paid vacations, holidays, and sick days; life and health insurance; and retirement benefits. These are usually paid by the employer

States with the Highest
Employment Level in this Occupation

State	Employment	Employment per thousand jobs	Annual mean wage
Texas	17,910	1.60	$158,770
Oklahoma	3,670	2.32	$148,550
California	2,150	0.14	$126,990
Colorado	1,850	0.78	$151,960
Louisiana	1,590	0.83	$128,230

Source: Bureau of Labor Statistics

EMPLOYMENT AND OUTLOOK

Petroleum engineers held about 38,500 jobs nationally in 2012, mostly in the fields of oil and gas extraction and petroleum refining. Most petroleum engineers work in Texas, Oklahoma, Louisiana, Alaska and California, including offshore sites as well as overseas in oil- producing countries.

Employment of petroleum engineers is expected to grow faster than the average for all occupations through the year 2022, which means employment is projected to increase 25 percent or more. Petroleum engineers will be needed to develop new resources for petroleum as well as discover new methods of extracting more resources from existing sources. Good job opportunities are expected for petroleum engineers because the number of job openings is likely to exceed the relatively small number of graduates. Some of the best job opportunities may be outside of the United States.

Employment Trend, Projected 2012–22

Petroleum engineers: 26%

Total, all occupations: 11%

Engineers (all): 9%

Note: "All Occupations" includes all occupations in the U.S. Economy. Source: U.S. Bureau of Labor Statistics, Employment Projections Program

Related Occupations
- Chemical Engineer
- Chemist
- Energy Engineer
- Environmental Engineer
- Environmental Science Technician
- Geologist and Geophysicist
- Metallurgical/Materials Engineer
- Mining and Geological Engineer

Conversation With . . .
CHRISTA LAWSON

Subsea Operations Manager, for major oil company
Petroleum engineer, 19 years

1. **What was your individual career path in terms of education/training, entry-level job, or other significant opportunity?**

   I have a B.S. in Mechanical Engineering. I began my career in oil and gas through an internship with a major oil company. That first summer, I spent many weeks going to offshore oil platforms that the company operated in the Gulf of Mexico. I got a great understanding of how oil and gas are produced and the incredible engineering that goes into bringing oil/gas from deep in the seabed, processing it and then transporting it onshore for refining.

   I spent two summers interning with the company that I accepted a full time position with upon graduation. In my current role, I manage a team of subsea engineers responsible for the maintenance and repair of equipment, pipelines and structures siting on the ocean floor that are used to control and transport oil and gas.

2. **What are the most important skills and/or qualities for someone in your profession?**

   Important skills for any engineer are logical and inquisitive thinking. You must be curious about how things work and want to problem solve. Also key to success is being a strong team player. I have seldom worked alone in this industry. Most work is done in dynamic teams, with each member bringing unique knowledge to the project.

   Writing skills are very valuable. Early in my career, I wrote operating procedures manuals for use by offshore technicians in their day-to-day operation of equipment. Turning engineering knowledge into easy-to-understand-and-follow instructions ensures a safe and long running operation.

   Lastly, you need initiative. You must be willing to stretch yourself and get outside your comfort zone to work on assignments that are unfamiliar. This industry has many challenges. It needs bright, ambitious engineers to secure its future.

3. What do you wish you had known going into this profession?

How much relationship building is required. I negotiate daily with my team and other teams. My ability to interface and to influence can affect the overall outcome. While these "soft skills" are necessary for success, they're not exactly cultivated in engineering school. Networking is important too. Take every opportunity to meet the leaders in your field. Talk to them, ask questions and don't be afraid to ask for assistance. My mentors have supported me and provided opportunities that took me further than I could ever have gone on my own.

4. Are there many job opportunities in your profession? In what specific areas?

The oil industry is largely driven by the price of a barrel of oil. When prices are high, there is ample opportunity for engineers of all backgrounds. When prices are low, opportunity shrinks. Some of the most interesting and well-paying jobs are in the "upstream"—or exploration and production—part of the petroleum sector.

5. How do you see your profession changing in the next five years? What role will technology play, and what skills will be required?

Technology is at the fore of all that we do. We are constantly trying to find new, safer, and environmentally conscious ways to produce oil and gas.

6. What do you enjoy most about your job? What do you enjoy least about your job?

My job is exciting. I get to travel on helicopters and large construction boats. I direct Remotely Operated Vehicles (ROV) working in water depths of over a mile. Rapidly changing technology and engineering advances mean there's always something new to learn. I like knowing that I help the world run. Energy and petroleum products— medical devices, plastic, fuel to heat homes and, of course, gasoline—are such an important part of everyone's day. In a small way, I know I am helping improve and make people's lives more comfortable.

Travel has been one of the most memorable parts of my work. I have travelled to Japan, the U.K., and many other interesting places. I even had a chance to live and work in Norway for two years as a part of an assignment.

Working in the petroleum industry can be exhausting. I don't always work 9 to 5. In the operations department, we're producing oil/gas 24 hours a day, seven days a week, including holidays. There are times you will need to go the extra mile, stay late, and even miss being with your family. I have spent several Thanksgivings on an offshore platform, but really I didn't mind because the cooks made an incredible feast!

7. **Can you suggest a valuable "try this" for students considering a career in your profession?**

Find the LinkedIn profile of someone working in the sector and email them for information. Also, oil services companies and major oil companies have cutting edge websites that give a glimpse into what they do.

By far the best "try this" would be to intern with an oil company. I knew after my first summer as an intern that this would be my lifelong career. It has been a great decision.

SELECTED SCHOOLS

A variety of colleges and universities offer programs in petroleum engineering. Some of the more prominent schools in this field are listed below.

Colorado School of Mines
1500 Illinois Street
Golden, CO 80401
Phone: (303) 273-300
www.mines.edu

Louisiana State University
Baton Rouge, LA 70803
Phone: (225) 578-3202
www.lsu.edu

Pennsylvania State University
University Park
State College, PA 16801
Phone: (814) 865-4700
www.psu.edu

Stanford University
450 Serra Mall
Stanford, CA 94305
Phone: (650) 723-2300
www.stanford.edu

Texas A&M University
401 Joe Routt Boulevard
College Station, TX 77843
Phone: (979) 845-3211
www.tamu.edu

Texas Tech University
2500 Broadway
Lubbock, TX 79409
Phone: (806) 742-2011
www.ttu.edu

University of Houston
4800 Calhoun Road
Houston, TX 77004
Phone: (713) 743-2255
www.uh.edu

University of Kansas
1450 Jayhawk Boulevard
Lawrence, KS 66045
Phone: (785) 864-2700
www.ku.edu

University of Texas Austin
Austin, TX 78712
Phone: (512) 471-3434
www.utexas.edu

West Virginia University
Morgantown, WV 26506
Phone: (304) 293-0111
www.wvu.edu

MORE INFORMATION

American Association of Drilling Engineers (AADE)
P.O. Box 107
Houston, TX 77001-0107
281.293.9800
www.aade.org

American Petroleum Institute
Communications Dept.
1220 L Street, NW
Washington, DC 20005-4070
202.682.8000
www.api.org

Independent Petroleum Association of America
1201 15th Street, NW, Suite 300
Washington, DC, 20005
202.857.4722
www.ipaa.org

National Action Council for Minorities in Engineering
440 Hamilton Avenue, Suite 302
White Plains, NY 10601-1813
914.539.4010
www.nacme.org

Society for Mining, Metallurgy and Exploration (SME)
12999 East Adam Aircraft Circle
Englewood, CO 80112
303.948.4200
www.smenet.org

Society of Petroleum Engineers
222 Palisades Creek Drive
Richardson, TX 75080
800.456.6863
www.spe.org

Technology Student Association
1914 Association Drive
Reston, VA 20191-1540
703.860.9000
www.tsaweb.org

Simone Isadora Flynn/Editor

Physicist

Snapshot

Career Cluster: Science, Technology, Engineering & Mathematics

Interests: Science, mathematics, designing and performing experiments, data analysis, numerical data

Earnings (Yearly Average): $117,300

Employment & Outlook: Average Growth Expected

OVERVIEW

Sphere of Work

Physicists research and explore the scientific laws that govern the behavior of the physical world. They design and perform experiments to study matter, energy, and the interaction of physical forces. The scope of their inquiry ranges from the smallest subatomic particles to the large forces governing the universe.

Physicists work for public and private research institutions, including universities, national space and defense agencies, and corporations engaged in primary or applied physics research. Physicists also teach in high schools, colleges, and universities.

Work Environment

A laboratory is the central workplace of a physicist. Laboratories vary in size, ranging from small individual laboratories to large international research facilities. Bigger laboratories house large equipment such as linear accelerators and space telescopes. Physicists plan and analyze their experiments in offices. They also work in an office setting when writing about their research and applying for grants. Physicists who are employed as teachers spend a considerable amount of time in classrooms. They also lead student experiments in laboratories. Physicists often work in teams that include specialists from other scientific disciplines.

Profile

Working Conditions: Work Indoors
Physical Strength: Light Work
Education Needs: Doctoral Degree
Licensure/Certification: Usually Not Required
Opportunities For Experience: Military Service, Volunteer Work, Part-time Work
Holland Interest Score*: IRE

* See Appendix A

Occupation Interest

Physics appeals to individuals who like to design, build, and perform physical experiments. A physicist must also have a good grasp of science and mathematics. Physicists have curious, inquisitive minds and like to articulate new questions about the rules of the physical environment and the universe. Aspiring physicists should be prepared for a long academic career, including undergraduate, postgraduate, and doctoral work.

A Day in the Life—Duties and Responsibilities

The day-to-day work of a physicist typically involves conducting experiments and analyzing data. Physicists work regularly with other scientists, technicians, and engineers in the design and implementation of experiments. While some physics experiments employ simple designs, others involve complex computer models and extensive scientific apparatuses. Once an experiment has been conducted, physicists perform data analysis, in which they and their colleagues pore over data generated by the experiment and attempt to interpret the results. While experiments take place in laboratories, data analysis is often conducted in an office environment.

Physicists in a high school or academic setting spend much of their time in classrooms, conducting lectures and monitoring student experiments. They also attend seminars and spend time grading student work. More experienced physicists spend some of their time conducting administrative tasks, including writing grant applications, academic articles, and research reports. Physicists involved in larger projects with teams of other researchers often travel to different locations around the world to conduct their work. However, some physics experiments can be conducted live or recorded on a digital feed, allowing the data to be analyzed and interpreted by scientists working in different locations and different time zones.

Physicists work in a variety of fields and specialties, including atomic physics, astronomy, astrophysics, biophysics, and mathematical physics. Other disciplines include nonlinear dynamics, quantum field theory, relativity, and cosmology.

Duties and Responsibilities

- Devising procedures for conducting research and physical testing of materials
- Determining physical properties of materials
- Relating and interpreting research
- Describing observations and conclusions in mathematical terms
- Developing theories/laws based on observation and experiments
- Developing mathematical tables and charts
- Supervising scientific activities in research

OCCUPATION SPECIALTIES

Nuclear and Particle Physicists

Nuclear and Particle Physicists study the properties of atomic and subatomic particles, such as quarks, electrons, and nuclei, and the forces that cause their interactions.

Atomic and Molecular Physicists

Atomic and Molecular Physicists study atoms, simple molecules, electrons, and light, and their interactions. Some look for ways to control the states of individual atoms, which might allow for further miniaturization, or contribute toward the development of new materials or computer technology.

Medical Physicists

Medical Physicists work in healthcare and use their knowledge of physics to develop new medical technologies and radiation-based treatments. For example, some develop better and safer radiation therapies for cancer patients. Others may develop more accurate imaging technologies that use various forms of radiant energy, such as magnetic resonance imaging (MRI) and ultrasound imaging.

Plasma and Condensed Matter Physicists

Plasma Physicists study plasmas, which are considered a distinct state of matter and occur naturally in stars and interplanetary space and artificially in neon signs and plasma screen televisions. Condensed Matter Physicists study the physical properties of condensed phases of matter, such as liquids and solids. They study phenomena ranging from superconductivity to liquid crystals.

Astrophysicists

Astrophysicists study the physics of the universe. Astrophysics is a term that is often used interchangeably with astronomy.

WORK ENVIRONMENT

Physical Environment

Physicists spend an equal amount of time in the laboratory and in the office, generally in urban or suburban environments. Those employed as teachers spend most of their time in schools and classrooms. Some academic positions may be located in rural settings.

Relevant Skills and Abilities

Organization & Management Skills
- Coordinating tasks
- Managing people/groups
- Paying attention to and handling details
- Performing duties which change frequently

Research & Planning Skills
- Analyzing information
- Developing evaluation strategies

Technical Skills
- Performing scientific, mathematical and technical work
- Working with machines, tools or other objects

Human Environment

Physicists often work in teams with other scientists. They also interact with nonscientists, such as politicians and education administrators, in order to acquire funding for their work, so good interpersonal skills are invaluable.

Technological Environment

Physicists work with cutting-edge technology, often devising innovative solutions for their experiments. They work at the forefront of scientific progress, using powerful computer systems and advanced software. Physicists also use a variety of laboratory equipment, including telescopes, amplifiers, chemical processors, spectrometers, and video equipment.

EDUCATION, TRAINING, AND ADVANCEMENT

High School/Secondary

Students interested in physics should enroll in science and mathematics classes. Classes in physics, applied physics, chemistry, and electronics are essential, as are math classes such as algebra, applied mathematics, calculus, geometry, trigonometry, and statistics. If possible, students should enroll in advanced placement (AP) courses. Students should conduct as many experiments as they can and spend as much time in the laboratory as possible. Writing and reading skills are also important, as physicists are routinely required to write reports, apply for funding, and communicate their findings. In addition to their course work, students interested in physics should consider attending science camps and participating in science clubs.

Suggested High School Subjects
- Algebra
- Applied Math
- Applied Physics
- Calculus
- Chemistry
- College Preparatory
- Computer Science
- Electricity & Electronics
- English
- Geometry
- Mathematics
- Physics
- Science
- Statistics
- Trigonometry

Famous First

The first physical manipulation of individual atoms was achieved in 1990 at the IBM research center in San Jose, Calif. Researchers Donald Eigler and Erhard Schweizer used a scanning tunneling microscope to position 35 individual atoms of xenon on a nickel surface, successfully spelling the initials "IBM."

College/Postsecondary

A person interested in a career as physicist should be prepared to pursue the field through the doctoral level. Aspiring physicists should earn a bachelor's degree in physics or a related science such as astrophysics. Key courses include classical and quantum mechanics, thermodynamics, optics, and electromagnetism. A double major in mathematics can be helpful. A bachelor's degree only qualifies a person to become a physics technician or research assistant. A job as a secondary or high school physics teacher is also possible, but opportunities for employment and career advancement in academia are greater for those with a master's degree.

Graduate students in physics usually specialize in a subfield of the science, such as particle physics, medical physics, or optical physics. A master's degree in physics can improve a candidate's eligibility for jobs in academia and a variety of positions in applied physics research and development in the corporate world. However, the successful completion of a doctoral program is required for those seeking to conduct research at the top level.

In the United States, there are approximately 190 universities and colleges with doctoral programs in physics. Doctoral students spend five to seven years doing course work and conducting research before earning a Ph.D. in physics. Typically, those who earn their Ph.D. spend two to three additional years training in a postdoctoral position, deepening their understanding of their specialty through work with senior physicists.

Related College Majors

- Anatomy
- Astrophysics
- Chemistry, General
- Earth & Planetary Sciences
- Engineering Physics
- Physics, General

Adult Job Seekers

Physicists are in high demand in both academia and business. Adult job seekers interested in physics should investigate undergraduate and graduate programs in a physics-related specialty. Newly trained physicists are encouraged to attended employer conferences and job seminars. The website for the Society of Physics maintains updated information about networking and employment opportunities in the field. Depending on their area of specialization, physicists can seek employment in engineering, science, and education.

Professional Certification and Licensure

Generally, physicists are not required to earn any special certificate or license. There are some exceptions for physicists employed in engineering jobs.

Additional Requirements

Physicists should enjoy both designing and performing experiments and have a solid understanding of mathematics. They are interested in complex, wide-ranging questions regarding the physical universe. Physicists should also be comfortable working with large quantities of numerical data.

Fun Fact

Physics majors earn the highest Law School Admission Test (LSAT) scores of any group.

Source: http://www.aps.org/programs/education/loader.cfm?csModule=security/getfile&PageID=235197

EARNINGS AND ADVANCEMENT

Earnings depend on the geographic location of the employer, and the employee's educational level and experience.

Mean annual earnings of physicists were $117,300 in 2014. The lowest ten percent earned less than $54,930, and the highest ten percent earned more than $184,650. Average annual salaries for physicists employed by the federal government were $114,750 in 2014.

Physicists may receive paid vacations, holidays, and sick days; life and health insurance; and retirement benefits. These are usually paid by the employer.

Metropolitan Areas with the Highest Employment Level in this Occupation

Metropolitan area	Employment	Employment per thousand jobs	Annual mean wage
Washington-Arlington-Alexandria, DC-VA-MD-WV	1,300	0.55	$119,740
Houston-Sugar Land-Baytown, TX	750	0.26	$143,130
Chicago-Joliet-Naperville, IL	750	0.20	$95,410
San Jose-Sunnyvale-Santa Clara, CA	740	0.76	$124,370
Bethesda-Rockville-Frederick, MD	590	1.05	$131,720
Boston-Cambridge-Quincy, MA	560	0.31	$108,450
Nassau-Suffolk, NY	520	0.42	$125,880
San Francisco-San Mateo-Redwood City, CA	510	0.47	$117,180
Boulder, CO	400	2.41	$92,990
San Diego-Carlsbad-San Marcos, CA	340	0.26	$84,360

Source: Bureau of Labor Statistics

EMPLOYMENT AND OUTLOOK

There were approximately 20,600 physicists employed nationally in 2012. Over one-third worked for scientific research and development services firms; about another one-fourth were employed by the federal government, mostly in the Department of Defense and the National Aeronautics and Space Administration (NASA). In addition, many physicists were employed in faculty positions at colleges and universities.

Employment of physicists is expected to grow about as fast as the average for all occupations through the year 2020, which means employment is projected to increase 8 percent to 12 percent. Federal funding for the physical sciences is on the increase and will result in more job opportunities for physicists. In addition, the need to replace physicists who retire or otherwise leave the occupation permanently will account for many job openings.

Employment Trend, Projected 2012–22

Total, all occupations: 11%

Physicists: 10%

Astronomers: 10%

Note: "All Occupations" includes all occupations in the U.S. Economy. Source: U.S. Bureau of Labor Statistics, Employment Projections Program

Related Occupations
- Astronomer
- College Faculty Member
- Medical Scientist
- Meteorologist

Related Military Occupations
- Nuclear Engineer
- Physicist

Conversation With . . .
CRYSTAL BAILEY

Careers Program Manager
American Physical Society, College Park, MD
Physicist, 19 years

1. What was your individual career path in terms of education/training, entry-level job, or other significant opportunity?

I grew up in Arkansas, not a rich state, and got the rare opportunity to attend the publicly-funded residential Arkansas School of Math and Science. I had a great time building things like electrical circuits and wanted to be an electrical engineer when I went to the University of Arkansas. After a year, I took a course taught by Gay Stewart, one of a group of educators that has pioneered a new way of teaching physics called Physics Education Research. PER encourages an inquiry-based approach, so students spend more time writing qualitative responses to questions rather than following a cookbook set of instructions. During that class, I had a profoundly moving experience in a lab. I attached one end of a wire to a battery, draped it through a U-shaped magnet, then touched the other end to the battery's second pole. The current created its own magnetic field; the wire behaved like a magnet. All of a sudden, I could see the magnetic field lines and the whole process, including the mathematics, clicked into place. The fact that we live on a physical plane that can be so perfectly described through mathematics struck me as just beautiful.

So I became a physics major, and went to work helping Gay Stewart with her research. I was interested in doing away with boring, "traditional" physics classes and making them cool, exploratory classes. After graduation, I went to Indiana University for graduate school. I entered grad school without a clear reason for being there. Not having your eye on a clear prize makes it really hard when you encounter adversity—which you will. So I quit and moved to Nova Scotia. I was 23 or 24 and interested in traditional Irish music. I stayed about six months. After that, I was ready to be grounded. I went back to the IU physics department —at that point I had a master's degree—and took a teaching job to pay the bills. I reconnected with how passionate I was when teaching, decided to focus on Physics Education Research as a career, and got my Ph.D. in nuclear physics. Knowing I needed the degree to do what I wanted to do in my career made the difference.

Now, I work on programs to inform students, early-career physicists, and faculty members about the employment picture for physics graduates, as well as develop resources such as the APS Webinars, the Online Professional Guidebook, and "Becoming a Physicist" Pages on our careers website to help prepare students and their mentors for the future.

2. What are the most important skills and/or qualities for someone in your profession?

A very sincere desire to help people. Unemployment is low for young physicists, about 4 percent, but I want to draw the connection between a physics major and a career, and draw even more people in. So, I also need communications skills.

Physics training will give you technical skills—understanding circuits, problem solving, and lab techniques—that overlap with a computer scientist or engineer. That said, these graduates think and approach problems differently, which is why employers recruit from each area. They make an effective team.

3. What do you wish you had known going into this profession?

I've had to learn to communicate in a very focused and succinct way.

4. Are there many job opportunities in your profession? In what specific areas?

Physics is one of the most employable majors. At the bachelor's level, about 35 to 50 percent go straight into the workforce, typically either in the private sector, as a high school physics teacher, or in a national or military lab. A similar proportion of master's degree recipients in the workforce are in the private sector. Of PhD's, 64 percent of those who go into permanent jobs are in the private sector. Many students are only aware of academic careers, but the majority will not have academic careers.

5. How do you see your profession changing in the next five years, what role will technology play in those changes, and what skills will be required?

I see biophysics and biomedicine becoming big: there's a lot of emphasis on collaboration among disciplines such as physics and biology. There's potentially so much money in building technologies to support health. I feel like it's going to explode.

6. What do you enjoy most about your job? What do you enjoy least about your job?

I most enjoy interacting with people: going to meetings, speaking to graduate students and our younger generation of scientists, and working with faculty who are dedicated to mentorship. I enjoy traveling. I least enjoy administrative-type work.

7. Can you suggest a valuable "try this" for students considering a career in your profession?

Science outreach events for high school students take place all the time. Check local universities for open houses held by physics departments, which are usually full of cool and interactive demos. Also check out Physics Central (http://www.physicscentral.com), APS' main website for cool physics demos, podcasts, or interviews with famous physicists and astronauts.

SELECTED SCHOOLS

Most colleges and universities offer programs in physics. Some of the more prominent schools in this field are listed below.

California Institute of Technology
103-33
Pasadena, CA 91125
Phone: (626) 395-4244
www.pma.caltech.edu

Cornell University
109 Clark Hall
Ithaca, NY 14853
Phone: (607) 255-6016
www.physics.corell.edu

Harvard University
17 Oxford Street
Cambridge, MA 02138
Phone: (617) 495-2872
www.physcis.harvard.edu

Massachusetts Institute of Technology
77 Massachusetts Avenue
Cambridge, MA 02139
Phone: (617) 253-4841
www.mit.edu/physics

Princeton University
210 Jawdin Hall
Princeton, NJ 08544
Phonc: (609) 258-4403
www.princeton.edu/physics

Stanford University
Varian Physics Room 108
Stanford, CA 94305
Phone: (650) 723-4344
www.stanford.edu/dept/physics

University of California, Berkeley
366 LeConte Hall
Berkeley, CA 94720
Phone: (510) 642-7166
www.physics.berkeley.edu

University of California, Santa Barbra
Broida Hall, Mail Coke 9530
Santa Barbara, CA 93106
Phone: (805) 893-3888
www.physics.ucsb.edu

University of Chicago
5720 S. Ellis Avenue
Chicago, IL 60637
Phone: (773) 702-7007
www.physics.uchicago.edu

University of Illinois, Urbana, Champaign
1110 W. Green Street
Urbana, IL 61801
Phone: (217) 333-3645
www.physics.uiuc.edu

MORE INFORMATION

American Association for the Advancement of Science
1200 New York Avenue NW
Washington, DC 20005
202.326.6400
www.aaas.org

American Association of Physics Teachers
1 Physics Ellipse
College Park, MD 20740-3845
301.209.3311
www.aapt.org

American Astronomical Society
2000 Florida Avenue, NW, Suite 400
Washington, DC 20009-1231
202.328.2010
www.aas.org

American Center for Physics
1 Physics Ellipse
College Park, MD 20740
301.209.3000
www.acp.org

American Institute of Physics
Education Division
One Physics Ellipse
College Park, MD 20740-3843
301.209.3100
www.aip.org

American Physical Society
Education Department
One Physics Ellipse
College Park, MD 20740-3844
301.209.3200
www.aps.org

Association for Women in Science
1442 Duke Street
Alexandria, VA 22314
703.372.4380
www.awis.org

National Aeronautics and Space Administration
Public Communications Office
Suite 5K39
NASA Headquarters
Washington, DC 20546-0000
202.358.0000
www.nasa.gov

R. C. Lutz/Editor

Veterinarian

Snapshot

Career Cluster: Health Science

Interests: Medicine, Biology, Science, Animal Husbandry, Animal Care

Earnings (Yearly Average): $98,230

Employment & Outlook: Average Growth Expected

OVERVIEW

Sphere of Work

A veterinarian is a licensed doctor of veterinary medicine (DVM) who evaluates, diagnoses, and treats various kinds of animals. A veterinarian also works to prevent animal diseases and injuries.

Although the majority of veterinarians work with household pets, some treat wild animals, livestock, and animals living in zoos, on farms, or in laboratories. A few veterinarians specialize in preventing the diseases spread by animals and others conduct research related to the medical science of animals.

Work Environment

Most veterinarians operate out of a private medical practice or clinic and specialize in one or two animal species. Veterinarians who work primarily with pets (such as cats, dogs, birds, ferrets, and reptiles) typically work more than forty hours per week. Their work environment, while indoors and private, is busy and noisy due to the constant animal traffic in their offices and noise from overnight boarding facilities Veterinarians who work with livestock or horses generally spend long hours outdoors and commute from their offices or homes to farms, barns, or ranches. Veterinarians whose jobs are research based or related to public health work in offices or laboratories and can expect to work regular hours.

Profile

Working Conditions: Work both Indoors and Outdoors
Physical Strength: Light Work, Medium Work
Education Needs: Doctoral Degree
Licensure/Certification: Required
Opportunities For Experience: Military Service, Volunteer Work, Part-time Work
Holland Interest Score*: IRS

* See Appendix A

Occupation Interest

Veterinarians genuinely care about the health and well-being of animals and should have a solid grasp of the sciences, anatomy, and general medicine. Since veterinarians work not only with animals but also with people, they should enjoy interacting with and, when necessary, consoling pet owners and handlers. Many veterinarians are perpetually "on-call" twenty-four hours a day as emergencies occur, so potential veterinarians must be wholeheartedly committed to treating animals.

A Day in the Life—Duties and Responsibilities

Most veterinarians are general practitioners who work in private medical practices and diagnose and treat pets, including dogs, cats, birds, reptiles, rabbits, hamsters, and other small animals. These veterinarians often perform spaying and neutering operations, orthopedic procedures, animal dentistry, and trauma surgery, as well as euthanize those animals they are unable to help. Some veterinarians have private animal practices where they treat ranch and farm animals like cattle, horses, and pigs. These veterinarians evaluate animal production, feeding, and housing, and perform cesarean sections on animals in labor. A few veterinarians in private practice focus solely on equine (horse) medicine. All veterinarians diagnose diseases, perform surgeries, vaccinate, euthanize, medicate, treat broken bones and open wounds, and counsel owners on the proper care, maintenance, and breeding of animals. All veterinarians also perform diagnostic tests, including ultrasounds, x-rays, and blood and stool tests. Some specialized veterinarians work with exotic and wild animals.

Some veterinarians have food safety practices and are employed by members of the food industry and government agencies. They generally work in offices, studying and researching methods of food illness prevention, food safety, and food inspection. Other veterinarians work in laboratory animal practices and are employed by a university or industrial laboratory. They collaborate with scientists and other physicians to examine the relationship among animals, the environment, and human health problems.

Veterinarians constantly interact with animal owners, often working with them to discover and diagnose problems and speed the recovery of their pets. Pet owners have increasingly shown a willingness to pay for more sophisticated health care procedures and treatments for their pets, and as pets' health care becomes more advanced, veterinarians must continue to learn new techniques and offer more choices to clients in order to remain financially competitive.

Duties and Responsibilities

- Treating animals by performing surgery, dressing wounds and setting bones
- Testing and vaccinating animals for disease
- Advising owners on care and breeding of animals
- Performing autopsies to determine the cause of an animal's death
- Inspecting animals to be used as food
- Performing research in areas of animal and human diseases

OCCUPATION SPECIALTIES

Clinical Practice, or Small Animal, Veterinarians

Clinical Practice, or Small Animal, Veterinarians treat pets and generally work in private clinics and hospitals. They most often care for cats and dogs, but also treat other pets, such as birds, ferrets, and rabbits.

Large Animal Veterinarians

Large Animal Veterinarians work with farm animals such as pigs, cattle, horses, and sheep. They spend much of their time at farms and ranches treating illnesses and injuries and testing for and vaccinating against disease.

Research Veterinarians

Research Veterinarians work in laboratories, conducting clinical research on animal health problems. These veterinarians may perform tests on animals to identify the effects of drug therapies. They may also research how to prevent, control, and eliminate food- and animal-borne illnesses and diseases.

WORK ENVIRONMENT

Physical Environment

Most veterinarians work indoors in clean, well-ventilated clinical settings. Veterinarians who travel to farms or ranches work outdoors, often in inclement weather and, often, in unsanitary conditions. Veterinarians who perform research usually work in sterile, well-lit offices or laboratories.

Relevant Skills and Abilities

Communication Skills
- Speaking effectively
- Writing concisely

Interpersonal/Social Skills
- Cooperating with others
- Working as a member of a team

Organization & Management Skills
- Paying attention to and handling details
- Performing duties which change frequently

Technical Skills
- Performing scientific, mathematical and technical work

Work Environment Skills
- Working with plants or animals

Human Environment

All veterinarians must work and interact with numerous other individuals, including office personnel, veterinary technicians, interns, farm or ranch owners and employees, and pet owners.

Technological Environment

Veterinarians must be comfortable handling surgical instruments, hypodermic needles, medications, and diagnostic, radiographic, and ultrasound equipment. Veterinarians who primarily perform research must use complex laboratory equipment.

EDUCATION, TRAINING, AND ADVANCEMENT

High School/Secondary

High school students who wish to become veterinarians should prepare by taking advanced mathematics and science courses, including chemistry, biology, physiology, algebra, trigonometry, and physics. They should also take courses in English, health, technology, and communications to supplement their primary studies. Outside of school, students can gain valuable experience with animals by working or volunteering at a local animal shelter, grooming facility, farm, pet store, or general veterinary medical practice.

Suggested High School Subjects
- Algebra
- Biology

- Chemistry
- College Preparatory
- English
- Geometry
- Health Science Technology
- Physical Science
- Physics
- Physiology
- Science
- Social Studies
- Trigonometry

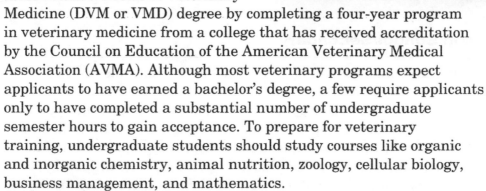

Famous First

In 2005, the Steffee Center for Zoological Medicine at the Cleveland Metroparks Zoo became the first zoo hospital to use a CT scanner.

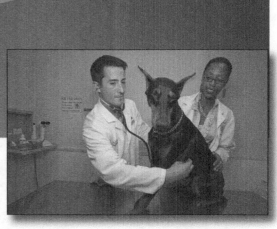

College/Postsecondary

In order to become a veterinarian, one must obtain a Doctor of Veterinary Medicine (DVM or VMD) degree by completing a four-year program in veterinary medicine from a college that has received accreditation by the Council on Education of the American Veterinary Medical Association (AVMA). Although most veterinary programs expect applicants to have earned a bachelor's degree, a few require applicants only to have completed a substantial number of undergraduate semester hours to gain acceptance. To prepare for veterinary training, undergraduate students should study courses like organic and inorganic chemistry, animal nutrition, zoology, cellular biology, business management, and mathematics.

Related College Majors
- Human & Animal Physiology
- Pre-Veterinary Studies
- Veterinary Medicine (D.V.M.)

Adult Job Seekers

Licensed veterinarians can begin to practice immediately; however, new veterinarians often choose to participate in internships at private medical practices. Internships usually last for one year and afford the new veterinarian excellent employment opportunities once finished. Other veterinarians apply directly to general medical practices. Those interested in research apply directly for research jobs with government agencies or private companies.

Professional Certification and Licensure

Before veterinarians can practice medicine, they must be licensed. Licensing requirements vary by state; however, all states require veterinarians to have received a DVM degree and to have successfully passed the North American Veterinary Licensing exam. In many states veterinary candidates must complete additional testing, which may include a state examination and the evaluation of clinical competency. Some veterinarians choose to specialize in a specific area of medicine; these doctors must be board certified and have successfully completed a residency program in one of thirty-nine AVMA-recognized veterinary specialties.

Additional Requirements

Generally, veterinarians love animals and care deeply about their health and welfare. As the situation arises, veterinarians must be comfortable counseling difficult or upset pet owners, demonstrating patience, and offering sympathy and understanding. At the same time, they should be highly analytical and exhibit an extreme proficiency in all things related to animal science and medicine. Excellent vision, as well as the ability to distinguish small changes in the appearance or color of specimens or body parts, is necessary for accurate and prompt diagnoses. Veterinarians should be able to manage and maintain a successful business to which customers want to return. They should have the leadership skills necessary to effectively run a team of health care professionals. A calm demeanor is extremely helpful when treating animals and when working collaboratively.

Fun Fact

Female horses have fewer teeth than male horses. The cat is the only domestic animal not mentioned in the Bible. A duck's quack does not echo. And cows cannot walk down stairs.

Source: http://www.veterinarians.com/articles/fun-and-useless-facts-about-animals.html

EARNINGS AND ADVANCEMENT

Earnings of veterinarians depend on the type, size, and geographic location of the practice and the individual's amount of experience. On the average, salaried veterinarians earn less than self-employed veterinarians.

Mean annual earnings of veterinarians were $98,230 in 2014. The lowest ten percent earned less than $52,530, and the highest ten percent earned more than $157,390.

Veterinarians in salaried employment may receive paid vacations, holidays, and sick days; life and health insurance; and retirement benefits. These are usually paid by the employer. Veterinarians in private practice must make their own arrangements for these fringe benefits.

Metropolitan Areas with the Highest Employment Level in this Occupation

Metropolitan area	Employment[1]	Employment per thousand jobs	Annual mean wage
Chicago-Joliet-Naperville, IL	1,480	0.40	$90,210
New York-White Plains-Wayne, NY-NJ	1,310	0.24	$131,550
Atlanta-Sandy Springs-Marietta, GA	1,160	0.49	$98,120
Los Angeles-Long Beach-Glendale, CA	1,140	0.28	$131,270
Philadelphia, PA	1,110	0.59	$137,170
Washington-Arlington-Alexandria, DC-VA-MD-WV	1,050	0.44	$130,180
Denver-Aurora-Broomfield, CO	990	0.74	$103,630
Phoenix-Mesa-Glendale, AZ	980	0.54	$79,250
Minneapolis-St. Paul-Bloomington, MN-WI	880	0.48	$83,710
Houston-Sugar Land-Baytown, TX	790	0.28	$106,600

[1]Does not include self-employed. Source: Bureau of Labor Statistics

EMPLOYMENT AND OUTLOOK

There were approximately 70,300 veterinarians employed nationally in 2012. Veterinarians are employed in many areas, such as solo or group practices, colleges of veterinary medicine, medical schools, research laboratories, animal food companies, pharmaceutical companies, and the federal government. Employment of veterinarians is expected to grow as fast as the average for all occupations through the year 2022, which means employment is projected to increase 9 percent to 15 percent. This is primarily because of a growth in the household pet population and pet owners' willingness to spend more money on caring for their pets.

Employment Trend, Projected 2012–22

Health diagnosing and treating practitioners (all): 20%

Veterinarians: 12%

Total, all occupations: 11%

Note: "All Occupations" includes all occupations in the U.S. Economy. Source: U.S. Bureau of Labor Statistics, Employment Projections Program

Related Occupations
- Microbiologist
- Veterinary Assistant/Technician
- Wildlife Biologist

Related Military Occupations
- Life Scientist

Conversation With . . .
RANIA LISAS, DVM

Tidewater Veterinary Hospital, Charlotte Hall, MD
Veterinarian, 15 years

1. What was your individual career path in terms of education/training, entry-level job, or other significant opportunity?

One of the laudable characteristics of Veterinary Medicine is that its practitioners come from every background you can imagine and often have taken circuitous routes to get there. I started out wanting to be a veterinarian because I grew up with animals, found a love and respect for them, and tagged along with our local vet, Dr. Herbert Howard in Leesburg, Va., every chance I got. Then I found I loved literature and teaching and went into that field, only to go back to vet school in my early 30s. A rotation in my senior year at a private practice led to my position at that same practice, where I am now an associate vet. We are a mixed animal practice, so we see all domestic and exotic pets as well as farm animals such as horses, cattle, sheep, goats, alpacas and pigs.

2. What are the most important skills and/or qualities for someone in your profession?

My English background has been invaluable because being able to listen, and to teach, are the most important qualities for a veterinarian. Our patients are animals, but our clients are people. Being able to take an animal's history and truly listen to what a client is telling you about her animal's problem will help you be a better vet. Teaching clients in a way they can understand how to help their own animals is key, whether monitoring a sick animal or using preventive medicine properly to improve herd health in beef cattle, or increase production in a goat dairy herd.

3. What do you wish you had known going into this profession?

I was very prepared after riding around with Dr. Howard all those years. Still, if you are thinking of going into this career, understand that you are dealing with life and death and therefore you will see people at their best and their worst. There is elation and sorrow. You are witness to sickness and pain and death, and to loving care and horrible cruelties. You will hold an owner's hand as they say goodbye to a loved one.

4. **Are there many job opportunities in your profession? In what specific areas?**

The field is wide open to enter private practice and to care for any species from farm animals to dogs and cats, to exotics and pocket pets, to birds and marine life. You can be a general practitioner or specialize in fields ranging from cardiology to pathology. As a vet, you can be involved with in lab medicine and research, be an animal and plant health investigator with the U.S. Department of Agriculture, join the Veterinary Corps to care for U.S. Army animals around the world, or research emerging or highly dangerous diseases in military labs.

5. **How do you see your profession changing in the next five years, what role will technology play in those changes, and what skills will be required?**

I sometimes worry about the cost of vetmed. Technology is wonderful and often gives us more opportunities to diagnose problems earlier and better, but it will be of no use if the tools are too expensive. I don't want to see an owner put a pet down because a corporate veterinarian can't adjust diagnostics and treatment to a client's budget because the boss is looking over his shoulder and insisting on ivory tower medicine that will show a profit. I also worry about there being fewer large animal veterinarians in areas where farmers need them.

6. **What do you enjoy most about your job? What do you enjoy least about your job?**

When a very sick animal that I seriously thought was not going to make it turns around, feels good, and will live a long and happy life, the owners and I have a very hard time containing our joy! I run into a woman whose dog we saved and she always hugs me and announces to anyone who will listen that I am the vet who saved her dog. The worst is dealing with stupidity, ignorance, and, sometimes, cruelty. These are totally avoidable disasters: people who didn't think antifreeze was so bad for their dog; people who leave a collar on a dog as a small puppy whose body grows, imbedding the collar in the neck like a tree engulfing a wire fence; and people who laugh and think it is cute when their dog lunges at another human or dog. Death or pain for an animal as a result of ignorance or cruelty always makes me feel terrible.

7. **Can you suggest a valuable "try this" for students considering a career in your profession?**

Volunteer at your local veterinarian, preferably your own vet! Think about widening your range of interests in different species by volunteering at different types of private practices or investigating opportunities at local stables, farms, zoos, natural history or marine museums, fisheries, poultry farms or aviaries.

SELECTED SCHOOLS

A variety of colleges and universities offer programs in veterinary science. Some of the more prominent schools in this field are listed below.

Colorado State University
1601 Campus Delivery
Fort Collins, CO 80523
Phone: (970) 491-7051
http://csu-cvmbs.colostate.edu

Cornell University
Ithaca, New York 14853
Phone: (607) 254-4636
www.cornell.edu

North Carolina State University
1060 William Moore Drive
Raleigh, NC 27606
Phone: (919) 513-6786
www.cvm.ncsu.edu

Ohio State University
1900 Coffey Road
Columbus, OH 43210
Phone: (614) 292-1171
www.vet.ohio-state.edu

Texas A&M University
402 Raymond Stotzer Parkway
College Station, TX 77845
Phone: (979) 845-5051
www.vetmed.tamu.edu

Tufts University
200 Westboro Road
North Grafton, MA 01536
Phone (508) 839-7920
http://vet.tufts.edu

University of California, Davis
1 Shields Avenue
Davis, CA 95616
Phone (539) 752-1011
www.ucdavis.edu

University of Pennsylvania
3800 Spruce Street
Philadelphia, PA 19104
Phone (215) 898-5434
www.vet.upenn.edu

University of Minnesota, Twin Cities
1352 Boyd Ave
St Paul, MN
Phone (612) 624-1227
http://www.cvm.umn.edu

University of Wisconsin, Madison
2015 Linden Drive
Madison, WI 53706
Phone (608) 263-6716
www.vetmed.wisc.edu

MORE INFORMATION

American Holistic Veterinary Medical Association
P.O. Box 630
Abingdon, MD 21009-0630
410.569.0795
www.ahvma.org

American Veterinary Medical Association
1931 N. Meacham Road, Suite 100
Schaumburg, IL 60173-4360
800.248.2862
www.avma.org

American Veterinary Medical Foundation
1931 N. Meacham Road
Schaumburg, IL 60173
800.248.2862
www.avmf.org

Association of American Veterinary Medical Colleges
1101 Vermont Avenue, Suite 710
Washington, DC 20005-3521
202.371.9195
www.aavmc.org

National Association of Federal Veterinarians
1910 Sunderland Place, NW
Washington, DC 20036
202.223.4878
www.nafv.net

National Board of Veterinary Medical Examiners
P.O. Box 1356
Bismarck, ND 58502
701.224.0332
www.nbvme.org

U.S. Department of Agriculture
Agricultural Research Service
5601 Sunnyside Avenue, Room 4-1139
Beltsville, MD 20705-5100
301.504.1074
www.ars.usda.gov

Zoologist

Snapshot

Career Cluster: Science, Technology, Engineering & Mathematics
Interests: Zoology, Biology, Animal Behavior, Research (field and laboratory), Environmental Studies
Earnings (Yearly Average): $63,230
Employment & Outlook: Slower Than Average Growth Expected

OVERVIEW

Sphere of Work

Zoologists study the structure, origin, epidemiology, behavior, and life processes of animals. In addition to studying animal anatomy and physiology, they monitor and inventory animal populations, study

the impact of industrial development on animals' natural habitats, and analyze the relationship between animal species and their immediate environments. Zoologists are usually classified by the animal groups they specialize in studying, such as mammals (mammalogy), birds (ornithology), fish (ichthyology), reptiles (herpetology), or the study of certain aspects of animal life, such as the development of animals from fertilized cell to birth or hatching (embryology). Zoologists conduct research and laboratory work. Most zoologists are college or university professors, although many are employed by government agencies, zoos, or private companies.

Work Environment

Zoologists work in offices, laboratories, academic buildings, government agencies, private companies, natural animal habitats, and zoological parks. Although they spend time in laboratories, offices, and classrooms, they must also spend a great deal of time outdoors conducting research, hiking rough terrain, and working in different weather conditions in order to study animals in their natural habitats.

Profile

Working Conditions: Work both Outdoors and Indoors
Physical Strength: Light Work
Education Needs: Doctoral Degree
Licensure/Certification: Usually Not Required
Opportunities For Experience: Internship, Volunteer Work
Holland Interest Score*: IRE

* See Appendix A

Occupation Interest

Most zoologists love the outdoors. Zoologists are highly educated experts in their particular sub-field of animal research. They also do important work to help the rest of the world understand and appreciate wildlife. Some are professors, teaching others while conducting their own research. Others work in zoos and animal sanctuaries, where they share their knowledge and love of animals with the general public. Still others contribute to efforts to protect the environment, working for not-for-profit or government agencies and providing input on policies that safeguard threatened species and their habitats.

A Day in the Life—Duties and Responsibilities

A considerable portion of the work performed by zoologists is research or laboratory work. In the field, zoologists set up observation camps from which to study animals in their natural habitats, taking photos, taking samples, and keeping daily records of animals' interrelationships, development, and health. In the laboratory, they dissect animals, prepare tissue slides, study samples, and classify species. They also write reports and articles for their employers and for publication in scholarly journals. As biological scientists, zoologists may be invited to present their findings at academic and environmental conferences.

When they are not in the field or laboratory, most zoologists are university or college professors, committed to both research and teaching responsibilities. Some zoologists work in zoos, animal sanctuaries, and nature preserves. Others are hired by government agencies to study how animals and their habitats are affected by pollution and industrial development, as well as make recommendations as to how better protect these species. Pharmaceutical and biological supply companies employ some zoologists to conduct applied research.

Duties and Responsibilities

- **Studying animals**
- **Performing research on animal behaviors, such as mating and eating habits**
- **Teaching courses at the secondary and college level**

WORK ENVIRONMENT

Physical Environment

When conducting research in the field, zoologists often travel to remote locations in all types of terrain and weather conditions, sometimes to areas where their research puts them in close proximity to a frightened animal. In the laboratory, zoologists work in a much more controlled and safe environment.

Relevant Skills and Abilities

Research & Planning Skills
- Analyzing information
- Gathering information

Technical Skills
- Performing scientific, mathematical and technical work

Work Environment Skills
- Working with plants or animals

Human Environment

Depending on their job specialization, zoologists interact with many different people. When traveling to animal habitats to do research in the field, they may work with guides and local residents; in the laboratory, they work with lab technicians, graduate students, and interns. At zoos, they work with zookeepers, veterinarians, and the general public. In government agencies, zoologists interact with elected as well as appointed officials, public administrators, and fellow scientists. In private organizations, they work with executives, other scientists, and administrators.

Technological Environment

In the field, zoologists use traps, nets, and other devices to capture live specimens. They also use special containers and other sampling equipment. In the laboratory, zoologists use microscopes, reactive chemicals, and other test equipment and substances. In addition, zoologists should be competent with modeling, map-generating, and database computer software.

EDUCATION, TRAINING, AND ADVANCEMENT

High School/Secondary

High school students interested in pursuing a career in zoology should take courses such as biology, physics, chemistry, physiology, and other sciences. They should also take math courses, including algebra and geometry. Computer science skills are critical to the recording and sharing of scientific data.

Suggested High School Subjects
- Biology
- Chemistry
- Computer Science
- English
- Geography
- Mathematics
- Physical Science
- Physics
- Physiology
- Science

Famous First

The first American zoologist to publish material for general readers was Benjamin Smith Barton (1766-1815). In 1796 he published a "Memoir Concerning the Fascinating Faculty Which Has been Ascribed to the Rattle-Snake" and later published "Facts, Observations and Conjectures relative to the Generation [i.e., Reproduction] of the Opossum of North-America."

College/Postsecondary

A doctoral degree is required for most positions in zoology, so it is critical to earn a bachelor's degree in a biological science and plan for continued study in master's and doctoral programs within the natural sciences.

Related College Majors
- Biology, General
- Human & Animal Physiology
- Zoology, General

Adult Job Seekers

Adult job seekers must follow the same academic path outlined above. Qualified individuals seeking zoologist positions should apply directly to universities, zoos, and other organizations with posted openings. The US Department of the Interior, for example, posts such positions. The American Zoo and Aquarium Association can be useful in networking.

Professional Certification and Licensure

Most zoologists hold doctoral degrees as a pre-requisite for their positions. Additionally, they may be required to be certified in the use of certain technology in the field depending on what type of animal they study (such as SCUBA equipment for zoologists specializing in the study of fish or dolphins).

Additional Requirements

Zoologists should demonstrate natural curiosity, a strong ability to analyze complex issues and problems, and strong written, research, and verbal skills. When and if necessary in the course of their work, they should be physically fit and prepared to travel to and stay in remote and potentially dangerous areas.

Fun Fact

There is no "zoo" in zoologist. The word is pronounced zo—(rhymes with toe)—ologist.

Source: http://dictionary.cambridge.org/us/pronunciation/english/zoology

EARNINGS AND ADVANCEMENT

Earnings depend on the type and geographic location of the employer and the employee's education and level of responsibility. Mean annual earnings of zoologists were $63,230 in 2014. The lowest ten percent earned less than $38,080, and the highest ten percent earned more than $96,720.

In 2014, zoologists employed by the federal government earned an average annual salary of $80,210.

Zoologists may receive paid vacations, holidays, and sick days; life and health insurance; and retirement benefits. These are usually paid by the employer.

States with the Highest Employment Level in this Occupation

State	Employment	Employment per thousand jobs	Annual mean wage
California	3,330	0.22	$68,600
Washington	1,780	0.61	$70,600
Florida	1,410	0.18	$50,180
Oregon	1,030	0.61	$64,840
Alaska	810	2.48	$71,790

EMPLOYMENT AND OUTLOOK

There were approximately 20,000 zoologists and wildlife biologists employed nationally in 2012.Zoologists are employed by state governments, the federal government, private research and consulting organizations, zoos, and colleges and universities, among others. Employment of zoologists is expected to grow slower than the average for all occupations through the year 2022, which means employment is projected to increase 3 percent to 8 percent. This growth will be due primarily to the need to study the impact of changing environments on animal populations and

Employment Trend, Projected 2012–22

Total, all occupations: 11%

Life, physical, and social science occupations (all): 10%

Zoologists: 5%

Note: "All Occupations" includes all occupations in the U.S. Economy. Source: U.S. Bureau of Labor Statistics, Employment Projections Program

Related Occupations
- Biological Scientist
- Microbiologist
- Wildlife Biologist

Conversation With . . .
TERESA M. TELECKY, PhD

Wildlife Department Director
Humane Society International, Washington, DC
Zoologist, 25 years

1. What was your individual career path in terms of education/training, entry-level job, or other significant opportunity?

I loved animals from the time I was a child. I really enjoyed biology in high school and decided to pursue it in college. I received three degrees in zoology: Bachelor of Science, Master of Science, and doctorate. I specialized in the study of ecology and animal behavior. I also did postdoctoral research in Japan. After that, I began looking for a job and thought I would become a university teacher and researcher. I never planned to work in animal protection, but when I saw an advertisement for a position in the wildlife department at the Humane Society International, I felt drawn to it and applied.

Humane Society International is the international arm of The Humane Society of the United States, the nation's largest and most effective animal protection organization. My department focusses on international threats to wildlife, especially wildlife trade. We do a lot of work in the context of a United Nations treaty called the Convention on International Trade in Endangered Species, the purpose of which is to ensure that wildlife are not over-exploited by international trade. We work to protect elephants from poachers who are after their tusks to supply the illegal ivory trade, rhinos who are threatened by poachers after their horns, and polar bears killed for the international fur trade, among many others.

We also work to reduce demand for wildlife parts and products, including demand for ivory in the U.S. and China, and for rhino horn in Vietnam. We advocate at local, national, regional and international levels for the strongest possible wildlife protection laws and policies.

2. What are the most important skills and/or qualities for someone in your profession?

Being knowledgeable about wildlife, being highly organized, having good social and managerial skills, and having excellent written and verbal communication skills.

3. What do you wish you had known going into this profession?

How to speak Spanish or French fluently! My job is to convince people who represent governments from around the world to protect animals. A second language—particularly one of those two languages—would have been very helpful to me. Since I don't have language skills, I rely on colleagues who speak these languages to help me with my work.

4. Are there many job opportunities in your profession? In what specific areas?

There are many jobs in animal protection and you don't have to be a scientist to work in this area. For example, people who work for The Humane Society of the United States are accountants, public relations experts, lawyers, veterinarians, lobbyists, human relations experts, fundraisers, artists, animal caretakers, building managers, writers, IT professionals, campaigners, executive assistants, and many others.

Job possibilities for zoologists are: doing research for a university, government or in the private sector; teaching and education; advocacy (such as what I do at HSI or with other local, state, national or international non-profits); working on governmental policy; at public zoos, aquaria, and wildlife rescue centers; and as a naturalist, which would typically be at a park.

5. How do you see your profession changing in the next five years? What role will technology play in those changes, and what skills will be required?

Every day someone is inventing new ways to use technology to protect wildlife. Recent examples include drones used for aerial surveys and phone apps that help wildlife officers identify the types of animals they have seized.

Things have really changed in the past 25 years in terms of the growth in the number of jobs in animal protection; the professionalization of this line of work, including involvement of people with a wide diversity of skills; and in communications. When I first began my work, the Internet hadn't even been invented, the only way to share documents was by fax or post, it was difficult to get more than five people on a phone line at one time for a discussion, and it was difficult to speak to someone from Africa or Asia on the telephone because of poor connections! Nowadays, communication is so much easier. And better communication helps us in our work. I think in coming years we will continue to see these trends.

6. What do you enjoy most about your job? What do you enjoy least about your job?

I enjoy the process of seeing a problem, developing a solution, convincing others that this is a good solution, and seeing the solution applied successfully. Sometimes, no matter how hard I try, I cannot get people to agree to my solution and so the problem persists; I don't like that part of my job!

7. **Can you suggest a valuable "try this" for students considering a career in your profession?**

Get involved in activist work in your school or community (it doesn't have to be animal related). Try your hand at identifying a problem to tackle, coming up with a solution, and convincing others that your solution will work.

SELECTED SCHOOLS

Many colleges and universities offer programs in zoology, animal science, or wildlife biology. Some of the more prominent schools in this field are listed below.

Brigham Young University
Life Sciences Building
Provo, UT 84602
(801) 422-2760
pws.byu.edu

Colorado State University
109D Wagar Building
1474 Campus Delivery
Fort Collins, CO 80523
(970) 491-5020
warnercnr.colostate.edu/fwcb-home

Michigan State University
480 Wilson Road, Room 13
East Lansing, MI 48824
(517) 355-4478
www.fw.msu.edu

Texas A&M University
TAMU 2258
College Station, TX 77843
(979) 845-5777
wfsc.tamy.edu

University of Arizona
Biological Sciences East, Room 325
1311 East 4th Street
Tucson, AZ 85721
(520) 621-7255
snre.arizona.edu

University of Florida
110 Newins-Zeigler Hall
PO Box 110430
Gainseville, FL 32611
(352) 846-0643
www.wec.ufl.edu

University of Maryland
Center for Environmental Science
PO Box 775
Cambridge, MD 21613
(410) 228-9250
www.umces.edu

University of Minnesota
135 Skok Hall
203 Upper Buford Circle
St. Paul, MN 55108
(612) 625-5299
Fwcb.cfans.umn.edu

University of Missouri
302 Anheuser-Busch Natural Sciences Building
Columbia, MO 65211
(573) 882-3436
www.snr.missouri.edu/fw

University of Tennessee
274 Ellington Plant Science Building
Knoxville, TN 37996
(865) 974-7987
fwf.ag.utk.edu

MORE INFORMATION

American Physiological Society
Education Office
9650 Rockville Pike
Bethesda, MD 20814-3991
301.634.7164
www.the-aps.org

American Society for Microbiology
1752 N Street, NW
Washington, DC 20036-2904
202.737.3600
www.asm.org

American Zoo and Aquarium Association
8403 Colesville Road, Suite 710
Silver Spring, MD 20910-3314
301.562.0777
www.aza.org

Biotechnology Industry Organization
1201 Maryland Avenue, SW
Suite 900
Washington, DC 20024
202.962.9200
info@bio.org
www.bio.org

Botanical Society of America
P.O. Box 299
St. Louis, MO 63166-0299
314.577.9566
www.botany.org

Society for Integrative and Comparative Biology
1313 Dolley Madison Boulevard
Suite 402
McLean, VA 22101
800.955.1236
www.sicb.org

The Wildlife Society
5410 Grosvenor Lane, Suite 200
Bethesda, MD 20814-2144
301.897.9770
www.wildlife.org

Wildlife Conservation Society
2300 Southern Boulevard
Bronx, NY 10460
718.720.5100
www.wcs.org

Zoological Association of America
P.O. Box 511275
Punta Gorda, FL 33951-1275
941.621.2021
www.zaoa.org

Michael Auerbach/Editor

What Are Your Career Interests?

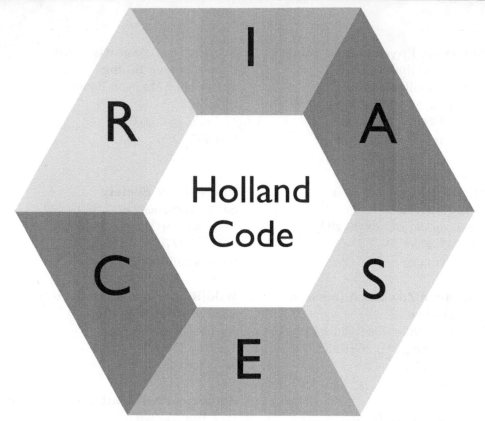

This is based on Dr. John Holland's theory that people and work environments can be loosely classified into six different groups. Each of the letters above corresponds to one of the six groups described in the following pages.

Different people's personalities may find different environments more to their liking. While you may have some interests in and similarities to several of the six groups, you may be attracted primarily to two or three of the areas. These two or three letters are your "Holland Code." For example, with a code of "RES" you would most resemble the Realistic type, somewhat less resemble the Enterprising type, and resemble the Social type even less. The types that are not in your code are the types you resemble least of all.

Most people, and most jobs, are best represented by some combination of two or three of the Holland interest areas. In addition, most people are most satisfied if there is some degree of fit between their personality and their work environment.

The rest of the pages in this booklet further explain each type and provide some examples of career possibilities, areas of study at MU, and co-curricular activities for each code. To take a more in-depth look at your Holland Code, take a self-assessment such as the SDS, Discover, or a card sort at the MU Career Center with a Career Specialist.

<u>R</u>ealistic *(Doers)*

People who have athletic ability, prefer to work with objects, machines, tools, plants or animals, or to be outdoors.

Are you?
practical
straightforward/frank
mechanically inclined
stable
concrete
reserved
self-controlled

independent
ambitious
systematic

<u>Can you?</u>
fix electrical things
solve electrical problems
pitch a tent
play a sport
read a blueprint
plant a garden
operate tools and machine

Like to?
tinker with machines/vehicles
work outdoors
be physically active
use your hands
build things
tend/train animals
work on electronic equipment

Career Possibilities
(Holland Code):

Air Traffic Controller (SER)	Dental Technician (REI)	Laboratory Technician (RIE)	Property Manager (ESR)
Archaeologist (IRE)	Farm Manager (ESR)	Landscape Architect (AIR)	Recreation Manager (SER)
Athletic Trainer (SRE)	Fish and Game Warden (RES)	Mechanical Engineer (RIS)	Service Manager (ERS)
Cartographer (IRE)	Floral Designer (RAE)	Optician (REI)	Software Technician (RCI)
Commercial Airline Pilot (RIE)	Forester (RIS)	Petroleum Geologist (RIE)	Ultrasound Technologist (RSI)
Commercial Drafter (IRE)	Geodetic Surveyor (IRE)	Police Officer (SER)	Vocational Rehabilitation
Corrections Officer (SER)	Industrial Arts Teacher (IER)	Practical Nurse (SER)	Consultant (ESR)

<u>I</u>nvestigative *(Thinkers)*

People who like to observe, learn, investigate, analyze, evaluate, or solve problems.

Are you?
inquisitive
analytical
scientific
observant/precise
scholarly
cautious

intellectually self-confident
Independent
logical
complex
Curious

Can you?
think abstractly
solve math problems
understand scientific theories
do complex calculations
use a microscope or computer
interpret formulas

Like to?
explore a variety of ideas
work independently
perform lab experiments
deal with abstractions
do research
be challenged

Career Possibilities
(Holland Code):

Actuary (ISE)	Chemical Engineer (IRE)	Geologist (IRE)	Physician, General Practice (ISE)
Agronomist (IRS)	Chemist (IRE)	Horticulturist (IRS)	Psychologist (IES)
Anesthesiologist (IRS)	Computer Systems Analyst (IER)	Mathematician (IER)	Research Analyst (IRC)
Anthropologist (IRE)	Dentist (ISR)	Medical Technologist (ISA)	Statistician (IRE)
Archaeologist (IRE)	Ecologist (IRE)	Meteorologist (IRS)	Surgeon (IRA)
Biochemist (IRS)	Economist (IAS)	Nurse Practitioner (ISA)	Technical Writer (IRS)
Biologist (ISR)	Electrical Engineer (IRE)	Pharmacist (IES)	Veterinarian (IRS)

Artistic *(Creators)*

People who have artistic, innovating, or intuitional abilities and like to work in unstructured situations using their imagination and creativity.

Are you?
creative
imaginative
innovative
unconventional
emotional
independent
Expressive

original
introspective
impulsive
sensitive
courageous
complicated
idealistic
nonconforming

Can you?
sketch, draw, paint
play a musical instrument
write stories, poetry, music
sing, act, dance
design fashions or interiors

Like to?
attend concerts, theatre, art
  exhibits
read fiction, plays, and poetry
work on crafts
take photography
express yourself creatively
deal with ambiguous ideas

Career Possibilities
(Holland Code):

Actor (AES)
Advertising Art Director (AES)
Advertising Manager (ASE)
Architect (AIR)
Art Teacher (ASE)
Artist (ASI)

Copy Writer (ASI)
Dance Instructor (AER)
Drama Coach (ASE)
English Teacher (ASE)
Entertainer/Performer (AES)
Fashion Illustrator (ASR)

Interior Designer (AES)
Intelligence Research Specialist
  (AEI)
Journalist/Reporter (ASE)
Landscape Architect (AIR)
Librarian (SAI)

Medical Illustrator (AIE)
Museum Curator (AES)
Music Teacher (ASI)
Photographer (AES)
Writer (ASI)
Graphic Designer (AES)

Social *(Helpers)*

People who like to work with people to enlighten, inform, help, train, or cure them, or are skilled with words.

Are you?
friendly
helpful
idealistic
insightful
outgoing
understanding

cooperative
generous
responsible
forgiving
patient
kind

Can you?
teach/train others
express yourself clearly
lead a group discussion
mediate disputes
plan and supervise an activity
cooperate well with others

Like to?
work in groups
help people with problems
do volunteer work
work with young people
serve others

Career Possibilities
(Holland Code):

City Manager (SEC)
Clinical Dietitian (SIE)
College/University Faculty (SEI)
Community Org. Director
  (SEA)
Consumer Affairs Director
  (SER)Counselor/Therapist
  (SAE)

Historian (SEI)
Hospital Administrator (SER)
Psychologist (SEI)
Insurance Claims Examiner
  (SIE)
Librarian (SAI)
Medical Assistant (SCR)
Minister/Priest/Rabbi (SAI)
Paralegal (SCE)

Park Naturalist (SEI)
Physical Therapist (SIE)
Police Officer (SER)
Probation and Parole Officer
  (SEC)
Real Estate Appraiser (SCE)
Recreation Director (SER)
Registered Nurse (SIA)

Teacher (SAE)
Social Worker (SEA)
Speech Pathologist (SAI)
Vocational-Rehab. Counselor
  (SEC)
Volunteer Services Director
  (SEC)

<u>E</u>nterprising *(Persuaders)*

People who like to work with people, influencing, persuading, leading or managing for organizational goals or economic gain.

Are you?		**Can you?**	**Like to?**
self-confident	ambitious	initiate projects	make decisions
assertive	agreeable	convince people to do things	be elected to office
persuasive	talkative	your way	start your own business
energetic	extroverted	sell things	campaign politically
adventurous	spontaneous	give talks or speeches	meet important people
popular	optimistic	organize activities	have power or status
		lead a group	
		persuade others	

Career Possibilities
(Holland Code):

Advertising Executive (ESA)
Advertising Sales Rep (ESR)
Banker/Financial Planner (ESR)
Branch Manager (ESA)
Business Manager (ESC)
Buyer (ESA)
Chamber of Commerce Exec
  (ESA)

Credit Analyst (EAS)
Customer Service Manager
  (ESA)
Education & Training Manager
  (EIS)
Emergency Medical Technician
  (ESI)
Entrepreneur (ESA)

Foreign Service Officer (ESA)
Funeral Director (ESR)
Insurance Manager (ESC)
Interpreter (ESA)
Lawyer/Attorney (ESA)
Lobbyist (ESA)
Office Manager (ESR)
Personnel Recruiter (FSR)

Politician (ESA)
Public Relations Rep (EAS)
Retail Store Manager (ESR)
Sales Manager (ESA)
Sales Representative (ERS)
Social Service Director (ESA)
Stockbroker (ESI)
Tax Accountant (ECS)

<u>C</u>onventional *(Organizers)*

People who like to work with data, have clerical or numerical ability, carry out tasks in detail, or follow through on others' instructions.

Are you?		**Can you?**	**Like to?**
well-organized	practical	work well within a system	follow clearly defined
accurate	thrifty	do a lot of paper work in a short	procedures
numerically inclined	systematic	time	use data processing equipment
methodical	structured	keep accurate records	work with numbers
conscientious	polite	use a computer terminal	type or take shorthand
efficient	ambitious	write effective business letters	be responsible for details
conforming	obedient		collect or organize things
	persistent		

Career Possibilities
(Holland Code):

Abstractor (CSI)
Accountant (CSE)
Administrative Assistant (ESC)
Budget Analyst (CER)
Business Manager (ESC)
Business Programmer (CRI)
Business Teacher (CSE)
Catalog Librarian (CSE)

Claims Adjuster (SEC)
Computer Operator (CSR)
Congressional-District Aide (CES)
Cost Accountant (CES)
Court Reporter (CSE)
Credit Manager (ESC)
Customs Inspector (CEI)
Editorial Assistant (CSI)

Elementary School Teacher
  (SEC)
Financial Analyst (CSI)
Insurance Manager (ESC)
Insurance Underwriter (CSE)
Internal Auditor (ICR)
Kindergarten Teacher (ESC)

Medical Records Technician
  (CSE)
Museum Registrar (CSE)
Paralegal (SCE)
Safety Inspector (RCS)
Tax Accountant (ECS)
Tax Consultant (CES)
Travel Agent (ECS)

BIBLIOGRAPHY

Science

Bloomfield, Victor A. and Esam E. El-Fakahany. *The Chicago Guide to Your Career in Science: A Toolkit for Students and Postdocs*. Chicago: University of Chicago Press, 2008.

Feibelman, Peter J. *A PhD Is Not Enough! A Guide to Survival in Science*. New York: Basic Books, 2011.

Ghosh, Abhik, ed. *Letters to a Young Chemist*. Hoboken, NJ: Wiley, 2011.

Hälgren, Markus, ed. *Reflection on a Scientific Career: Behind the CV*. Copenhagen: Copenhagen Business School Press, 2014.

MacRitchie, Finlay. *Scientific Research as a Career*. Boca Raton, FL: CRC Press, 2011.

Mohanty, Sanat and Ranjana Ghosh. *Planning a Scientific Career in Industry*. Hoboken, NJ: Wiley, 2010.

Roth, Wolff-Michael and Pei-Ling Hsu. *Talk about Careers in Science*. Boston: Sense, 2010.

Schwartzkroin, Philip A. *So You Want to Be a Scientist?* New York: Oxford University Press, 2009.

Shewfelt, Robert L. *Becoming a Food Scientist: To Graduate School and Beyond*. New York: Springer Science + Business Media, 2012.

Strauss, Anselm L. and Lee Rainwater. *The Professional Scientist: A Study of American Chemists*. New Brunswick, NJ: Aldine, 2011.

Wilson, Edward O. *Letters to a Young Scientist*. New York: Liveright, 2014.

Engineering & Technology

Brittian, L.W. *Audel Electrical Trades Pocket Manual*. Hoboken, NJ: Wiley, 2012.

Dorr, Barry L. *Ten Essential Skills for Electrical Engineers*. Hoboken, NJ: Wiley, 2014.

McDowell, Gayle L. *Cracking the Tech Career*. Hoboken, NJ: Wiley, 2014.

Millar, Dean C. *Ready for Takeoff! A Winning Process for Launching Your Engineering Career*. Upper Saddle River, NJ: Pearson Prentice Hall, 2011.

Oakes, William, et al. *Engineering Your Future: A Brief Guide to Engineering*. New York: Oxford University Press, 2011.

Pond, Robert J. and Jeffrey L. Rankinen. *Introduction to Engineering Technology*. Upper Saddle River, NJ: Prentice Hall, 2014.

Mathematics

Mathematical Association of America. *101 Careers in Mathematics*. Washington, DC: The Association, 2014.
Wood, Leigh N., et al. *Becoming a Mathematician*. New York: Springer, 2012.

Women and STEM

Bilimoria, Diana, et al. *Women in STEM Careers: International Perspectives*. Northampton, MA: Edward Elgar, 2014.
Bush, Pamela McCauley. *Transforming Your STEM Career through Leadership and Innovation: Inspiration and Strategies for Women*. Boston: Elsevier, 2013.
Koch, Janice, et al. *Girls and Women in STEM: A Never Ending Story*. Arlington, VA: Information Age, 2014.

INDEX